The
GORBACHEV
REGIME

Consolidation to Reform

The GORBACHEV REGIME

Peter Juviler and Hiroshi Kimura

editors

ALDINETRANSACTION
A Division of Transaction Publishers
New Brunswick (U.S.A.) and London (U.K.)

First paperback printing 2009

Copyright © 1988 by Transaction Publishers, New Brunswick, New Jersey.

Library of Congress Catalog Number: 2009003713
ISBN: 978-0-202-36269-4
Printed in the United States of America

Library of Congress Cataloging-in-Publication Data

The Gorbachev regime : consolidation to reform / Peter Juviler and Hiroshi Kimura, {editors].

     p. cm.

   Originally published: Gorbachev's reforms : U.S. and Japanese assessments. New York : A. de Gruyter, c1988.

Includes bibliographical references and index.

ISBN 978-0-202-36269-4 (alk. paper)

    1. Soviet Union--Politics and government--1985-1991. 2. Gorbachev, Mikhail Sergeevich, 1931- 3. Soviet Union—Foreign public opinion, American. 4. Soviet Union—Foreign public opinion, Japanese. 5. Public opinion—Japan. 6. Public opinion—United States. I. Juviler, Peter H. II. Kimura, Hiroshi.

DK288.G6635 2009
947.085'4--dc22

To John N. Hazard

Mentor and Friend

CONTENTS

This book is about reforms meant to revitalize and redefine Soviet socialism, and to break Stalinism's death-hold on the system. The authors of this book work in centers of Soviet study across Japan and the United States. Our topic is Gorbachev's "revolutionary" *perestroika*—restructuring or transformation. It envisages the most sweeping changes in the Soviet economy, society, and politics since Stalin's "revolution from above" of the late 1920s and early 1930s.

What does *perestroika* bode for the USSR and the outside world? Can it work within the present Soviet system? Is it simply an image-making stunt by a politician talented in public relations who enjoys more popularity and prestige abroad than he may at home, judging from opinion polls and his designation by *Time* as 1977 Man of the Year? How secure in power is Gorbachev? However that turns out, what are the forces for and against a revitalizing Soviet reform? What are its short- and long-run prospects? And what are its implications for relations with the rest of the world?

People's views about a phenomenon like reform in the USSR reflect their particular location and concerns. For the Soviet people, the reforms mean changes that will impinge directly on their work and quality of life in ways that are yet uncertain. Americans tend to be preoccupied with arms agreements, human rights, and Third World tension, and to wonder whether a more productive Soviet Union is a good thing. The Japanese and their Asian neighbors have particular reasons of history, territorial issues, and the shadow of growing Soviet power in the area, to view with caution *perestroika*, "new thinking," and Soviet–U.S. nuclear arms reduction agreements.

Hence was the value of a U.S.–Japanese interchange, such as that preceding the writing of this volume, for stringently testing out each author's assumptions about Gorbachev's reforms. The interchange leading up to this symposium occurred at the Third U.S.–Japan Sapporo Summer Slavic Studies Seminar (S-5 '87) meeting July 27–28, 1987 in Sapporo, on Hokkaido Island in Japan, that part of the country closest to the USSR and to the "Northern Territories" which the USSR took from Japan during World War II.

The contributions to this volume are revised and updated versions of the papers discussed at the seminar, which was attended by the contributors and by other Japanese participants from varying academic, military, business, and media affairs backgrounds.

The editors acknowledge valuable insights provided by the participants at S-5 '87. They are grateful for the assistance of members of the Slavic Research Center, Hokkaido University, Sapporo, Japan. They are grateful also to the S-5 Executive Committee, headed by Mr. Takei Tojo, for generous assistance, without which the Seminar would not have been organized. They thank the Northern Region Center, Sapporo, for making available to the seminar its conference facilities with excellent devices for simultaneous translation, and they thank the interpreters, Mr. Tomi Naga, Mr. Doi, and Ms. Kobata, as well as the United States Information Service's Washington office, its Press and Cultural Section in Tokyo, and its American Center in Sapporo. The editors and participants assume responsibility for their contributions to this volume; opinions expressed are entirely our own, and do not necessarily reflect those of any of the organizations so graciously assisting us.

Peter Juviler
Hiroshi Kimura

INTRODUCTION

This book conveys both sides of Gorbachev's reforms—the extent of their dramatic changes, and the sobering evidence of their limits and obstacles. Its narrators are not such that "nothing short of instant systemic change, revolution, or destabilization" would satisfy them as tokens of meaningful change.[1] Our assessments are no more cautious than those we have encountered among Soviet supporters of reform. They are no less torn between wonder at the new atmosphere and expressive possibilities, on the one hand, and recognition of reform's reversibility, increasing difficulty, and long road ahead, on the other.

Whether an individual contributor's assessment of the reforms is unqualified or cautious depends, in most cases, not on whether the author is American or Japanese, so much as on the extent to which the theme of his or her chapter looks beyond principle to the complexities of implementation and the pull of traditional interests which confront domestic and foreign policy reforms, or breed inherent contradictions in them.

The facets of Gorbachev's reforms treated in this book, viewed in the context of other thinking on the Soviet Union, suggest conclusions about the intent behind the reforms, the forces favoring and hampering them, and their prospects and implications.

Intentions. The evidence seems pretty clear that Gorbachev intended his reforms not to be primarily a public relations stunt, for all the media ballyhoo about them, but rather, a means to preserving the status of the USSR as a world power into the 21st century.

Gorbachev did capitalize abroad on the positive features of *perestroika* which he defined as a "revolutionary" restructuring or transformation of the Soviet economy, society, and politics. He peddled assiduously "the new thinking" for foreign policy, and its picture of an interdependent rather than an ideologically polarized world.

His book, a best seller in the U.S., painted a rosy picture of reforms and their prospects, and their meaning for world peace.[2] *Time* designated Gorbachev as 1977 Man of the Year. Public opinion polls placed him above the president in the proportion of "favorable" to "unfavorable" ratings. *Perestroika* entered the English language; it gained entry into the second edition of a leading dictionary.

Still, the reforms are meant to be much more than propaganda. They are a high-risk gamble. Gorbachev doggedly urged them forward at possible cost to his own length of tenure in office. As the reforms went into effect, they stirred up rising opposition, in the latest stage of a long struggle over the future of Soviet socialism waged between "friends and foes of change"[3] (see chapters 1 and 2).

Forces favoring reform included Gorbachev's leadership. Gorbachev followed the typical path of the successful post-Bolshevik leader, rising from modest birth, March 2, 1931, in a peasant family of Southern Russia, through the youth and Party apparatus of his native Stavropol Territory, to become a Central Committee secretary in 1978, nonvoting Politburo member in 1979, full member in 1980, and general secretary on March 11, 1985, at the age of 54.

In other ways, Gorbachev's background represented something new and promising in Soviet leadership. His Politburo patrons during his rise to power stood for vigorous and uncorrupt leadership. Gorbachev represented the first post-Stalin political generation. A law degree from Moscow University in 1955, supplemented by an agricultural institute degree in 1967, made him the most educated leader since Lenin.[4] Gorbachev brought with him a sense of domestic crisis matching or surpassing his ally, and predecessor, Iurii Andropov, the general secretary for 15 months between Brezhnev's death in 1982 and Chernenko's even briefer interregnum, and uncommon talent at public relations and diplomacy both before and after he became Secretary General. Gorbachev then turned out to be a leader of "formidable energy and consummate political skill" (chapter 1) in a climate favoring strong leadership.

That climate originated in frustration with stagnation and demoralization under Brezhnev, and the existence of a large, new politically dissatisfied middle class of professional people who were appalled at their country's growing crisis of economic and civic decline. Also the critics, unlike their bureaucratic targets, stood to gain from reform. Between Khrushchev's "full-scale building of communism," and Gorbachev's call in April 1965 for "accelerated social and economic development" there had elapsed 21 years of falling growth rates. The gaps widened between productivity and needs, between Soviet technology and the technology of the West, and the "NICS," the newly industrialized Asian-Pacific countries. Japan had supplanted the USSR as the world's second ranking economic power. Soviet socialism had all but run out of steam.

As a third force favoring reform, there had grown since Khrushchev's time a loose cluster or reform movement of academics, journalists, and Party officials, augmented by dissidents and the underground publishing of *samizdat* which supplied ideas, support, and pressures for reform, which Gorbachev synthesized into his reform program (chapters 2, 4, 6, 7). Economic critiques go back more than 20 years; Gorbachev quoted one of them to the assembled Party elite a quarter century later (chapter 5). In sum: "The web of reformist connections and thinking stretches over time and space. It was not something improvised in 1985, and it crosses the line between Party work and academia" (chapter 4).

Fourth among the forces favoring reform was Gorbachev's ideological revision of the socialist model, an essential legitimizing and orienting prelude to fundamental shifts in policy. Gorbachev propounded, among other revisions, the non-class sources of interests, global oneness, the noninherence of socialist superiority which may fade without a revolutionary renewal, and the centrality of market devices to that renewal (chapters 3, 4, 7).

This impressive list of forces favoring reform should not distract attention away from the obstacles to reform.

Obstacles confronting reform reflect remnants of Stalin's legacy. They add up to, first, a disharmony of interests between reformers, on the one hand, and the bureaucratic apparatus and some working people and national minorities, on the other; second, the absence of a rallying appeal and common belief. Together, these lacks of common interest and motivating belief deprive the reform movement of a broad mass social base. Gorbachev hinted at this difficulty in his domestic speeches,[5] but spared his American readers details of such difficulties, claiming "grass roots movement" support.[6]

Ironically, Stalin's "revolution from above" beginning in 1928 could lay greater claim to a "grass roots" support than could Gorbachev's, because Stalin had four means of harmonizing interests in the cause of accelerated development which Gorbachev lacked: first, mass terror;[7] second, nationalist appeals to build "socialism in one country" and to save the fatherland in danger; third, conditions made so bad by 1930 due to forced collectivization and unemployment that millions had much to gain by joining in the "revolution from above" to speed up industrialization whereas under Gorbachev, they tended to cling to the security of its legacy, fearing to be the losers in reform (chapters 1, 2); and fourth, new leadership posts to offer young supporters, the *vydvishentsy*, or ones promoted up, rather than the old posts Gorbachev seeks to take away from those who fear being promoted down.[8]

Stalinism (1928–1953), the defeat of Khrushchev (1955–1964), and the Brezhnev era (1964–1982) left a "swollen" bureaucratic state, and Party machine ruling over a "spent society."[9] Those parts of the Stalinist legacy remaining no longer favor reform, but, in Gorbachev's words make up a braking or "retarding mechanism." This means not only obsolete economic *structures*, but also a "human factor" quite compatible with the Brezhnev era but unsuited to radical reform.

Because of that legacy, there is a long way to go to enlist, as Gorbachev has tried to do, "the talents and energies of the Soviet population" (chapter 1). To do this will mean to change what many Soviets, including Gorbachev, have noted as a subservient and dependent political culture among Soviet officials and working people, a culture of vested interest in stagnation, avoidance of risk, dependency on central command, bail-outs, and general demoralization (chapters 1, 2, 5).

The obstacles to reform include not simply conflicts of interest, but also a lack of belief in a common cause. Stalin's broken promises of life after World War II, Khrushchev's unfulfilled promises of plenty, the fall of the Stalinist idol, and the stagnation and continued privations under Brezhnev have turned Soviet people from believers to skeptics, leaving the USSR without a central, rallying myth.[10] Hence the disparity between the "enormity of the change he has launched and the limited support on which it is based" (chapter 1). "We are pragmatists these days," two Soviet social scientists told one of the editors. Into the void pour competing ideologies, yearnings for small truths and self-expression, and a pop-*glasnost'* youth culture.

Obstacles in the form of contradictions within the reforms relate mainly to Lenin's legacy. The contradictions have begun to show up in signs of possible conflict between Lenin's legacy of centralized rule by one vanguard Communist Party and the nature of economic and political reform. During reforms' first implementation, Party guidance may be needed to hold things together while old and new economic systems coexist. Eventually the Party tutelage will become superfluous and even counterproductive. The Party will then face the prospect of sponsoring reforms which mean a substantial erosion in its role as the all-guiding vanguard (chapters 2, 5). By rejecting that outcome, the Party might be rejecting also the completion of economic *perestroika*.

If Stalin's legacy were completely removed, the Leninist legacy would remain, as would its inherent contradictions between principles of Party tutelage, and workplace autonomy and grass roots activism.[11] Lenin's political legacy binds the Soviet Union together, but maybe too tightly, as now interpreted, for the success of a decentralizing reform which relies on the work force's motivation and initiative.

Stalin's legacy might not be dispelled and reforms taken to completion unless the Soviet leadership carries its revision of Soviet socialism farther, and changes to a less authoritarian and exclusive interpretation of political Leninism. Party leaders show no signs of acceding to that, as yet (chapters 1, 2).

Glasnost' and democratization have brought an openness for which there is as yet no suitable legal or institutional framework. They remain possibilities rather than rights. The regimes's ambivalence extends to attitudes on human rights. But human rights came to stay, as reforms got under way, both in Soviet public discourse, and in diplomatic exchanges with the U.S. and other concerned countries signatories of the 1975 Helsinki Final Accord on Security and Cooperation in Europe.[12]

Glasnost' and democratization are a double-edged sword to be used with care, with "potential for turbulence and conflict" as nationalist and other demonstrations have shown (chapters 1, 2, quotation from chapter 2). *Glasnost'* has its limits. Top Party leaders are not to be criticized in public or at meetings, for example, nor may the process of leadership selection.

Part of the inner-Party and inter-elite debate in the USSR seems to be on the issue of how far to open up the slow-starting "democratization," and the more rapidly unfolding process of *glasnost'*, how far the Party should carry its uncertain tolerance for former "dissidents" and present "informal" groups. These have proliferated to bring together peace activists, environmentalists, advocates of social democratic reform, petitioners for a monument to Stalin's victims, seekers of an expose of Stalin, national minority representatives, preservers of historical monuments, supporters of *perestroika*, human rights advocates, refuseniks, religious believers, and ethnic chauvinists (chapter 2).

Gorbachev promoted democratization as a way to advance his supporters and his reform policies. But genuinely democratic elections could bring to power not only supporters of Gorbachev but all sorts of undesirables like the demoted D.A Kunaev, former First Secretary of Kazakhstan (chapter 1).

With democratization has come the wider exercise of the possibility (not yet a right) of demonstration. But there are perils and limits here. The relatively liberal commentator, Fedor Burlatskii lamented, "how quickly the interpenetration of democracy and mob rule occurs!" He wrote that the people demanding unlimited rights to demonstrate are "local nationalists, extremists from Pamyat [a Russian nationalist, largely anti-semitic group—P.J.] and several groups of similar orientation, people pursuing selfish interests, so called 'refuseniks,' who want to go abroad, etc." If given the chance, he claimed, opposing groups like "local nationalists and great power [Russian—P.J.] chauvinists, anti-semites and zionists" would come to blows, and promote "anarchy, disorder, and a miserable, uncivilized political culture." This selective depiction of groups in the article of an important analyst and spokesperson, along with *Pravda*'s editorial line, illustrate the anxieties arising from above when movements from below take sponsors of democratization at their word.[13] "The genie is out of the bottle. We can't put him back," a Moscow journalist told one of the editors.

Implementing "new thinking" has its own contradictions. New thinking in foreign policy teaches global interdependence and the importance of a mutually acceptable regime of security. It makes an essential complement to internal reform. It heralds changes in Soviet foreign policy assumptions, strategies, and ultimate goals. But it is a doctrine yet to be fully tested abroad, and accepted at home (chapters 6, 7).

Two contradictions accompany the implementation of new thinking. The first contradiction poses the long run, militarily significant priorities of economic modernization against the shorter run priorities of ongoing military growth (chapter 7).

The second contradiction arises between the new thinking's vision of an interdependent, cooperating world, and traditional regional strategic aims reflecting the balance-of-power system now with us more or less since 1648. Regional diplomacy reveals a limited strategic price the Soviet Union is willing to pay for improving relations (chapters 1, 6, 8).

A case in point is Soviet policy toward the Asia-Pacific area, analyzed in this book (chapter 8), but probably applicable, at least in part, to Soviet policy throughout the third world. The new thinking is a doctrine applied more to relations with the U.S. (and the United Nations), and to a lesser extent, with China, than it is applied to relations with Japan and other countries of the Asia-Pacific area. Moscow thinks it is applying new thinking through existing improvements in its relations with an economically, and increasingly re-armed ally of the U.S.; Japan does not think so, given its limited, nonnuclear military power, and the Soviet occupying force and bases on islands lying off Hokkaido—the so-called "Northern Territories."

A certain flexibility has appeared vis-à-vis China and the rest of the region. The Soviets are working to expand foreign trade and commerce with the region, even opening up Vladivostok to visits by businessmen. The ultimate Soviet objective remains the same, in the analysis here: to increase political and diplomatic influence in the region. New thinking has changed the balance of military and nonmilitary means but has not caused the abandonment of a military buildup. Military escalation and economic flexibility "are not contradictory but complementary, both serving the objective of increasing Soviet influence in Asia and the Pacific" (chapter 8).

Prospects for reform depend on the outcome of the present, crucial first phase of implementing the shift from an administrative to a limited market economy lasting into the 1990s. This stage is crucial for Gorbachev's political future as well. Technical problems, conflicts of interest, loss of motivation in a skeptical populace, and inner contradictions between centralism and spontaneity in the new political economy of Soviet socialism point to a very difficult road out of what Seweryn Bialer calls the present Soviet "crisis of effectiveness." A "crisis of survival" that could stir up a more widespread sense of urgency is a not looming tomorrow.[14]

The General Secretary finds among his officialdom a widespread belief that his sense of crisis means a crisis for *them*, and that they had better sit tight. He lacks the reassurance of a fixed term (serving at the pleasure of the Politburo and Central Committee) and the power to compel the reforms which will end the crisis of effectiveness. His own vision is fraught with contradictions between Party tutelage and grass roots initiatives. He has given his country a vision of crisis and opportunity which neither it, nor in another sense, he, are yet ready to accept.

The next, entirely post-Stalin generation, in both education and service, may be ready, though. Gorbachev is himself an example of change in generational outlook.

Reform in the USSR should be viewed not as a cut-and-dried process over a defined, and short time period, with simple criteria of "success" and "failure" but as an involved and protracted technical and political struggle lasting into the 21st century. It will be a struggle over how to reconcile legacy, urgent need, and limited circumstances—a process of innovation and partial reaction: two steps forward, one back.

Pressures on any leadership for change will come from setbacks to living standards (in the form of increased prices and other impingements on living costs or job security, the pressures can, of course, go against change too), the incipient maturation and growing assertiveness of Soviet society, changes in the present political culture of dependency and subordination, and the widening technical gap between the USSR and capitalist countries of Europe, Asia, and even the faltering Northern hemisphere.[15]

Implications of reform for the rest of the world. If the reforms achieved their original sponsor's stated goals, *and stuck to means heralded by the program for perestroika and "new thinking,"* they would be a good thing for the world. They would mean a more economically potent Soviet Union, but at the same time a more open Soviet polity (probably an unavoidable precondition for the success of reform anyway); growing Soviet-Western interdependence; greater possibilities for shifting resources from arms to development and global coping and a lower risk of world nuclear war. Conversely, failure of reform could bring a harsher regime and a more aggressive Soviet foreign policy, probing for "targets of opportunity" in vulnerable parts of the world, at least in the view of Andrei Sakharov.[16]

Politics rarely work out in ideal absolutes. New thinking, our contributors suggest, is not necessarily either an absolute or an unchanging guideline for Soviet foreign policy. Moreover, one's view on the implications of Soviet reforms may depend in part on where one lives, and one's country's relations with the USSR, outstanding issues included. The view of reform from Japan is likely to differ from the U.S. view because of Japan's location, and especially because of the unresolved issue of the Soviet-occupied Northern Territories lying right off Hokkaido. Chapter 8 expresses a regional-realist skepticism about Soviet motivations behind "new thinking," when it applies to Japan. Outside Japan, realism finds proponents of realist doctrines, like the former Secretary of State and National Security adviser, Henry Kissinger, who see in successful Soviet reforms the making of a formidable Soviet challenge, one to be met by active and firm, though not necessarily unfriendly, diplomacy to maintain the world balance of power.

Between skeptical realism (still willing to negotiate) and roseate optimism lies the cautiously positive view that the total dynamic of reform may well cement irreversible ties and dependencies between the Soviet Union and the West.

Western diplomatic and economic responses to Soviet reform could make a substantial difference to their pace and timing, even though the responses probably cannot overcome deep conflicts of interest or inherent contradictions in reform. Arms reduction agreements and settlements of regional disputes, including a Soviet withdrawal from Afghanistan, and a more open door to trade on both sides, all on the basis of mutual benefit and due regard to mutual security, could bolster the leaders' authority at home, and free resources for consumption, an immediate prerequisite of popular support.

No high level meetings should occur without human rights being mentioned or being on the agenda. Directions of political change, and of Soviet-Western cooperation, which result in the enhancement of human rights, are to be encouraged as a way to greater international trust, more successful reform, and a greater popular oversight in Soviet foreign policy.

This welcoming of successful Soviet reforms presupposes a careful Western diplomacy. There is no absolute guarantee that the "new thinking" might not turn out to be a tactic one day, possibly because of different leadership or circumstances. Soviet foreign policy is influenced by countless factors, both domestic and international.[17] Balance of power considerations remain in evidence in regions of vital Soviet interest.

Nevertheless, the only way to know the proper limits and forms of interaction with the Soviet Union is to keep up the interaction. In other words, an international, Soviet-Western harmony of interests in Soviet reform exists, as long as it remains a liberating reform, not a re-Stalinizing one, and as long as Western security concerns are safeguarded. The "Soviet paradox" combines internal stagnation and external expansion conducted to provide a compensating legitimacy. If stagnation begins to dissipate, and expansion continues to falter, then a fundamental shift in Soviet foreign policy priorities and political legitimation would be taking place.[18]

The ambivalent, but not unpromising implications for Western policy may be summed up this way: "Western responses to Soviet foreign policy under new thinking should be guided by the principle of our own interests. Our own interests themselves, however, will be ultimately influenced by the outcome of this conflict in the Soviet Union. To this extent, new thinking expresses the truth—interdependence and mutual security" (chapter 6).

Notes

1. During that period a close observer of Soviet politics, Archie Brown, wrote that "To ignore many important changes and to dismiss others on the grounds that they are 'within the system' or 'do not challenge basic Soviet values' is to be guilty of a dangerous ethnocentrism. It would be ironic if, at a time when many in the Soviet Union are discovering or rediscovering the virtues of reform and evolutionary change—concepts that have such an honorable place in the Western tradition—nothing short of instant systemic change, revolution, or de-stabilization should satisfy their Western critics." Archie Brown, "Soviet Political Developments and Prospects," *World Policy* (Winter 1986–87), p.85.

2. Mikhail Gorbachev, *Perestroika: New Thinking for Our Country and the World* (New York: Harper & Row, 1987).

3. Stephen F. Cohen, "The Friends and Foes of Change: Reformism and Conservatism in the Soviet Union," in Stephen F. Cohen, Alexander Rabinowitch, and Robert Sharlet, eds., *The Soviet Union Since Stalin* (Bloomington, IN: Indiana University Press, 1980), pp. 11–31.

4. On Gorbachev's biography, see Zhores A. Medvedev, *Gorbachev* (New York: W.W. Norton & Company, 1986).

5. See, for example, his complaints about unfavorable aspects of public culture in his 70th Anniversary speech, *Pravda*, November 3, 1987.

6. "*Perestroika*," said Gorbachev, "began as à 'revolution from above' but then gained support from below. Yes, the Party leadership started it. The highest Party and state bodies elaborated and adopted the program. True, *perestroika* is not a spontaneous, but governed process . . . it would not have acquired its present scope, nor would it have had any firm chance of success if it had not merged the initiative from 'above' with the grass roots movement; if it had not expressed the fundamental, long-term interests of all the working people. . . ." Gorbachev, *Perestroika*, p. 56.

7. Roy A. Medvedev, *Let History Judge: The Origins and Consequences of Stalinism* (New York: Alfred A. Knopf, 1971), p. 313.

8. Party history covered in this introduction and the changes and continuities in rule are recapitulated in Merle Fainsod, *How Russia Is Ruled* (2nd ed.; Cambridge, MA: Harvard University Press, 1963), passim, especially useful for the vision of coexisting terror and revitalization. For more recent analyses, into the Brezhnev period, see Jerry E. Hough and Merle Fainsod, *How the Soviet Union Is Governed* (Cambridge, MA: Harvard University Press, 1979), pp. 38–274; and Seweryn Bialer, *Stalin's Successors: Leadership, Stability and Change in the Soviet Union* (New York: Cambridge University Press, 1980).

9. Robert C. Tucker, "Swollen State, Spent Society: Stalin's Legacy to Brezhnev's Russia," *Foreign Affairs* (Winter 1981/82), pp. 417–424.

10. Ibid, pp. 423–427.

11. Over the longer run the need for popular creativity and initiatives may collide with Leninism's and its four key political principles, forged between 1900 and 1921, as a way to end spontaneous or pluralist political participation. First, the political monopoly of a vanguard party, the guiding and directing force of Soviet society" and the "nucleus of its political system," works against independent political organization and other group initiatives. Second, democratic centralism—more centrist than democratic—embodies a contradiction between enterprise autonomy, and the structures and habits of central planning and administrative controls (Chapters 2, 5). Third, *nomenklatura* or the list of Party-approved jobs at once sustains Party power and thwarts it through resistance of the privileged job holders. Fourth, the ban on Party factions (groupings with a separate platform) cripples inner-

Party democracy and competition within the externally monolithic vanguard.

12. William Korey, "Helsinki, Human Rights, and the Gorbachev Style," in *Ethics and International Affairs*, 1, 1987, pp. 113–134; "Secondly, we must in practice teach people to live in the conditions created by a deepening democracy; broaden—broaden and strengthen—human rights." M.S. Gorbachev 70th Anniversary speech, *Pravda*, November 3, 1987.

13. Fedor Burlatskii, "Uchit'sia demokratii," *Pravda*, July 18, 1987; "Demokratiia i initsiativa, *Pravda*, December 27, 1987.

14. Seweryn Bialer, *The Soviet Paradox: External Expansion, Internal Decline* (New York: Alfred A. Knopf, 1986), pp. 169–170.

15. Loren Graham, "The Limits of Change: Science and Technology," *The Nation*, June 13, 1987, pp. 804–808. Our system is too rigid, plan-bound," according to one leading computer specialist. "It takes us years to apply a computer discovery. It takes Western economies, with their small private companies, a few months."

16. Peter G. Peterson, "Gorbachev's Bottom Line," *The New York Review of Books*, June 25, 1987, p.33.

17. On the domestic determinants of Soviet foreign policy, see Seweryn Bialer, ed., *The Domestic Context of Soviet Foreign Policy* (Boulder, CO: Westview Press, 1981), particularly, Alexander Dallin, "The Domestic Sources of Soviet Foreign Policy," pp. 335–408; and *Politicheskie sistemy sovremennosti* (Moscow: Nauka, 1979) pp. 14, 20, and 21.

18. Bialer, *The Soviet Paradox*.

Gorbachev's Agenda: Domestic Reforms and Foreign Policy Reassessments

Gail Warshofsky Lapidus

CHAPTER 1

Introduction

The succession of Mikhail Gorbachev to the Soviet leadership has prompted significant new departures in Soviet domestic and foreign policies. While the style and sophistication imparted by the vigorous and dynamic leader have been dramatic and visible, Gorbachev's initiatives in internal and international affairs extend far beyond matters of style: they encompass changes in underlying assumptions, in institutional structure and personnel, and in the substance of policy itself.

Clearly, the scope of change on the Soviet domestic scene has far surpassed that in the realm of foreign policy. Equally evident is the fact that in neither area have we seen such fundamental discontinuities as to call into question the basic economic, political, and strategic commitments of the Soviet leadership, or the overarching values of the Soviet system. Nonetheless, Gorbachev's campaign for *perestroika* (restructuring) is a call for far-reaching departures from prevailing practices and norms across virtually every area of Soviet life. Its success would entail radical changes not only in the way the economy functions, but in social and cultural policy, in Soviet political life, and ultimately, in the way in which the Soviet Union deals with the larger international community. Consequently, it would be a mistake to reject as without significance reforms that may fall short of a fundamental structural transformation of the Soviet system. In most political systems, most of the time, significant changes occur within the framework of existing institutions.

Gorbachev's foreign policy strategy is a direct outgrowth of his domestic priorities. Economic and political reform is not only the key to domestic revitalization in Gorbachev's view; it is essential to sustain the Soviet Union's role as an international power. Gorbachev himself described the connection between his domestic and foreign policy programs: the success of efforts at internal reform will determine whether or not the Soviet Union will enter the twenty-first century "in a manner worthy of a great power."

1

There is not only an intimate connection between Gorbachev's domestic and foreign policies, but striking parallels between the two. They share a demand for "new political thinking." They reflect a growing recognition within important segments of the Soviet elite that in a number of key areas previous policies have proved sterile and counterproductive, that they are ill-suited to the needs of the 1980's and beyond, and that a price must be paid to liquidate them. They reflect as well a recognition that the rigidity and dogmatism of past practices have alienated potential sources of domestic and international sympathy and support, depriving the Soviet model of any genuine appeal. Thus there appears to be a determination to reorient Soviet domestic and foreign policies to generate approval from the real sources of dynamism in both the domestic and international arenas.

This chapter will present an overview of Gorbachev's emerging strategy in domestic and foreign policy by focusing on three broad themes: the impetus for reform in the Soviet system, the evolution of Gorbachev's reform agenda, the impact of domestic reform on Soviet foreign policy and the prospects for reform.

The Impetus for Change

Gorbachev's strategy has its roots in what the Soviet poet Andrei Voznesensky called a "revolution in consciousness" within an important segment of the Soviet elite. Growing malaise and even alienation, increasingly visible by the late 1970's, were the product of two mutually reinforcing trends: an objective deterioration in the performance of the Soviet economy, which brought in its wake a mounting array of social and political problems, and a growing demoralization within the Soviet elite, reflecting a subtle but profound shift in perceptions of regime performance. The effects of these trends were exacerbated by the immobilism of an aging political leadership unable to reverse the decline.

The deteriorating performance of the Soviet economy was the critical catalyst in the growing perception of failure. For the first time since Stalin's death, slowing rates of economic growth made it impossible to guarantee, by the late 1970's, a simultaneous increase in per capita consumption, investment and military spending. As the competition for increasingly scarce resources intensified, a growing gap between mass expectations of continued improvement in living standards and the leadership's capacity to satisfy them threatened the implicit "social compact" that had replaced the extensive reliance on mass terror and coercion and served as the cornerstone of stability in the post-Stalin era.[1]

The economic slowdown was compounded by technological backwardness, creating yet a second gap of profound political and psychological importance: the gap that increasingly separated the Soviet economy from those of other advanced industrial societies, as well as from the dynamic newly industrializing countries of Asia, from South Korea to Singapore. As Japan overtook the Soviet Union, to become the world's second economic power, and as a new industrial revolution transformed the international economy, placing a high premium on rapid technological innovation, speedy communication, and high-quality products, the Soviet system increasingly appeared to be relegated to marginality, a comparative backwater whose economic performance was increasingly incommensurate with its political ambitions. This gap became even more alarming as it began to impinge on future Soviet military prowess, a concern heightened by the collapse of détente, the buildup of American and allied military forces, and the inauguration of the U.S. Strategic Defense Initiative (SDI).

Economic slowdown and diminished international competitiveness might not otherwise have generated a sense of urgency, but they coincided with and contributed to a crisis of confidence within the Soviet elite. The optimism of the 1950's and 1960's gave way to an increasingly negative assessment of regime performance, a growing sense of failure, and profound pessimism about the future.

The dramatic shift in attitudes was rooted in broader social and demographic changes in the post-Stalin era which transformed the passive and inarticulate peasant society of the Stalin era into an urban industrial society with an increasingly articulate and assertive middle class. By the mid 1980's, two thirds of the Soviet population lived in cities, twenty-two of which had populations of over one million; almost two thirds had completed secondary school; and twenty-two million had a higher education. In short, a large urban middle class, including a substantial professional, scientific-technical, and cultural intelligentsia had emerged on the Soviet scene, bringing with it new aspirations and values, and resentment of an authoritarian, patronizing, corrupt, and exclusionary pattern of rule.[2]

The spiritual alienation of important segments of this intelligentsia as well as of Soviet youth was in some respects accelerated by détente itself. By increasing the exposure of Soviet citizens to the outside world, détente provided new criteria and reference points for evaluating Soviet achievements and shortcomings. Judged by these standards, Soviet performance was increasingly found wanting, and previous official explanations of failure no longer seemed convincing. In the face of mounting domestic and international problems and the virtual paralysis of an aging and infirm leadership, the demoralization of an influential segment of the Soviet elite constituted an important impetus for reform. By the early 1980's, not only Western observers but key Soviet officials were themselves, in a fashion unprecedented since the early 1920's, beginning to use the term "crisis" to convey the urgency of the situation.[3]

Gorbachev's Strategy for Reform

When he finally succeeded to power in 1985, Gorbachev brought to the Soviet leadership neither a compelling vision of the future nor a detailed blueprint for moving toward it. Neither a "true believer" like Khrushchev, disposed toward egalitarian, utopian and populist programs, nor a conservative bureaucrat like Brezhnev, concerned with protecting the status and privileges of fellow members of the elite, Gorbachev is the first *modern* Soviet leader. Vastly more attuned than his predecessors to the imperatives of a scientific-technological age, pragmatic rather than ideological in his approach to problems, he is concerned with rationalizing and streamlining the system he inherited.[4] He is confident of its basic stability and of its legitimacy in the eyes of the Soviet population, sharply critical of its performance, impatient with the heavy weight of inherited dogma and bureaucratic inertia, but with no ready answers as to how it should be improved.

Gorbachev came to power, moreover, as the head of a reform-oriented coalition, united around a critical assessment of past policies and performance and agreed on the need to move more vigorously and decisively to break with the Brezhnevite past, yet lacking in a shared consensus regarding a strategy of reform or its scope. The common denominator of the coalition was support for energetic leadership, greater discipline, a revival of the asceticism and civic virtue associated with the heroic periods of Soviet history, and a reassertion of effective control of the strategic levers of power by the center. Beyond this common core, however, the coalition encompassed divergent views on how to move from discipline to revitalization, and varying degrees of willingness to sacrifice traditional forms of control for the sake of stimulating greater popular initiative.

The evident contradictions in the policies pursued over the past three years are also the result of a process of learning. Beginning with the summer of 1986, Gorbachev's speeches reveal a growing realization that the problems he inherited were more complex and the obstacles to reform more daunting, than he initially thought. They are marked by a perceptible radicalization, a gradual shift from an emphasis on acceleration *(uskorenie)*—a speeding up of the tempo within a basically stable framework—to a focus on restructuring *(perestroika)*, which contemplates more radical and even fundamental change. Indeed, Gorbachev himself described restructuring in July 1986 as nothing short of revolution, encompassing "not only the economy but all other sides of society's life: social relations, the political system, the spiritual and ideological sphere, the style and work methods of the party and of all our cadres. Restructuring is a capacious word. I would equate restructuring with revolution . . . genuine revolution in the minds and hearts of people, in the psychology and understanding of the present period and, above all, in the tasks engendered by rapid scientific and technical progress."[5] The striking evolution of Gorbachev's thinking during his first two years was manifested in his dramatic speech to the January 1987 plenum of the Central Committee, which argued that economic progress and social renewal were ultimately dependent on political democratization.

Gorbachev initially came to power with three rather traditional reformist priorities: to consolidate his political power; to arrest the deterioration of civic morale, restore discipline, and launch a process of social renewal; and to undertake reforms that would reverse the stagnation and technological backwardness of the Soviet economy and inject a dynamism now largely absent.

To these tasks Gorbachev brought considerable personal assets, most notably his comparative youth, formidable energy and consummate political skill. He also brought to the leadership a strong commitment to reform, shaped by his years as a law student at Moscow University during the early part of the Khrushchev era and by his subsequent continuing association with reform-minded intellectuals and professionals. He benefited from a psychological climate favorable to strong and decisive leadership—an understandable reaction to the long period of indecision and drift that characterized the succession of aging and infirm leaders—and from a demographic situation that gave him considerable opportunity to speed the retirement of an entire generation of leaders from the party, state, military, and ministerial apparatuses and thus to fill an exceptionally large number of vacancies with his own appointees.

But Gorbachev also came to power with some real liabilities: a limited political base of his own, particularly outside the Russian republic, and the presence of numerous well-entrenched regional leaders who had taken advantage of the stability and security afforded by Brezhnev's cadre policy to strengthen their own positions and build protective networks of informal ties based on patronage, nepotism and corruption. Moreover, the evolution of the Soviet political system itself in the years since Stalin's death had eroded many of the bases of power and authority associated with Stalin's rule. Terror and violence were no longer available as political tools, nor was a reliance on personality cults; and even the personnel weapon had been weakened by expectations of security within the elite. Thus, while Gorbachev has succeeded in forcing considerable turnover in key political positions, in using lateral transfers to bring "outsiders" into critical posts, and in forging alliances with powerful political associates, the changes so far are clearly insufficient to provide him with a broad and secure political base for his policy initiatives.

A second priority in Gorbachev's initial strategy was his drive for social renewal. In a dramatic effort to arrest and reverse a widespread and snowballing atmosphere of decay, corruption and cynicism, the new leadership sought to command the attention of the Soviet population and vigorously assert its authority, utilizing three highly visible campaigns—one directed against violations of work discipline, the second against alcoholism, and the third against corruption, particularly within the elite. In the short term, the campaigns would serve to boost economic performance by increasing productivity and tapping unused reserves of labor and capital. Moreover, the highly publicized attack on corrupt officials would assure the working class it was not the only target of renewed social discipline and simultaneously provide the new leadership with a device for replacing political opponents. However unpopular specific measures might have been, they succeeded in their larger purpose: to mobilize elite and popular support by creating from the onset an image of strong and decisive leadership determined to confront widely acknowledged social problems.

Gorbachev's third priority was to carry out an economic reform to arrest the stagnation in growth rates and introduce a self-sustaining process of technological innovation that would create the essential foundation for superpower status. The urgent need to shift from an extensive to an intensive pattern of economic growth had long been recognized, but bureaucratic inertia and political resistance had thwarted earlier, halfhearted attempts to reform under Brezhnev. Notwithstanding Gorbachev's clear commitment to significant economic reform, his dispositions are only slowly being translated into a coherent reform program; critical decisions concerning price reform, the supply system, or the relative roles of plan and market remain to be made. Nonetheless, the broad outlines of his approach can be discerned.

First, Gorbachev's strategy would simultaneously strengthen central control over strategic planning decisions and enhance initiative and responsibility at the management level by striking at the middle strata of the stifling economic bureaucracy. Management would enjoy greater latitude as well as increased responsibility; profitability would become the main criterion of performance; and bankruptcy would become the penalty for failure.

The work force as well as each enterprise will face a more competitive environment if the economic reform proceeds. A major revision of the wage structure allowing increased wage differentials, combined with a reduction in job security, will simultaneously increase the rewards for initiative and productivity as well as the penalties for failure.

The proposed reforms also seek to encourage private initiative in agriculture and in the services, where centralized planning has proved least effective, where poor quality and limited availability of desired goods and services has been a perennial source of complaints, where dependence on supplies from other sectors is lower than in much of industry, and where the precedent of Lenin's Economic Policy of 1921 makes ideological constraints less inhibiting. The expansion of collective farm markets selling agricultural produce in urban areas, the spread of private or cooperative restaurants, the encouragement of cooperative housing construction, and the creation of a network of establishments providing needed consumer services are seen as a modest contribution to improving the living conditions of the Soviet population, much as similar measures have done in Hungary. The success of such initiatives, however, depends on the cooperation of local authorities, and complaints abound of their resistance to new proposals.

Finally, Gorbachev's economic strategy also involves new international economic policies. Not yet clearly defined, they would rely on the limited use of joint ventures with capitalist firms and on greater involvement with international economic institutions to attract Western and Japanese capital, technology, entrepreneurship and managerial skills to Soviet enterprises. Moreover, by obliging joint ventures to produce for an international market as well as an internal one, economic policymakers are seeking to challenge Soviet enterprises to meet international standards of quality. What all these Soviet economic initiatives have in common is an increased reliance on the discipline of the marketplace to make Soviet products more competitive and to challenge the influence of a protectionism that has long insulated the Soviet economy from outside influences and protected enterprises and workers from the consequences of failure.

The effort to expand the role of market relationships in the framework of what remains a socialist command economy and to utilize economic levers in place of administrative control mechanisms is fraught with difficulty on technical grounds alone. Moreover, the challenge such change poses to habitual norms and practices evokes political and ideological resistance as well. Gorbachev has explicitly criticized those who view changes in the economic system as a retreat from the principles of socialism. He has, in effect, called into question the identification of Stalinism with socialism, and the assumption that socialism's features are immutable.[6] Challenging the relevance of the Stalinist economic model to contemporary needs, Gorbachev has insisted that "there will be no progress if we seek answers to new economic and technological questions in the experience of the 1930's, the 1940's, the 1950's, or even of the 1960's and the 1970's. . . ."[7]

But the novelty and significance of Gorbachev's strategy go beyond the three priorities described so far. They lie in Gorbachev's recognition that Soviet society has reached a level of maturity that requires a new approach to its governance, that the Soviet people, and particularly the educated middle classes, can no longer be treated as objects of official policy but must be regarded as genuine subjects. They express his growing realization, in short, that successful reform rests on redefining the relationship between state and society.

Khrushchev had launched the process of inclusion—a shift, however erratic, from the centralized, coercive statism of the Stalinist system to a more conciliatory and flexible approach to social forces.[8] Gorbachev seeks to extend it further. His advocacy of *glasnost'*, of cultural liberalization, and of democratization is not merely a tactical device to secure the support of the intelligentsia for his economic and political programs, or a public relations effort aimed at world opinion. It reflects a profound recognition that an embryonic civil society of autonomous political interchange has begun to emerge in the Soviet Union, and an unprecedented willingness to lend the process official encouragement.

The endorsement of *glasnost'*, with its simultaneous connotation of both candor and publicity, stands at the center of this effort to include the educated middle class in public life. It is, of course, a policy of preemption, intended to reduce the reliance of the Soviet population on foreign and unofficial sources of information—from foreign television and radio broadcasts to gossip—to fill the voids created by Soviet silence. The Chernobyl experience gave enormous impetus to this effort. The fact that the Soviet people first learned of a major domestic catastrophe with far-reaching implications for their own welfare from foreign broadcasts, and that the news was initially denied by their own government, was a major political embarrassment. It dramatized as never before the high costs of traditional Soviet secretiveness, both domestically and internationally, and it strengthened Gorbachev's determination to expand the flow of information and communication in order to enhance the leadership's credibility among its citizens.

Glasnost' is also a symbol of trust. To the extent that *glasnost'* is permitted, it reflects a recognition by the Soviet leadership of the maturity of the Soviet people, and a partial repudiation of the patronizing notion that only a small elite could be entrusted with truth. It marks at least a partial break with the entire Bolshevik conception of a vanguard party, premised as it was on the need for tutelage over backward masses.

It is equally an expression of confidence in the basic legitimacy of the Soviet system and in its leadership, a recognition that the pretense of infallibility is no longer necessary to command popular allegiance and support. Indeed, greater publicity for shortcomings and problems—be they the shoddy construction of nuclear power plants or the spread of drug addiction—is an indispensable precondition for successfully addressing them.

The case for *glasnost'* and its intimate connection to the prospects for reform was most eloquently put by Tatyana Zaslavskaya, the reformist sociologist, who argued in a remarkable article in *Pravda:* "If we continue to keep from the people information about the conditions under which they live, say the degree of environmental pollution, the number of industrial accidents, or the extent of crime, we cannot expect them to assume a more active role in economic or in political life. People will trust and support you only if you trust them."[9] It goes without saying that the issue of trust has important international as well as domestic ramifications.

Finally and of potential significance for the future, *glasnost'* is linked to accountability. An expanded and more independent role for the media—including serious investigative reporting—is an important instrument for exposing abuses of power and position and for holding officials accountable for their actions. Needless to say, it also offers a convenient weapon to use against political opponents. It is nonetheless of great importance that *glasnost'* has extended, in however tentative a manner, to the first gingerly exposés of abuses by the police and the KGB.

Even military affairs still largely exempted from public discussion have begun to receive closer scrutiny.[10] In a round table discussion reported in *Literaturnaia gazeta*, a group of scientists criticized the drafting of university students, arguing that "our society does not need soldiers more than it needs . . . physicists, biologists, engineers and social scientists."[11] Even the morality of nuclear weapons has been openly challenged in the press, with a well-known Belorussian writer, A. Adamovich, arguing that "for me there are no military men more courageous and worthier than those who . . . give their military expertise to the antiwar movement." The future treatment of such issues will be a key barometer of the scope and limits of official candor.[12]

Dramatic new departures in Soviet cultural policy—the most far-reaching and tangible of Gorbachev's reforms thus far—reflect a similar redefinition of the role of the state in the arts and an orientation toward inclusion and trust. The publication of long suppressed poems and novels, and the public screening of controversial films long kept from public view, are not only a form of reconciliation with the intelligentsia but an expression of a more tolerant and encompassing approach to Soviet culture. The reappraisal of the contributions of writers and poets such as Mikhail Bulgakov, Boris Pasternak, Marina Tsvetaeva, and Anna Akhmatova, once scorned for their deviation from "socialist realism," extends the boundaries of licit literature to include figures previously outside them. And in contrast with the cultural thaw of the Khrushchev era, current approaches also involve a partial devolution of cultural decisionmaking from the center.

In the historical and social sciences as well as in culture, darker aspects of Soviet life have been brought to the forefront, and the positive hero of "socialist realism" has moved off center stage. It is above all the Stalin era that is emerging as a central subject, as well as a major source of controversy. Two important cultural events of recent months—the announced publication of Anatoly Rybakov's *Children of the Arbat* and the screening of Tengiz Abuladze's powerful film *Repentance*—involve unprecedently frank and powerful evocations of the crimes of the Stalin era, with clear lessons for the present. At the same time, the literary and cultural journals that review these works have become a forum for major public debates, with clear political ramifications. A recent review of *Repentance* vividly captured its mood:

> Don't we sometimes hear, even from young people, the proposition, at bottom a monstrous one, that in the past, under Stalin, there was greater order? But what kind of order was it? The people's life took its normal course, to be sure, and many people still retain bright memories of that time of economic development and construction. They are pages of our life, of our history. But as far as the order that supposedly reigned during the repressions is concerned, the film gives an exhaustive answer on this score. The silent line, crushed by grief, that forms in front of the barred window from which an abrupt voice, totally unlike that of a human being, barks

out something rather than speaking it. . . . So many mistakes, so many personal tragedies and painful lessons are hidden in the past that this scene cannot slake our thirst for retribution and repentance in one sitting . . . we know too many cases in which an exposed evil was, after a while, declared to be a good again, and the graves of criminals were once more decorated as seemly monuments. That is why you want this frame to be repeated again and again, until there is not one person left among us who dares to say that "when you chop wood, the chips will fly" and that the bright edifice of the future can be built on the blood of innocent ruined people. . . .[13]

Renewed attention to the crimes of the Stalin era also invites reexamination of the alternatives to Stalin, and one result has been the emergence of Lenin's associates and the victims of Stalinism—Bukharin, Trotsky, Zinoviev, and others—from decades of oblivion. A more forthcoming and accurate treatment of early Soviet history received the endorsement of Gorbachev himself, who urged that "forgotten names and blank spots" in Soviet history be filled in, although others within the leadership have been notably less sympathetic to what they view as an unwarranted tendency to minimize the achievements of the past.

Indeed, a real transformation of Soviet ideology is itself under way, most visibly in the Party's ideological journal, *Kommunist,* wherein Lenin's conception of a single truth and an infallible approach to problems no longer holds sway; its articles present diverse and even conflicting approaches to current problems, and readers' letters often include sharp critiques of key points. The introduction of formal debate on Soviet television, with its presentation of two diametrically opposed positions on major issues of the day—including the desirability of reform or whether Gorbachev should go to Reykjavik—without any final resolution, is also a dramatic departure from long-standing behavior.

Gorbachev clearly aligned himself with the advocates of ideological change at the January 1987 Central Committee plenum when he criticized what he called a "schematic and dogmatic approach" to Party ideology. He attacked the persistence of theoretical concepts that had remained unchanged since the 1930's and the 1940's while the country's needs had fundamentally changed, the disappearance of vigorous debates and creative ideas, the absence of competition and conflict, and the absolutizing of particular authors and particular points of view which, Gorbachev implied, ought to have been treated as contingent and context-dependent. And he explicitly criticized portrayals of Soviet society that denied the diversity of groups and interests, and the possibility of conflicts among them, as a denial of social dynamism itself.

Gorbachev's speech echoed a striking article that had appeared in late 1986 in *Izvestiia* calling for greater debate and controversy on major issues of the day. "We must get used to the idea that a multiplicity of voices is a natural part of openness," its author, Aleksandr Vasinsky, had argued.

> We must treat diversity normally, as the natural state of the world; not with clenched teeth, as in the past, but normally as an immutable feature of social life. . . . We need in the economy and other areas of Soviet life a situation where multiple variants and alternative solutions are in and of themselves development tools and preconditions for obtaining optimal results, and where the coexistence of two opposing points of view on a single subject is most fruitful.

Reminding his audience of the high price paid in the past for intolerance toward other opinions, he concludes: "We must learn to live under democratic conditions."[14]

All of these themes come together in the issue that has emerged as the most fundamental—and the most explosive—dimension of Gorbachev's strategy: his advocacy of democratization. In recent months Gorbachev appears to have concluded that the success of the entire reform effort ultimately depends on whether the Soviet population can be actively engaged in the process, and whether a greater sense of participation will at least partially compensate for the absence of other immediate payoffs. His campaign for democratization seeks to encourage more extensive grass roots involvement in economic and political life, more candid discussions of problems in the workplace and in local, state and Party organizations, and greater accountability by leaders.

In a succession of speeches to workers and Party officials, Gorbachev has repeatedly called for open competition in elections of factory managers, members of local soviets and Party leaders, and the media have sought to provide concrete illustrations of how such novel elections might work in practice. Although Gorbachev's proposals for the competitive election of Party officials were not formally approved by the January 1987 plenum—and indeed their controversial nature was underlined by Gorbachev's admission that the plenum itself had to be postponed three times—he has pressed ahead with his campaign, has encouraged local and republic Party organizations to experiment with such elections, and has made it clear that electoral reform is high on his political agenda. It is equally evident that his efforts are encountering fierce resistance, and numerous accounts abundantly illustrate the way in which such reforms can be subverted.

Gorbachev's increasing focus on the need for democratization has brought to the forefront a fundamental tension that runs through virtually the entire reform effort: the desire to enhance initiative versus the fear of loss of control. Responding to widespread concerns that democratization would weaken discipline and undermine Party and government control, Gorbachev has insisted that "democracy is not the antithesis of order. . . . On the contrary, it is order on the higher level, based not on unthinking obedience and the blind execution of directives but on the full-fledged and resourceful participation of members of society in all undertakings."[15] Acknowledging that the effort will encounter serious difficulties, Gorbachev expressed the ultimate source of his confidence: "There is no need to fear if some things don't run smoothly at first. . . . We have a mature society and a strong Party. The socialist system rests on an extremely strong foundation of the people's support. . . ."[16] Nonetheless, the potential for turbulence and conflict is very real; indeed, Kunaev might well have been the first beneficiary of genuinely free elections in Kazakhstan!

The enormity of the challenge he has launched and the limited support on which it is based have compelled Gorbachev to seek new instruments of leverage. In the effort to overcome the resistance and inertia of the Party and state bureaucracies and to mobilize broader support for his programs, both domestically and internationally, Gorbachev has turned to the media as a major political resource. Indeed, one of the most intriguing features of the recent Soviet scene is the way in which the media have emerged as a novel and influential instrument of political power. Mass access to television has, in a very short time, rendered obsolete the entire *agitprop* system that was long the linchpin of Soviet political socialization, and Gorbachev is the first Soviet leader to appreciate fully and utilize this development. By placing supporters in key positions in ideological and cultural institutions—for example, as head of the ideological and cultural department within the Central Committee, or as the editors of influential journals such as *Kommunist* and *Pravda*—he has sought to shape the terms of the debate over reform to his political advantage and to compensate for his relative weakness in the more traditional organs of power.

The Impact of Reform on Foreign Policy

In foreign as in domestic policy, Gorbachev's succession has prompted a serious reassessment of previous assumptions and policies, and has brought with it a number of new departures in substance as well as style. Although the foreign policy changes thus far remain modest compared with domestic ones, the new flexibility manifest in Moscow—reinforced by changes of personnel in key positions—carries the potential for fresh approaches in a number of areas.

Gorbachev's foreign policy, as he himself has argued on several occasions, is a direct outgrowth of his domestic priorities. The two are more closely entwined at this juncture than at any previous time in postwar Soviet history. Reform is not only the key to domestic revitalization, in Gorbachev's view; it is essential to sustain the Soviet Union's international role. To gain the time necessary to consolidate his power and carry out his domestic programs, Gorbachev urgently needs both a respite from external pressures and evidence of external success. He has therefore centered his efforts on shaping an international environment that will be compatible with domestic reform, and a foreign policy that recognizes the nonmilitary dimensions of security. The key challenge he confronts is to reframe Soviet policies without jeopardizing the major strategic and political gains of the 1970's—and his own position with them.

Gorbachev's approach has two key features. The first is his effort to revive the atrophied instruments of Soviet diplomacy to project a more positive and dynamic Soviet image abroad, to convey an image of moderation, good neighborliness and willingness to seek political settlements to outstanding issues, while reducing the costs and risks of Soviet involvements in the international arena. The second is to extricate the Soviet Union from dead-end positions where this can be accomplished without threatening Soviet geostrategic interests and alliance systems.

As in domestic affairs, the bases of a more dynamic and flexible Soviet foreign policy were created by a series of organizational and personnel changes that altered the foreign policymaking process itself. The replacement of the veteran foreign minister, Andrei Gromyko, by Eduard Shevardnadze, signaled Gorbachev's determination to assert direct control over foreign as well as domestic policy, and to distance the new Soviet leadership from some of the liabilities of its predecessors. Equally significant in laying the foundation for new initiatives was the shift of responsibility for policy planning from the Foreign Ministry to the International Department of the Central Committee, and the replacement of its veteran and ideological head, Boris Ponomarev, by Anatoly Dobrynin, assisted by a knowledgeable staff with substantial experience abroad. The Foreign Ministry was reorganized to make it more responsive to new international trends, and in a personnel shake-up new ambassadors were appointed to the United States, China and Japan.

Changes in the leadership of key foreign policy institutes and publications, and the call for "new political thinking," further signaled Gorbachev's apparent interest in fresh approaches, or at least his desire to distance himself from the policies of his predecessors.

Gorbachev's initial strategy has focused above all on an effort to reduce tensions simultaneously with the United States and China and to reap the domestic political benefits of that achievement. It rests on the recognition that the military buildup and confrontational foreign policy pursued by his predecessors not only failed to enhance Soviet security but may have endangered it by provoking military countermeasures and greater political coordination in both Western Europe and Asia. As in the lesson of the famous children's fable, "North Wind and the Sun," Gorbachev understands that threats and pressure are less likely to elicit the outcomes he desires than an accommodating and flexible posture. Without as yet offering far-reaching and fundamental concessions to either country, Soviet policy has demonstrated a strikingly greater responsiveness to the long-standing concerns of both.

The United States remains the central Soviet preoccupation, and arms control its primary focus. Soviet policy in the past two and a half years has been marked by new initiatives across the entire range of arms control negotiations, as well as by an unprecedented willingness to address the thorny problem of verification. When important Soviet concessions on strategic arms limitations failed to alter the Reagan administration's commitment to SDI, Gorbachev swiftly refocused the negotiations on an International Nuclear Forces (INF) agreement instead, and added short-range systems to the package. The INF accord signed December 8, 1987 in Washington by Reagan and Gorbachev marked the first Soviet-American agreement to reduce stocks of nuclear weapons.

Apparent shifts in Soviet doctrine toward an emphasis on sufficiency rather than on parity may well be intended to reduce internal pressures to "keep up with the U.S." In an effort to blunt possible political challenges, Gorbachev has accused advocates of stepped-up military spending of playing into American efforts at economic warfare.

Soviet policy under Gorbachev has also demonstrated an exceptionally subtle appreciation of the domestic forces affecting American foreign policy, both in its recognition that extreme Soviet secretiveness helped feed Western mistrust and fear of Soviet intentions and in its readiness to modify some of the more odious previous practices concerning human rights and Jewish emigration. The return of Andrei Sakharov from exile and the release of a number of prominent dissidents and refuseniks were important gestures in this effort, as were the decisions to allow a group of American scientists to monitor Soviet underground nuclear tests, and a Congressional delegation to visit the controversial Krasnoyarsk radar site.

The improvement in Soviet relations with China, which had taken its first halting steps under Brezhnev in 1983, was similarly given new impetus following Gorbachev's accession to power. Gorbachev's own commitment to reform contributed to a more positive view of developments in China than had previously prevailed within the Soviet leadership, and an acknowledgment that, like the Soviet Union, China was engaged in an effort to build "a socialist society worthy of a great people."[17] Indeed, generally greater tolerance for diversity within the socialist community has been a hallmark of the Gorbachev era.

Several concrete overtures to the Chinese leadership offered modest concessions to longstanding Chinese positions, including a reduction of Soviet troop deployments in Mongolia, and the demarcation of the disputed Amur River border, itself a departure from the traditional Soviet refusal to cede territory. While the Soviet position has not significantly changed on the one issue of central concern to the Chinese leadership—the Vietnamese occupation of Cambodia—and although important differences divide the two countries on a number of issues, the expansion of Sino-Soviet economic, cultural, and political ties has brought tangible benefits to the USSR, and has considerably diminished what was once a serious security threat.

Soviet efforts to repair strained relations with Japan are yet another manifestation of Gorbachev's desire to create a more benign environment for domestic reform. A new recognition of Japan's economic and strategic importance, as well as a desire to extricate Soviet diplomacy from the antagonistic and unproductive posture it had assumed under Gromyko, prompted a visit to Tokyo by Shevardnadze and hints of possible Soviet flexibility concerning the northern territories, although no significant concessions have thus far been proferred.

These and other Soviet initiatives around the globe nonetheless constitute a concerted and ambitious effort to overcome the political isolation and economic marginality of Moscow in the early 1980's, particularly in the vital and dynamic Asian region, to regain the diplomatic initiative, and to win breathing space for domestic revitalization. But it remains unclear whether Gorbachev's strategy entails only marginal and essentially tactical shifts, leaving unchanged core features of traditional arrangements and policies, or whether a new calculus of Soviet interests will ultimately lead to more far-reaching changes in Soviet international behavior.

The Prospects

Gorbachev's reforms have already brought important changes to the Soviet system, but they are by no means irreversible. Indeed, all the evidence suggests that Gorbachev is pursuing a high-risk strategy that confronts deep-seated obstacles to success.

Although significant policy changes across a wide range of areas are already evident, as these changes increasingly impinge on core institutional arrangements the obstacles, and the resistance, mount. This is especially true of efforts at economic reform, where key features of the Soviet economy are not only closely intermeshed, but tightly bound to the nature of the Soviet political system and ultimately to the role of the Party itself. To shift from the administrative allocation of resources to an increased reliance on market mechanisms is ultimately to challenge the very raison d'etre of the Party, in the USSR as well as in China. It is equally the case in foreign and security policy, where Gorbachev's unsettling initiatives have challenged the status of two key institutions: the KGB and the military.

Thus, reform is not only a technical process but a highly political one, involving fundamental changes in the allocation of resources, status and power. It has already brought latent and long-repressed conflicts of interest in the USSR to the surface, and is likely to trigger further manifestations of working class and nationality grievances, in particular. The effort to promote competition, to increase the rewards for success and the penalties for failure, and to reduce the scale of state subsidies by, in effect, shrinking the economic safety net would deprive important segments of the working class of what by now are perceived as customary entitlements. Similarly, just as the comparative immobilism of the center during the Brezhnev era allowed regional elites to enhance their economic and political power, Gorbachev's efforts to regain central control over cadre policy, to redirect resources away from Central Asia, and to challenge the preferential treatment of indigenous nationalities, not only represent a more assertive, if not coercive, nationality policy; they are clearly a serious challenge to local prerogatives.

The demonstrations in Kazakhstan, and the workers' protests that erupted when the new system of quality control resulted in the rejection of such volumes of shoddy goods that wages were reduced, provide but two examples of the way in which these new policies threaten long-standing expectations. Cultural liberalization, political democratization and *glasnost'* are a potent recipe for ever greater expression of grievances and for unprecedented manifestations of social and political conflict in a system long unaccustomed to dealing with them openly, as the demonstrations by Crimean Tatars and Baltic nationalists make clear. Managing these tensions effectively will pose a major political challenge.

Another source of resistance lies in the bureaucracy itself, a largely passive resistance of established routines, of inertia, but one which has demonstrated a formidable capacity over the years to absorb and domesticate reforms rather than be transformed by them.

Beyond passive resistance Gorbachev confronts outright political opposition, not yet highly visible, not yet organized, and without as yet an alternative program of its own, but an opposition that draws sustenance from the widespread anxiety that the changes have already provoked by blurring familiar boundaries, eroding stable expectations, and bringing long-repressed conflicts to public attention. Abundant evidence is available, if any is needed, of bitter antagonism to many of Gorbachev's domestic initiatives, including the relase of prominent dissidents, what is perceived as an excessively critical assessment of the Stalin era, the attack on elite privileges, and the potential challenge of democratization to the very role of the *nomenklatura* (holders of high posts subject to Party approval). Opposition to a number of measures in the foreign policy and security domain, while less visible, may be equally real.[18]

Finally, Eastern Europe constitutes a significant constraint on the prospects for reform in the Soviet Union. The irony of Gorbachev's triumphal visit to Prague—accompanied by the Czech Party leader who owed his position to the defeat of Alexander Dubcek—and his lukewarm reception in Romania, was hardly lost on Eastern Europe. Gorbachev and his colleagues have learned the lessons of 1968, and may well be determined that instability in Eastern Europe will never again be permitted to halt the reform of the Soviet system. But the situation is inherently unstable, and a serious eruption in Eastern Europe is bound to reverberate in Moscow.

Gorbachev's reforms seek to tap the sources of vitality and dynamism that have increasingly developed outside the Soviet system, to draw back into the official economy, polity and culture individuals and activities that had deserted it or been excluded from it. At home, it is an effort to enlist the talents and energies of the Soviet population—from Andrei Sakharov to avant-garde writers and artists, from second economy entrepreneurs to alienated workers and youth—in the revitalization of the Soviet system by supporting more genuine participation by them in managing its affairs. It is an effort to alter the Soviet role internationally as well, by identifying Moscow with support for peace, for nuclear disarmament, for political accommodation, and for interdependence, and by cultivating ties to a wider range of movements and actors abroad.

Whether or not Gorbachev's far-reaching effort to reform the Soviet system will prove successful, and indeed how to measure success, remains an open question. But in domestic as in foreign policy, it has introduced new approaches and a new degree of fluidity that deserve to be welcomed as well as tested at home and abroad.

Notes

1. For a more detailed analysis of these trends, see the author's chapter in *After Brezhnev: Sources of Soviet Conduct in the 1950's,* ed. R. Byrnes (Indiana University Press, 1983), pp. 186–249.

2. A more extensive treatment can be found in Gail W. Lapidus, "Gorbachev and the Reform of the Soviet System," *Daedalus,* Spring 1987.

3. K. U. Chernenko, *Kommunist,* no. 13, September 1981, pp. 10–11; Gorbachev in *Pravda,* January 28, 1987.

4. The Party program adopted in 1961 was the quintessential expression of Khrushchev's unbounded optimism, with its extravagant prediction that in twenty years Soviet economic output would outstrip that of the United States, and its promise that the Soviet population would enjoy material abundance. The most striking features of the new Party programs adopted under Gorbachev are the modesty and lack of concreteness of their goals.

5. Khabarovsk speech in *Pravda,* August 2, 1986.

6. *Pravda,* February 6, 1987.

7. *Pravda,* August 2, 1986. For a coherent statement of Gorbachev's economic and ideological approaches, see *Pravda,* June 26, 1987. On private economic initiative, see chapter 2.

8. The most original treatment of this theme is Kenneth Jowitt's "Inclusion and Mobilization in Marxist-Leninist Political Systems," *World Politics,* XXVIII, 1 (October 1975), pp. 69–97.

9. *Pravda,* February 6, 1987.

10. It is significant that the continuing presence of such "forbidden zones" has itself become a subject of discussion in the Soviet media.

11. *Literaturnaia gazeta,* May 13, 1987. Sharp responses to this discussion by military figures were carried in *Literaturnaia gazeta,* June 8, and *Krasnaia zvezda,* May 22, 1987.

12. FBIS, Soviet Union-Daily Reports, March 24, 1987, pp. AA 13. An account of this exchange is offered by Stephen Foye, "Intellectuals Attack the Military," *Sovset Newsletter,* Vol. III, No. 9, July 30, 1987, based on a Radio Liberty analysis by Thomas Nichols. On the military see also chapters 5 and 7.

13. T. Khlopiankina, in *Moskovskaia pravda*, February 4, 1987, p. 4.

14. Aleksandr Vasinsky, in *Izvestiia*, October 28, 1986.

15. Speech to the Trade Union Congress, *Pravda*, February 26, 1987.

16. Ibid.

17. Vladivostok speech, *Pravda*, July 29, 1986.

18. For example, the military's concerns over the Soviet moratorium on nuclear testing were openly expressed, and questions raised by a leading political analyst about Soviet SS-20 deployments in Europe were sharply refuted by a military spokesman. For a useful discussion of the attitude of the military to economic reforms, see George G. Weickhardt, "The Soviet Military-Industrial Complex and Economic Reform," in *Soviet Economy*, Vol. 2, No. 3 (July–September 1986), pp. 193–220 and the comments by Julian Cooper and Timothy Colton.

Prospects for *Perestroika:* New Goals, Old Interests

Peter H. Juviler

Mikhail Gorbachev wasted no time in summoning his country to a renewal, after assuming the office of General Secretary on March 11, 1985. He subsequently intensified the drive for reform until all but the most cynical Soviet watchers saw his program of *perestroika*, or reconstruction of Soviet economic, social and political life, as more than a public relations stunt. Even many doubters of its feasibility saw in *perestroika* a vision of the most far-reaching transformation since Stalin's "revolution from above" of the late 1920's and early 1930's.

What are the prospects for *perestroika?* Will it justify the hope that liberals and reformers saw in Gorbachev before he assumed power? Will the reform effort Gorbachev initiated serve to end the Soviet economic decline and social demoralization that spread during Leonid Brezhnev's eighteen years as General Secretary, briefly slowed during Yuri Andropov's fleeting term (November 1982 to February 1984), and resumed under the "living corpse," Konstantin Chernenko?[1]

The ultimate test of Gorbachev's transforming vision will not be whether the USSR literally attains the unlikely goals he set at the 27th Party Congress in 1986—solving the housing problem, doubling the Soviet national product and growth rates, and developing a world-class, high-tech economy by the year 2000.[2] A fairer and more meaningful test will be the pace and success of such goals' prerequisite, *perestroika*.

According to Gorbachev and his advisers,[3] Soviet economic revitalization depends on the pace and success of what Gorbachev has termed "no less than a revolutionary *perestroika*," or transformation, of Soviet society and economic relations, "the key to all our problems immediate and long term, economic and social, political and ideological." Nothing short of such radical change, in his view, would achieve his ultimate goal of "social and economic *uskorenie*"—acceleration—a speedup of growth and a rapid modernization of the antiquated, stagnating, and inefficient economy.[4]

21

Outright pessimists have deemed *perestroika* to be impossible because of the formidable resistance to reform of the sort that brought Khrushchev down in 1964,[5] and because of the inherent contradiction between Party control and the liberated social and political spontaneity essential for reform.[6]

On the other side of the discussion were those who viewed the bitter struggle over the future of the USSR as undecided. From this perspective, *perestroika* has never been certain to succeed, nor has it been doomed inevitably to failure. Aware of obstacles to reform, the cautiously expectant observers have given more weight to positive factors than have the outright pessimists. They see the time as ripe for forward movement, given the confluence of urgency, determined leadership by the man "with a nice smile but iron teeth,"[7] and a Soviet society structurally ready for change—urbanized, and well informed—if not yet enamored of reform.[8]

After these assessments were made, *perestroika* encountered growing difficulties and complexities in all spheres.[9] The time may seem ripe for *perestroika* to those like Gorbachev who believe that "*perestroika* is mandated by burning and urgent necessity" so great that "the costs of marking time, of stagnation, and of indifference are far more telling and great than the costs which we incur for a time in the process of creating new forms of social life." But it does not seem so ripe to "conservative forces who see in *perestroika* nothing but a threat to their own selfish interests and goals," and whose resistance, said Gorbachev, is "intensifying."[10]

Perestroika, if it continues, will likely be, in Gorbachev's words, "a comparatively prolonged process . . . with its own logic and stages."[11] As Abraham Brumberg has concluded "healthy skepticism is justifiable but not to the point of dismissing the possibility of change."[12]

The ultimate prerequisite for a successful *perestroika* appears to be a shift from centralized controls to autonomy and spontaneity in Soviet public life—in expression, participation and motivated individual initiative at work.

That is why, from the beginning of his leadership, Gorbachev has emphasized that the success of reform lay not only in the technical-financial side of development, though there are many problems in this area, but also in the "human factor."[13] This will mean drawing the public into the national effort—hence the particular importance of, first, overcoming conflicts of interest over reform that recall the context of Khrushchev's failures, and, second, promoting *glasnost'*, democratization and social justice. The rest of this chapter touches on these aspects of the quest for *perestroika*.

Fatal Parallels?

Sobering and instructive, though not necessarily fatal, parallels have been drawn between *perestroika* and past reform efforts in Russia, the Socialist orbit, and the USSR after Stalin.

Perestroika, Gorbachev recalled, comes as the latest historical instance of "revolution from above." This he said means "profound and essentially revolutionary changes implemented on the initiative of the authorities themselves but necessitated by objective changes in the situation and in social moods."[14] In this case, "the authorities" were the Communist Party,[15] the latest manifestation of "autocratic power" bringing revolution from above to Imperial Russia and the USSR.[16]

But Gorbachev of himself is no autocrat. His task is all the more complicated for the lack of such terror and compulsion rulers such as Ivan the Terrible or Peter the Great used to first "weaken the grip of the ruling elite that he had inherited, and then shape it to his own will."[17]

Moreover, domestic revolution and reform could lead to retreat by triggering upheaval in Eastern Europe. Unease with *perestroika* and fear of unrest haunt the leaders of some East European countries.[18] Soviet East European policy faces choices between the possibility of unrest due to economic stagnation, or unrest due to the dislocations and opening up of reform.[19] Present Soviet dilemmas in Eastern Europe, however, have not yet reached the level of revolutionary crisis, which dogged Khrushchev's domestic reform efforts almost from the start.[20] Also lacking today is Khrushchev's calamitous and costly ideological race with China to be the first to enter into communism. On the contrary, Sino-Soviet relations have been gradually improving, while China heads in the same general direction of economic reform as the USSR.

Watchers of the home front have espied "remarkable parallels between Khrushchev and Gorbachev." Both leaders pursued vigorous and bold strategies disproportionate to the limitations of their power in the face of dogged resistance.[21] Gorbachev, too, faced a clash of interest with the Soviet bureaucracy that tended to obstruct the implementation of reform in a manner well known to the Russian tsars.[22]

For Gorbachev, the primary problem was to resolve the contradiction between the "present state and the needs of Soviet development," and the now-obsolete, overcentralized, bureaucratized "mechanism braking progress" that stifles spontaneous initiative and encourages inertia and mediocrity.[23] The "mechanism braking progress" is the vast bureaucratic apparatus and habits of command and obedience, patronage and dependency that worked Stalin's will for a powerful USSR, but years ago became an obsolete impediment to modernization.

Just one of many signs of Gorbachev's problems with his government and Party machinery came in a Central Committee report during which Gorbachev criticized for their lack of initiative, incompetence, or excessive dependence on the center no fewer than fifteen ministries or state committees, thirteen of their heads, including the powerful heads of Gosplan and Gossnab (the State Committee for Supplies), whom he had appointed himself, delinquent Party organizations, and thirty republics or regions.[24] Gorbachev leveled his scorn against officials who wanted to "tinker" ineffectually with the system rather than change it. *Perestroika,* said Gorbachev, has brought out the contradiction between "conservatism, inertia, and selfish interests" on the one hand, and "needs for renewal, innovation, and creative initiative" on the other.

The administrators cannot but be aware of commentator Fedor Burlatskii's article calling "the 18 million people in the administrative apparatus . . . too high a price for carrying centralization to extremes." Informed Soviets point out that, including the Party, trade union, and youth league bureaucrats, the total may run to twenty-five million. That is almost one fifth of the Soviet work force. Burlatskii suggests that the administrative apparatus could usefully be cut to one half or one third its present size.[25] When asked if the bureaucrats can be expected to remove themselves, high Soviet officials conceded that the visitor had a "good point."[26] But unless the reform wave can sweep out opposition and incompetents among ministers and managers, an old chestnut of an anecdote will still apply: a peasant is asked, what do you think of Gorbachev's reforms? The peasant scratches his head and replies, "It's like the *taiga* [Siberian forest], with lots of rustling noises at the top, but everything quiet and still at the bottom."

Viktor Chebrikov, head of the KGB, depicted the extremes of *glasnost'* as the result of imperialist agents' subversive influence on susceptible Soviet writers.[27] The more far-reaching openness, *glasnost'*, turns out to be, the more resentment it could generate in the KGB[28] and the more crucial could be Gorbachev's firm control of that agency and a friendly military. Yet as Tsuyoshi Hasegawa writes in Chapter 7, Gorbachev has mixed support from the military. It is divided over disapproval of nuclear strategy, and the benefits of diverting funds from arms to modernize Soviet industrial technology.[29] Arms reduction agreements are likely to have opponents in the military, especially if they think that the U.S. is getting away with too much latitude concerning development of the SDI, with all the new offensive threat this may pose from a Soviet perspective.[30]

Luck, timing and determination, however, may have increased Gorbachev's authority with the military in the wake of the West German

Mathias Rust's unscheduled penetration of Soviet airspace and subsequent landing in his Cessna light airplane on Red Square on May 28, 1987. As luck would have it, this was the Soviet "Day of the Border Troops," and the morrow of a successful undetected flight out to Swedish asylum by a Soviet crop dusting pilot. A special Politburo communiqué lambasted the military publicly for its "laxness," "indecisiveness," and "lack of necessary vigilance." The same communiqué announced the dismissal of the commander-in-chief of the air defense forces and "the strengthening of the leadership of the Ministry of Defense."[31] Gorbachev obtained the prompt retirement of Minister of Defense, Marshal Sergei Sokolov, and replaced him with an officer of his choice, General Dmitri T. Yazov, who was subsequently promoted to nonvoting membership in the Politburo.[32] The humiliation of the military continued when, in his report to the Central Committee, Gorbachev called Rust's successful flight and landing in Moscow "uprecedented from all points of view," an example of how persistent and strong, "even in the army," are the sort of "indiscipline," "irresponsibility," and "disorganization" that the Party has been trying to expose and eliminate.[33]

In sum, Gorbachev's important relationship with the Soviet military shows gains for Gorbachev as well as the possibility of future disagreements. Chebrikov has been an ally, and a powerful one, but he and Yegor Ligachev, the Party's virtual second-in-command, seem to be pushing to limit the pace and scope of *perestroika*.[34] It seems that millions of bureaucrats will be only too happy if they succeed, though for many bureaucrats, it is doubtful that Chebrikov's and Ligachev's reservations about *perestroika* go far enough.

Significant Differences?

Any comparison of Khrushchev and Gorbachev should consider the significant differences in their timing and circumstances, and in the leaders' styles and strategies.

The first difference between Khrushchev and Gorbachev is that Gorbachev had a longer start with reform than did Khrushchev. Gorbachev had been a Party Central Committee secretary since 1978, nonvoting Politburo member since 1979, full member since 1980 when projects for reform circulated. The best-educated of Party leaders, and the first university graduate since Lenin, Gorbachev belonged to an innovative group around Andropov that could draw on the experience of thirty years' thinking and efforts to promote economic reform.[35]

Timing can help explain Alexei Kosygin's failures at reform in 1965, early in Brezhnev's leadership. In addition, Kosygin was prime minister; he lacked the power of a general secretary, and he faced a Party head who was at best indifferent to reform if it rocked the boat in any way, which of course it must do.[36]

Second, the overall economic picture had seriously deteriorated since Khruschev's day. The ailing Andropov barely had time during his 15 months as general secretary, in between Brezhnev's 18 years and Chernenko's 13 months, to begin to crack down and experiment with reform.[37] Economic advisers who later moved into prominence under Gorbachev prepared, during Andropov's time, frank analyses of the obsolescence of the 50-year-old command economy inherited from Stalin. They showed a drop in GNP growth by the early 1980's to 2.5%, or only one third the growth rate of 7.5% in the period 1966–1970, early Brezhnev years. Moreover, the analyses ran, economic reform should deal not only with the economic administrative mechanism, but with the human problems of a resisting ministerial bureaucracy and a work force dispirited and demoralized by being too long treated as mere "cogs in the economic mechanism," and who "behaved accordingly—almost as obediently (passively) as machines and materials."[38]

Gorbachev could blend such dire information and pointed advice into a case reinforcing his argument that the risks of *perestroika* were less than the risks of allowing the contradiction to fester between the needs of development and the obsolete system of economic administration.[39]

The third difference between past and present lies in the personality and style of the two Party leaders. Khrushchev behaved more impulsively and inconsistently than Gorbachev did. He lacked Gorbachev's patience and skill.[40]

A fourth difference between Gorbachev and Khrushchev is that on the agricultural front, Gorbachev turned in a better record than Khrushchev, who brought devastation to grasslands with his mania for corn planting (earning him the contemptuous sobriquet "Nikita Kukuruznik," Nick the corn man), and who damaged food production with his dogmatic drive against private garden plots.

Fifth, Gorbachev's relationship with his allies among writers and artists and professionals lacks the stormy, unpredictable, love–hate element that alienated Khrushchev's liberal supporters.[41]

A sixth difference between Gorbachev and Khrushchev concerns the thrust of reform. Khrushchev saw economic development as a way of winning a peaceful competition with the West, to which he said, "We will bury you." This meant large aid packets to nonaligned third world countries. They were curtailed after Khrushchev left office. Gorbachev, on the other hand, judging from the findings of Lapidus, Dallin and Hasegawa in this volume (Chapters 1, 5, and 7, respectively), looks to foreign policy to help divert resources into funding *perestroika* and to preserve Soviet superpower status, not to create expensive new foreign military or economic commitments. Undoubtedly, a less tense rivalry with the U.S., better relations with other noncommunist countries, especially in Asia, and successful arms reduction agreements following the INF reduction agreement of December 8, 1987, could make easier the allocation of resources among consumption, investment and defense, thus greatly assisting reform while enhancing Gorbachev's authority and popularity at home.[42]

In sum, alongside the ominous similarities between Khrushchev and Gorbachev, significant differences are discernible as well. Moreover, with all his failings and failures, Khrushchev remained General Secretary for 11 years (1953 to 1964). Whatever Khrushchev's repressions, especially in the area of religion, it should not be forgotten that his version of *glasnost'*, his attack on the Stalin cult, his significant curbs on secret police powers and massive rehabilitations of Stalin's victims, living and dead, paved the way for Gorbachev's *perestroika* 30 years later. That may be why Khrushchev, after 23 years of being a nonperson, ceased being a nonperson.

Glasnost

Beginning in 1986, domestic issues moved ahead of foreign relations in the list of the Party's May Day slogans, perhaps reflecting the shift in priorities inherent in *perestroika*. A recent addition to the slogans heralds *glasnost'* for the first time.[43] And why not? Of all the aspects of *perestroika*, *glasnost'* is the most advanced, in fact the only great change apparent in the USSR since *perestroika* began. The long lines for goods and food and the general and depressing dowdiness remain. But new lines now form at the kiosks to buy once-boring papers and magazines.

Glasnost' met a deep moral and occupational need of its intellectual proponents, some of whom had been testing the limits of a narrower toleration under Brezhnev.[44] The new openness pushed far back the existing limits of permitted public expression. It flourished after a campaign in 1985 by writers, poets and theatrical people for freedom from bureaucratism.[45]

Reservations some share about the purpose, depth, and stability of *glasnost'* do not take away from a sense of awe at its rapid flowering. Few if any could have foreseen in early 1985 that a cultural thaw would melt back controls under Gorbachev so extensively and rapidly that, among other things, the publication of long banned works by novelists such as Nabokov and Bulgakov, poets such as Gumilev and Akhmatova, would be possible. Other changes include the near-liberation of the film industry from ministerial control; the new frankness and diversity of television— *the* Soviet mass medium;[46] the public airing of once-taboo subjects ranging from calamities like the Chernobyl atomic plant disaster to an excursion boat's fatal collision and social evils like drug abuse and prostitution; the desirability of a free economic market, even with unemployment; the need for the truth about Stalin and his victims who are still not rehabilitated; published reports of the prosecution of KGB and Party officials for persecuting inquiring reporters; and exposés of psychiatrists for abuse of their power to commit a complaining medical patient or resident. The high point of it all, in February 1986, was Gorbachev's personal telephone call to academician Andrei Sakharov inviting him and his wife Elena Bonner back from their 5-year exile in Gorky without conditions, followed by releases of other political prisoners.

The openness went so far in 2 years, raised expectations so high, that Gorbachev's address on the occasion of the 70th anniversary of the October Revolution seemed an anticlimax. Yet, for such a public and solemn occasion, the speech was unprecedented in its handling of the past, with its "great achievements and bitter failures" and Stalin's "guilt for mass repressions and lawlessness." Equally unprecedented was its sober treatment of the present, when reform efforts confront a "lack of culture" resulting in "abuse of power, undue reverence for rank, bad management, and irresponsibility." To sense the effect (for the time at least) of *glasnost'* compare Gorbachev's sober and ground-breaking reflections with Brezhnev's unrelieved boasting to honor the 60th anniversary of the October Revolution 10 years earlier.[47]

Even harsh émigré critics of their former government have seen in no less than the Party organ, *Pravda,* "criticisms of Soviet reality that only a few years ago would have been branded as 'anti-Soviet slander' and rewarded accordingly."[48] *Glasnost'* has enabled Gorbachev to forge an alliance with the liberal intelligentsia "with notable success."[49] *Glasnost',* as Gorbachev sees it, permits the writers and journalists to lay bare problems needing urgent attention, providing feedback to the Party, protecting it from "mistakes in policy."[50] It mobilizes opinion and action against all those bureaucrats and people on the job who deliberately, or through inertia or corruption, threaten the process of restructuring.

We need more light now more than ever so that the Party and the people know everything, so that we have no dark corners where the mold can settle, and everything against which we now carry on a determined but far from completed struggle. Therefore—more light![51]

There is no reason to disagree with Andrei Sakharov's opinion about *glasnost'*: "It's not right to say that it's only propaganda or window dressing. Indeed, the rehabilitation of Nikolai Bukharin, champion of NEP, and other purge victims begins to lend an air of permanence to *glasnost'*.[52]

But respondents met in the USSR remain unsure that *glasnost'* cannot be decreed away, unlike the pop-*glasnost'* of Soviet youth culture, which flourishes outside the creative establishment and appears to be deeply institutionalized in living mores.[53]

Glasnost' proper is the result of patronage from on high no less than pressure from below. Its Communist Party sponsors face challenges from both friends and foes of change. On the one side comes bitter criticism from within the Party and from literary elites.[54] A champion of *glasnost'*, the poet Andrei Voznesensky, sees its champions "in a spiritual revolution, a fight to the death between the 'new thinking' and the still very powerful reactionary system that defines our society."[55]

The Party sponsors of *glasnost'* find themselves in conflict on their other flank with independent groups, advocates of everything from environmental protection and disarmament to democratic socialism, human rights, Russian national chauvinism, and in most cases a greater freedom of activity than the Party sponsors can comfortably entertain without possible threat to political order and to their relationship with the KGB. A banner carried at a quickly disbanded demonstration in Moscow summed up the issue: "We Demand Permission for the Free Activity of Public Organizations!" Defining the limits of that "free activity" will go on for years to come. Significantly, though, the struggle for "free activity" surfaced more in 1986–1987. It encompasses hundreds, perhaps thousands of independent groups across a spectrum of causes and political acceptability.[56]

The most deeply rooted, mass manifestation of aboveground, spontaneous group political expression has come from the nationalities, Russian and non-Russian. Nationality unrest may pose the gravest threat to *glasnost'* and to Gorbachev's power. The violent riots in Alma Ata in December 1986 came after the replacement of the Kazakh first secretary, Brezhnev's old crony, D. V. Kunaev, with a Russian. Gorbachev responded with firm condemnation of the Alma Ata riots as manifestations of "national chauvinism and parochialism." The riots in Alma Ata, Gorbachev said, should remind Party officials that "we cannot resolve a single basic issue . . . without recognizing that we live in a multinational society."[57]

Many national demonstrations, such as those of Baltic nationalists, Russian national extremists in the Pamyat (memory) organization, Crimean Tatars seeking to end their exile from their homeland (which began with the 1944 deportations due to their alleged collaboration with the Germans), and Armenians seeking unification with their nearly national republic have occurred not in response to Party political moves but in response to the opportunities presented by *glasnost'*.[58]

Soviet reaction to unofficial advocacy and demonstrations has been varied and unpredictable, ranging from noninterference (beyond surveillance) to violence, vituperation, and arrests.[59] It is not surprising that the authorities are inconsistent in their responses to unofficial demonstrations. They are busy trying to redefine their system's limits of tolerable spontaneity under the Party vanguard.

Glasnost' is a Party instrument of reform no less than it is the cherished goal of writers. As Hiroshi Kimura said at our seminar, supporters of it sleep in the same bed, but dream different dreams. For Gorbachev, *glasnost'* has served the political purpose of stimulating the rest of *perestroika*, thus speeding up Soviet economic and social development. Only time will tell how liberally Gorbachev or his successors will continue to interpret the "Leninist" guiding principles that mark a difficult course between defending *glasnost'* and defending the vanguard party. Gorbachev himself seems to lean toward openness. He avowed that excesses outside "the framework of socialism" will be countered "inside the framework of democracy and openness," and conceded to media people, uncharacteristically for a General Secretary, that "I may be mistaken about some things—I lay no claim to the absolute truth. We must look for the truth together." Moreover, Gorbachev warned enemies of *glasnost'* not to take his criticism of "demagogues . . . in some editorial offices of newspapers and magazines" who are "particularly vicious in their attacks on Party cadres" as a sign that they may demand "the end of all criticism."[60]

On the side of tolerance, even enthusiastic support, for the writers' truths about the past and the present, a political commentator of *Kommunist*, the theoretical journal of the Central Committee, I. Dedkov, came out with eloquent praise of "new thinking in literature." He cited with approval writers seeking frankness about repressions under a certain "person of less than medium height" [Stalin]. He welcomed the publication of long banned writers' works and the "new thinking" in literature that was bringing "both a new sensitivity and a new level of humaneness," allowing for real heroes who, unlike the "positive heroes" of more repressive recent periods in literature, could experience unhappiness. He called on writers to create the tide, not simply to float on it.[61] This strong plea for creative freedom might have been acceptable to Gorbachev, but not to all Party leaders.

The most notable opponents of expressive freedom early on were two powerful Politburo members: Central Committee Secretary Yegor Ligachev, and KGB head Viktor Chebrikov. Ligachev appeared to be a rigid, conservative proponent of "positive heroes" and "socialist realism." Chebrikov warned against Western efforts to subvert the Soviet system by encouraging openness in writing and the arts.[62]

Another cause for uncertainty about *glasnost'*, beyond pressures from independent advocacy and nationality groups and Party opposition, is that it lacks institutionalization of even the informal kind that sustains pop-*glasnost'*, let alone legal guarantees for freedom of expression, organization, and publishing, and for the inviolability of the person.[63] *Glasnost'* has been rooted in particularly shallow soil of the party line and needs of the moment. It can be easily displaced, to the detriment of *perestroika* in both domestic and foreign contexts. Gorbachev proclaimed Party free expression early in 1987:

> At plenums it is necessary to assure to every member of the Central Committee the right to raise issues and participate in their collective discussion. In the Party—and all the more so at Central Committee plenums—there cannot be persons who do not have the right to criticize.[64]

Yet Party openness and *glasnost'* generally were called into question when Boris Yel'tsin, staunch supporter of reform, spoke up at the Central Committee plenum of October 21, 1987, to criticize the slow pace of reform and leaders holding it back. This (unpublished) outburst precipitated events leading to Yel'tsin's dismissal from the post of First Party Secretary (boss) of Moscow. That came November 11, at a meeting of the Moscow City Party Committee presided over by Gorbachev, and featured a hail of (published) attacks on Yel'tsin by Party subordinates and colleagues, including Gorbachev, for his alleged willfulness, ambition and other shortcomings in leadership. The meeting was topped by Yel'tsin's apology for his arrogance. Subsequently, Yel'tsin was appointed deputy head of the State Committee on Construction, hospitalized with a heart attack, and then released from candidate membership of the Politburo.[65]

Yel'tsin's fall evoked widespread doubt and questions. How deep *was* Gorbachev's commitment to openness and reform? Yel'tsin's October 21 speech was unpublished (as usual for plenum discussion nowadays), but the attacks on him and his apology were published, so was not the whole affair a sign of the fragility of *glasnost'* and the dangers of speaking out? Was Yel'tsin's humiliation a show of strength by conservative foes of reform? An act of revenge by demoted or threatened foes of the crime-busting and housecleaning Yel'tsin? Both apologists and critics ask whether personal shortcomings of Yel'tsin, the arbitrariness and impetuousness of his leadership style and the intemperance of his speech, contributed to his downfall. One scholarly advocate of a two-party system in the USSR ventured that "Yel'tsin broke the rules of how you speak in such meetings. He personally attacked people, yes, including Ligachev. He thought he was still king, as he had been back in Sverdlovsk. You don't act that way in Moscow." There appear to be some truth in all these interpretations. Whatever the case, Yel'tsin's October 21 speech provided everyone who wanted it with the occasion to rid themselves of him.[66]

This listing of progress, conflicts, limits and perils reveals both striking changes resulting from *glasnost'*, as well as its dependence on the dictates of Party politics and needs. In Sakharov's words: "Objectively, something real is happening. How far it's going to go is a complicated question."[67]

Democratization

One of the influences on the future of *glasnost'* will be the nature of "democratization," another part of Gorbachev's strategy. Will democratization serve simply to rally support for *perestroika*, as Gorbachev intended?[68] That would mean not pluralism but participatory monism, if such a thing is possible. Or will it go so far as to permit electoral competition and other political activity by independent groups, or by factions within the Party? That would mean not simply democratization, but elements of pluralist democracy and, therefore, a departure from the principle that the only permitted political spontaneity is that organized under the vanguard party.

Gorbachev's proposal for democratizing the Party does not promise pluralism. But it does mean competitive election of local leaders, the Party secretaries, by contested and secret balloting within the local Party committees. It has met with resistance, stalemated Central Committee meetings, and numerous postponements of decisions. "Certain comrades," Gorbachev said, "have shown a lack of understanding and fear of democratic change."[69] What Party cadres must fear most is not a fragmentation of the Party into factions, not pluralism, but a determined leadership's use of elections to smoke out and shunt aside opponents of *perestroika*, in a "renewal of leading cadres."

Gorbachev broached the idea of multicandidate Soviet elections and of workplace elections at the 27th Party Congress.[70] He promoted them persistently thereafter.[71] Democratization has introduced competitive elections into the system of Soviets, or government councils. Multicandidate elections took place for the first time on June 21, 1987, as an experiment at the town, district and village level, in about 5% of all electoral districts.[72] All over the country, nomination processes opened up to unprecedented preelectoral contests among potential candidates.

Do not expect lively contests to sweep the country tomorrow. These new election procedures pose for the Party the difficult task not of restraining popular initiative, but of breathing life, on orders from above, into contests marked by long-standing formalism. Voters and the officials running elections are used to seeing elections as "some theatrical, artificially created performance."[73] The Soviet people have never experienced a meaningful electoral contest. Of his people's lack of feel for democracy, Gorbachev said, "Many are still afraid, act cautiously, are wary of responsibility, and remain unquestioningly obedient to outmoded rules and orders. The task is to instill in people a taste for independence and responsibility."[74] How is this to be instilled in Party-managed elections? In 1918, the revolutionary Marxist, Rosa Luxemburg, wrote about the Communist Party control of the Soviets:

> Without general elections, without unrestricted freedom of press and assembly, without a free struggle of opinion, life dies out in every public institution, becomes a mere semblance of life, in which only the bureaucracy remains as an active element.[75]

Even a competitive election may not bring Soviets to life, unless there is an organized opposition. Some moderate Soviet professionals agree that "a game with only one team is a dull one," or one that won't work.

Advocates of workplace democracy see it as a logical and essential part of enterprise autonomy. "At one time not only the directives but the managers too used to come from the top," said economist Abel Aganbegyan. "Now in a system based on autonomy, obviously directors must be elected by labor collectives."[76] Workplace autonomy, or self-management, exists legally only within the framework of democratic centralism. The 1987 Law on the State Enterprise asserts that the administration of an enterprise rests on the principle of democratic centralism, or "the combination of centralized control with socialist self-government of the work collective."[77] Time will show how much democracy will grow alongside what remains of the old centralism.

Self-government means, first, the participation of working people in the affairs of their unit through consultation and the process of voting for leaders at all levels up to the director; and second, the autonomy of the unit as a whole. Elections run up against several limitations under democratic centralism. Voting may be by open as well as by secret balloting. The superior ministries, or state committees, may intervene to cancel the results of an election and schedule new elections. Administrators resist the free play of an electoral process that threatens their jobs and authority.[78] The competition leading up to selection of candidates gives the higher agencies opportunities for advancing preferred candidates.

Input by "working collectives" and their councils occurs in the context of one-person management by the director, and that, in turn, occurs in the context of the involvement of the Party organization in plant administration and personnel policy, according to the venerable principles of the Party's guiding role and of *nomenklatura*—Party approval of appointments to most important posts.

Whereas *glasnost'* speedily established itself, at least at the center, even ahead of explicit Party approval, democratization moves slowly, despite the General Secretary's fervent blessings. *Glasnost'* mobilizes a willing community of pro-reform people of literature and the arts. Democratization has no such large constituency to give it life. Meanwhile, its foes argue that democratization subverts discipline and undermines the socialist system. Or they feign democratism while repressing critics.[79]

For some years yet, the Party will be the indispensable vanguard Gorbachev asserted it to be. "Both the old and new methods of management will be operating simultaneously."[80] The Party organizations will provide mediation and coordination during times of considerable chaos. But assume that the semblance of a real market economy emerges in the USSR toward the year 2000. The decentralization and appearance of new interests involved in that will then indeed call into question the compatibility of Party control with initiative and spontaneity at the level of entrepreneurial decisionmaking in the state and private sectors.

At that point, the question could arise of moving from a political system similar to that of NEP, the New Economic Policy of 1921–1928, to a pluralist one. Roy Medvedev wrote in his *samizdat* [unofficially circulated—literally, self-published] work of 1974, *On Socialist Democracy*, that Leninism left room for political pluralism—that is, competition among autonomous groups for influence and power. Medvedev tactfully omitted mention of the "Prague spring," but what he advocated was in effect a version of the ill-fated 1968 Czech experiment in "socialism with a human face," under the liberal communist leadership of Alexander Dubcek. After Dubcek fell in August 1968, loyal Soviet socialist intellectuals wept because the Warsaw Pact forces had put down what had seemed to be a promising model for demanded change in the USSR.

Medvedev's vision is shared by a new group, The Movement for a Socialist Renewal. The market economy will not work, they say in their manifesto of November 1985, without "a degree of political pluralism, a freedom for alternative political organizations to present their different programs to the citizens, all within the framework of a socialist Soviet system."[81] Andrei Sakharov, too, in his 1968 memorandum, "Progress, Coexistence, and Intellectual Freedom," urged that the Soviet leadership open up the system to social democracy. With time, as a new Soviet generation matures into leadership, yet another redefinition of Soviet socialism could occur, only this time in the political rather than in the economic-administrative sphere. An intellectual token of this trend would be the initiation of discussion on the history of the short-lived, pre-Bolshevik Provisional Government of 1917, when Lenin called Russia the freest country in the world.

Social Justice

The transition from small economic experiments to national economic reorganization has brought the USSR to "the most crucial period of *perestroika.*" This is the period of transition from "primarily administrative to primarily economic forms of guidance." All enterprises are to have shifted to self-management by the end of 1989. The process of shifting to a partial market economy is supposed to reach completion by 1992.[82]

The success of economic reform will depend heavily on whether new incentives serve to motivate the demoralized and suspicious Soviet labor force, only one third of which is found to be working to full capacity and most of which is habituated to obedience, up to and including managers, ministers and local Party secretaries who learned long ago to favor plan fulfillment over initiative, creative innovation and risk-taking. One reason for this has been the "web of compulsion" of hierarchical command and subordination, patronage and dependency, spun for decades in the USSR.[83]

A second reason for apathy in the Soviet workplace, leaders have heard from their advisers, is the distortion of the principle of socialist equity: "from each according to their ability to each according to their work." Due to widespread wage leveling, that principle has become, in practice: from the state in its indifference to each regardless of their work. Remedying this will require a reassessment of wage, pricing and welfare policies.[84]

From the beginning of his term Gorbachev heeded his advisers' warnings about the importance of the "human factor"—labor's ability and motivation.[85] He named "the central question in the theory and practice of socialism" as being "how to create more powerful socialist stimuli than exist under capitalism. . . ." He argued, against ideological conservatives, that devices like profit, competition, self-management, variable prices, and stimuli tied to efficiency constitute a "new form of socialist economic administration," even though these are characteristics of capitalism. Under socialism, stimuli can be used in ways that reflect the parallel interests of the working person, enterprise, and society. Working people, then, are not exploited under such a system, but are "masters" of production. Their work input, along with the performance of their enterprise, and the progress of society as a whole, determines their reward. They have a voice in production decisions, and a growing responsibility over economic property.[86]

Gorbachev was really engaged in trying to persuade his audience, rather than in reporting the way working people actually feel about *perestroika*. Their concept of social justice does not agree with the antileveling slant of socialist equity. On the whole, they appear to prefer their present lot, inadequacies and all, to the mounting pressures and risks of a reformed economic system. Real socialist equity will mean a stricter connection between reward and work. It will violate a long-standing social contract between workers and their government: labor loyalty and peace in exchange for more or less secure jobs, stable real pay not particularly sensitive to work performance, and a purchasing power guaranteed by free or subsidized services and staples, such as education, health care, rent, bread, meat and milk products, and children's clothing.

Perestroika brings the possibility of job loss owing to redundancy or plant closing, deprivation of part of one's present real pay due to an end to subsidies, rising prices, tighter quality controls, and more stringent work rules. Working people may not be satisfied with the Party's ambiguous reassurance that "changes in retail prices not only should not cause a worsening in the working people's standards of living, but should on the contrary raise those standards for certain categories of working people, and to a fuller realization of social justice."[87] Soviet workers' skepticism about reform parallels that of U.S. workers when their companies switch, as increasingly more do now, to productivism—that is, to tying at least part of workers' pay to their performance or that of their group or company. U.S. workers tend to see productivism as passing on to workers part of the risk for what are ultimately management decisions.[88]

Already displeased with Gorbachev for his disciplinary crackdowns and restrictions on sales of wine and liquor (to men, that is, not to women, as a rule), working people wonder what is in it for them. As Gorbachev recognizes, they will judge his policy of *perestroika* "by its tangible results in better working and living conditions" as well as health care. Sickness cost the economy ten times more in 1986 than did absenteeism and work stoppages (associated often in the USSR with shortages of supplies).[89]

It will not be easy, says political analyst Fedor Burlatskii, to convince the population that reform will benefit them, as it has already the intelligentsia, who have "already had our dividends in the form of openness."[90] Soviet working people will be particularly dubious about socialist equity if they read any of the intellectuals' articles advocating stimuli like unemployment as a cure for laziness,[91] or an end to free and subsidized goods and services above a welfare "minimum."[92]

The workers' view must be: the squeeze definitely now, and benefits maybe sometime later. The Party has promised to bring supplies of goods and availability of services in line with demand by 1990. That is a familiar sort of promise. Now among the new measures to fulfill it is the promotion of private enterprise, called, in Soviet parlance, individual and cooperative labor activity.[93]

Here is another example of self-limiting reform, possibly reflecting the mixed feelings of its sponsors. They find expression in contradictory laws. For example, one law, in effect May 1, 1987, legalizes or affirms the legality of a range of small-scale private enterprises, such as dresses made at home, the services of a tutor, doctor, plumber and other home or car repair person, tourist board and lodging, taxi service, secretarial work, and instruction of art and music. However, the law carries built-in restrictions. It limits individual labor activity to spare time for employable people, leaving full-time individual activity to pensioners and housewives. It levies progressive taxes up to 65% for private earnings over 6000 rubles a year, which is far above the maximum income tax of 13%. Under such conditions, a private entrepreneur may be discouraged, or prompted to slip into the shadow economy.[94]

License fees are high. During a taxi ride in Moscow (five rubles across town), the driver, a physicist on his way home from the lab, said he is still driving "on the left" because the 560 rubles taxi fee will soak up his profits from spare-time driving, given costs of maintaining his car.

The local Soviet [government] finance departments and executive committees in charge of licensing and permitting individual labor activity spin red tape and at times exude hostility to applicants for permits, licenses and space. Gorbachev explained that expansion of individual and cooperative economic activity is vital to meeting needs for goods and services, yet it is progressing "with very great difficulty and very slowly" owing to bureaucratic obstruction.[95] The ideological fear of "letting the capitalist genie out of the bottle" threatens to get in the way of satisfying the consumer, and thus to retard reform.[96]

To further complicate matters, a 1986 Party–government decree of May 15, 1987, and USSR Surpreme Soviet Presidium edict of May 23, 1987, provide for an intensified crackdown on "persons receiving unearned income." Aimed primarily at people stealing state and personal property and padding plan fulfillment reports, the decrees also add to the climate of state intervention and coercion that hem in private enterprise. The measures single out "speculation"—purchase and resale for profit, labor hiring, and forbidden individual economic activity. They put tighter, damaging limits on the activities of the *shabashniki* (seasonal farm construction workers), on heavy equipment operators, and on drivers of trucks that carry farmers' produce to market—illegally but indispensably.[97]

More promising at this stage is the government's encouragement of cooperative ventures into private economic activity—for example, in the spheres of public catering, the making of consumer goods, and provision of essential services like repairs and laundering. Problems remain with getting supplies (legally), space and bureaucratic cooperation rather than interference and red tape.[98]

Only one sector of private enterprise—the farming sector, Gorbachev's former area of Party responsibility—evoked his full enthusiasm. He enthused over the successes of the newly organized family or small group teams working on contract. They pay fixed fees in produce and money for inventory and land use, and may dispose of the rest of their harvest on the open market. Gorbachev also championed garden plot farming, the leasing of unused village plots to city dwellers, and greater freedom from administrative controls for collective and state farms, including the right of the farmers to sell their products on the open market.[99] Controls remained almost intact, however, and the freely marketable share of farm produce is restricted to 30% of farm output.[100] It is not yet clear whether Gorbachev shares one analyst's sense of urgent need to preserve a remnant of a resourceful peasantry before it is too late by liberating them and their farms from bureaucratic controls.[101]

An improved food supply is central to the improved quality of life that may convince working people that their interests and those of the Party reformers do coincide, and that they can feel comfortable with the message of socialist equity: we demand more of you working people, and we give you more too.

Conclusions

Gorbachev encountered three mountainous obstacles that will beset any Soviet leader seeking *perestroika*. First, there is a gap between the material and technical needs of reform, and the available proposals, skills and resources. The second obstacle is the conflict of interests over reform. The third is the conflict between spontaneity and control within *perestroika* itself.

The second obstacle pits a Soviet reform coalition of Party officials and professionals against the opposition or indifference of much of the rest of the political apparatus and working class. The laggards on reform don't want to give up their concept of social justice and its limited but more or less secure benefits for the reformer's concept of "social justice"—pay according to work and more graduated incentives—and all the risk and exertion of change.

The reformist leadership rests on a narrow social base of Party supporters in the Central Committee Secretariat, some reforming administrators and supportive military commanders, the professional and artistic community, and a scattering of enthusiasts in the general work force. To broaden that base, to win over the working masses, as it must, the leadership needs to heal the rift over social justice that is threatening to widen between itself and much of the rest of the population. Leadership's foregoing some of the special privileges of status, such as special stores, schools and hospitals, would narrow the gap, but is unlikely. Two breakthroughs will help: one, international détente and arms reduction, where gains have been made, is important for Gorbachev's authority and resource management; second, the populace's perception that reform somehow benefits them. It's not a matter of the motherland in danger anymore. People seem to be saying, we're pragmatists today, though you may not think so.

The third obstacle to *perestroika* is the conflict between spontaneity and control within the reformers' own definition of socialism. Conflict stands out most vividly where *perestroika* has made its greatest strides, that is, within *glasnost'*.

"Compulsory *perestroika* cannot compete with liberating *perestroika*," someone has written to *Novy mir* magazine.[102] How liberating can it get? An idea floats among reformers of returning to a modernized form of NEP, the market-oriented and more open New Economic Policy of 1921–1928. But that begs the question of independent political activity, which cannot be said to have characterized NEP. For a Russian political model of the Soviet socialist future, one must turn to the period of the Provisional Government and earlier, eras marked by growing political initiative.

Glasnost' encourages spontaneous activism—for and against reform, for and against various individual and nationality rights, for and against the right to spontaneous expression and association. This spontaneous activism outside channels under Party control gravely tests the limits of a dramatic but shaky openness. When Americans expressed distrust and uncertainty about *glasnost'* at a meeting with Soviet visitors, Nikolai Shishlin of the Communist Party Central Committee found this understandable. "We ourselves are not certain about the depth and breadth of the changes in our country, so how can we expect Americans to be any different?"[103]

Perestroika can be viewed as a prolonged, four-phase process of reform. The process is likely to be marked by alternations of radicalism and retreat. The first three phases lie within Gorbachev's political vision of socialism; the fourth phase goes beyond it.

The first phase of *perestroika*, up to 1986, brought (a) the passage of experimental and piecemeal measures of reform and social discipline, as outlined in Chapter 6 by Tatsuo Kaneda; (b) a strengthening, if not ensuring, of Gorbachev's power; and (c) the expanding conceptualization of *perestroika*.

The second phase of *perestroika*, beginning in late 1986, brought the passage and implementation of a series of comprehensive measures of economic and procedural reform, ranging from the Law on Individual Labor Activity, in effect May 1, 1987, to the Law on the State Enterprise, in effect January 1, 1988, to cover 60% of Soviet enterprises by 1988, and nearly all by 1989. The formal completion of reform was scheduled to take place by 1991–1992, with the inauguration of a wholesale market in producer goods. "Informal" (independent) political activity and protest will continue to challenge the limits of *glasnost'* and democratization. The first years of this phase are bringing a struggle over reform that could be decisive for its short-term outcome, and for Gorbachev's political survival.

Assuming that *perestroika* keeps going, or if interrupted, then when it resumes, its third phase will bring efforts to straighten out the chaos created by the transition from a centralized to a partially market economy, and to continue dealing with the ideologically and socially sensitive policies of wage incentives, price subsidies and reform, plant bankruptcies, unemployment and reemployment, and the whole Pandora's box of "social justice."

The fourth phase of *perestroika* lies outside Gorbachev's political concept of one-party socialism. This phase could bring to the forefront, from the present unofficial fringes of debate, the issue of the role of the Communist Party and the possibilities of legal opposition within or to the Party. It may begin as an aspect of *perestroika* even during the second and third phases in the 1990's.

Perestroika is therefore not necessarily doomed to extinction, though at times it may seem to be. Rather, it will be, as Gorbachev said, a "comparatively lengthy process . . . with its own logic and stages."

Central to the "logic" of change, as Gail Lapidus shows in Chapter 1, is the decline in Russia's place as an economic power, from second to third, behind Japan.

China has been entering the next phase of its reforms, with an 8-year start at expanding the private sector. Now it is directing attention to the daunting task of reforming the urban, state-owned industrialized sector. Imagine that eventually China produces a working variant of a market economy, and progresses in its efforts to join the Asian NICS (newly industrialized countries). There may be no greater incentive for the Soviets to push ahead with *perestroika* than that provided by an awakened socialist giant next door.

Notes

1. On the policies and atmosphere in the USSR before Gorbachev's accession to power, see Seweryn Bialer, *The Soviet Paradox: External Expansion and Internal Decline* (New York: Knopf, 1987), pp. 109–125.
2. *Pravda*, February 26, 1987.
3. On the reform movement, see Chapter 4 in this volume.
4. Gorbachev's calls for *uskorenie* and social change go back to the April plenum early in his leadership (*Pravda*, April 24, 1985), and to a speech made in December 1984 under Chernenko (Archie Brown, "A reformer in the Kremlin," *The Nation*, June 13, 1987, p. 793). By the twenty-seventh congress, Gorbachev called for an even more broadly defined "revolutionary" *perestroika* (Pravda, February 26, 1986).

5. Marshall Goldman, WCBS, 5/25/87; Peter Reddaway, "Gorbachev the Bold," *New York Review of Books*, May 28, 1987, pp. 21–25.

6. Vladimir Bukovsky, "Will Gorbachev Reform the Soviet Union?" *Commentary* (September 1986), pp. 19–21. The fullest analysis of the limits on *perestroika* is to be found in Marshall Goldman, *Gorbachev's Challenge: Economic Reform in the Age of High Technology* (New York: W.W. Norton & Company, 1987).

7. Dusko Doder, *Shadows and Whispers: Power Politics inside the Kremlin from Brezhnev to Gorbachev* (New York: Random House, 1986), p. 267.

8. Archie Brown, "How much change in the USSR?" *World Policy Journal*, 4, No. 1 (Winter 1986–1987), pp. 55–87; Robert C. Tucker, "Gorbachev and the Fight for Soviet Reform," Ibid., 4, No. 2 (Spring 1987), pp. 179–206; Martin Walker, *The Waking Giant: Gorbachev's Russia* (New York: Pantheon Books, 1986).

9. *Pravda*, February 26, 1986; January 29, 1987; February 26, 1987; June 26, 1987; Harald Hamrin cites Abel Agenbegyan on an "emotionally charged" June central committee plenum in *Dagens Nyheter*, June 28, 1987. FBIS-SOV-87-133, pp. R14–R16.

10. M. S. Gorbachev, "Oktiabr' i perestroika: revoliutsiia prodolzhaetsia," report to a joint session of the CPSU Central Committee, USSR Supreme Soviet, RSFSR Supreme Soviet, celebrating the 70th anniversary of the Great October Socialist Revolution, *Pravda*, November 3, 1987.

11. Ibid.

12. Abraham Brumberg, "Moscow Seen Clearly," *The New York Times*, September 2, 1987.

13. *Pravda*, February 26, 1986 and November 3, 1987.

14. Mikhail Gorbachev, *Perestroika: New Thinking for Our Country and the World* (New York: Harper & Row Publishers, 1987), p. 55.

15. "Yes, the Party leadership started it. The highest Party and state bodies elaborated and adopted the program." Ibid., p. 56. Gorbachev qualified his terminology by asserting that *perestroika* began thus, but is now joined with a grass roots movement of initiative from below. Here wish is father to the thought. Summary of talk by Peter Hauslohner "The Mass Response to *Perestroika*," *At the Harriman Institute*, 1:2, November 1987.

16. It echoes the "series of revolutions effected peacefully by autocratic power" in nineteenth century Russia. D. Mackenzie Wallace, *Russia* (New York: Henry Holt and Co., 1877), p. 225.

17. Martin Walker, *The Waking Giant: Gorbachev's Russia*, p. xviii.

18. Charles Gati, "Gorbachev and Eastern Europe," *Foreign Affairs* 65, No. 1 (summer 1987), pp. 958–975.

19. Ivan Volgyes, "Hungary: Before the Storm Breaks," *Current History* (November 1987), pp. 373–376, 389–390.

20. Michael Kraus, "Soviet Policy toward Eastern Europe," Ibid., pp. .

21. Reddaway, "Gorbachev the Bold," p. 22.

22. Marshall I. Goldman, "Even the Tsar Found Anchor-Draggers," *The New York Times*, June 28, 1987.

23. *Pravda*, June 26, 1987.

24. *Pravda*, June 26, 1987.

25. Fedor Burlatskii, "Uchit'sia demokratii," *Pravda*, July 18, 1987.

26. Peterson, Peter G. "Gorbachev's Bottom Line," *The New York Review of Books*, June 25, 1987, pp. 29–34.

27. *Izvestiia*, September 12, 1987. Earlier he spoke much in the same way about dissidence. *Pravda*, March 1, 1986.

28. Paul Quinn-Judge, "Head of Secret Police appears cool toward reform; Chebrikov joins Kremlin's No. 2 leader in voicing concerns about Gorbachev changes," *The Christian Science Monitor*, September 14, 1987.

29. Condoleezza Rice and Rose Gottmoeller, cited in *Meeting Report. Kennan Institute for Advanced Russian Studies*. May 13 and June 3, 1987.

30. Archie Brown, "A Reformer in the Kremlin," pp. 792–793.

31. *Pravda*, May 31, 1987.

32. *Pravda*, June 27, 1987.

33. *Pravda*, June 26, 1987; Alexander Rahr, "Why Yazov?" RL212/87, June 1, 1987.

34. For examples of Ligachev's ideological caution, see note 63 below and *Izvestiia*, August 28, 1987.

35. Gorbachev reminded his listeners of Academician V. S. Nem-chinov's attack in 1964 on the "commands and quotas" of the "ossified mechanism" which "will sooner or later be broken by the pressures from the real process of economic life." *Pravda*, June 26, 1987. See also Nobuo Shimotomai and Tatsuo Kaneda in Chapters 4 and 5, this volume.

36. Archie Brown, "How Much Change in the USSR?", p. 66.

37. Bialer, *The Soviet Paradox;* Timothy J. Colton, *Dilemma of Reform in the Soviet Union*, rev. & expanded edit. (New York: Council on Foreign Relations, 1986); Peter H. Juviler, "The Drive for Discipline: Andropov Makes His Mark," *Soviet Union/Union Sovietique*, 11, Pt. 3 (1984), pp. 296–300.

38. Tat'iana Zaslavskaia, "Doklad o neobkhodimosti bolee uglu-blennogo izucheniia v SSSR sotsial'nogo mekhanizma razvitiia ekonomiki . . . predstavlen na nauchnom seminare v Moskve aprel' 1983." *Arkhiv samizdata*. Radio svoboda. No. 35/83. AC No. 5042. Excerpts freely translated in *The New York Times*, August 5, 1983.

39. *Pravda*, June 26, 1987.

40. Archie Brown, "How Much Change in the USSR?" *World Policy Journal* (Winter 1986–1987), pp. 65–66; Peterson, "Gorbachev's Bottom

Line," p. 29; and virtually any Western personage of any persuasion who has met Gorbachev.

41. Roy Medvedev, *Khrushchev* (Garden City, NY: Anchor Press/ Doubleday, 1983).

42. Peterson, "Gorbachev's Bottom Line," p. 32.

43. *Pravda,* April 13, 1985, April 13, 1986. "Citizens of the USSR, increase your political participation. Development glasnost, criticism and self-criticism—time tested means of socialist democracy!" *Pravda,* April 19, 1987.

44. Chingiz Aitmatov, *A Day Lasts a Hundred Years;* Albert Leong, "Socialist Realism in Tarkovsky's *Andrei Rublev, Studies in Comparative Communism,* 17, No. 3–4 (Fall/Winter 1984–85), pp. 227–233; *Metropol:* Literary Almanac, ed. by Vasily Aksyonov *et al.* (New York: W.W. Norton, 1982); Harlow Robinson, "Russian Culture after Brezhnev: Music," *Soviet Union/Union Sovietique,* 12, Pt. 2 (1985), pp. 137–143.

45. Serge Schmemann, "Yevtushenko Plays Rebel Again, calling for Open Soviet Literature," *The New York Times,* December 16, 1985; "Bold Play (á la Gorbachev) Makes Audience Gasp," Ibid., January 8, 1986; Yevgenii Yevtushenko, "Talk by Yevtushenko in Its Entirety," *The New York Times,* December 19, 1985; Mark Zakharov, calling for unbridled theatres in *Literaturnaia gazeta,* July 31, 1985.

46. "Ispol'zovanie svobodnogo vremeni," *Vestnik statistiki,* No. 2 (1987), pp. 62–63; Ellen Mickiewicz, "Soviet Viewers Are Seeing More, Including News of the US," *AAASS Newsletter,* 27, No. 3 (May 1987), pp. 1–3; Mark Koenig, "Media and Reform: The Case of Soviet Television," draft report, Harriman Institute for the Advanced Study of the Soviet Union (New York: Columbia University, April 1987).

47. Compare the pap that made up Brezhnev's speech, *Pravda,* November 3, 1977, with Gorbachev's speech, *Pravda,* November 3, 1987: praise of NEP, the New Economic Policy of 1921–1928 (with criticism too), ·of Bukharin, and Khrushchev's "no small courage" for de-Stalinization; the first public linking by a Soviet leader of Stalin with the excesses and blood guilt of his rule; the complexities of the tasks facing the Soviet Union. One of the few U.S. editorials I know to see Gorbachev's speech as anything but a capitulation to conservatism (which it may well have been in parts) said incorrectly that Gorbachev omitted the theme of Party democratization. "One Step Forward," *The Nation,* November 14, 1987, pp. 544–545.

48. Vasily Aksyonov *et al.* "Is Glasnost' a Game of Mirrors?" *The New York Times,* March 22, 1987.

49. Peter Reddaway, "Gorbachev the Bold," *The New York Review of Books,* May 28, 1987, p. 24. Among his allies appeared Andrei Sakharov after his release and the February prisoner releases, saying that he supports Gorbachev's agenda for change "wholeheartedly." Howell

Raines, "Sakharov Tells Thatcher of Need for West to Back Soviet Changes," *The New York Times*, April 1, 1987.

50. *Pravda*, January 28, 1987; Fyodor Burlatsky, interview in *Al Hawadith*, February 6, 1987.

51. *Pravda*, January 28, 1987.

52. *News from Helsinki Watch*, No. 1 (March 13, 1987), p. 2; on rehabilitations, see *Pravda*, February 6, 1988.

53. An opponent of pop-*glasnost'*, the writers union notable, Sergei Mikhalkov, compared rock to AIDS, "an infection that unfortunately cannot be cured." Michael R. Benson, "Back in the U.S.S.R.," *The Nation*, June 13, 1987, pp. 824–826.

54. *Pravda*, August 2, 1986; Fyodor Burlatsky, interview in *La Repubblica*, March 27, 1987; Vera Tolz, "Attacks on Glasnost' Intensify," Radio Liberty Research Bulletin RL150/87, April 8, 1987; and see note 24, above.

55. Yuri Bondarev, a well-known writer, recently described Russian literature as being besieged by destructive criticism, comparing it to the Red Army under attack by the Nazis in 1941. Andrei Voznesensky, "A Poet's View of *Glasnost*," *The Nation*, June 13, 1987, p. 811.

56. *From Below: Independent Peace and Environmental Movements in Eastern Europe & the USSR* (New York: Helsinki Watch Committee, October 1987).

57. *Pravda*, January 20, 1987.

58. Bill Keller, "Soviet Ethnic Minorities Take Glasnost into the Streets," *The New York Times*, August 30, 1987; Ann Sheehy, "Crimean Tatars Demonstrate for Restoration of Autonomous Republic in Crimea," RL(Radio Liberty Research Bulletin)305/87, July 17, 1987; Paul Quinn-Judge, "Nationalist Clashes in USSR Test Gorbachev's Tolerance," *The Christian Science Monitor*, February 26, 1988; Philip Taubman, "Gorbachev Urges Armenians to End Nationalist Furor," *The New York Times*, February 27, 1988.

59. Helsinki Watch Committee, "Documents from the Moscow Trust Group. Excerpts from *Day by Day*, the Trust Group's monthly information bulletin (No. 5, May 1987), and from other recent documents;" "*News from Helsinki Watch*, No. 2 (June 15, 1987), passim.

60. *Pravda*, July 15, 1987.

61. I. Dedkov, "Literatura i novoe myshlenie," *Kommunist*, No. 12 (August 1987), pp. 57–65.

62. Report on Yegor Ligachev's speech at the offices of *Sovetskaia kul'tura*, July 7, 1987, *Pravda*, July 15, 1987 and transl. in FBIS-Sov-87-132, pp. R11–R17; Paul Quinn-Judge, "Head of Soviet Secret Police appears cool toward reform;" Philip Taubman, "No. 2 Soviet Official Puts in a Bad Word Against Glasnost," *The New York Times*, September 24, 1987.

63. On this see Peter H. Juviler, "Law and Individual Rights: The Shifting Political Ground," forthcoming in *Soviet Restructuring through*

Law, eds. Albert Schmidt, Don Barry, George Ginsburgs, and William Simons.

64. *Pravda*, January 28, 1987.

65. *Pravda*, November 13, 1987, February 19, 1988.

66. Philip Taubman, "The Real Gorbachev?" *The New York Times*, November 14, 1987; Celestine Bohlen, "Gorbachev's Reforms Hit Heavy Weather," *The Washington Post National Weekly Edition*, November 30, 1987; Marshall I. Goldman, "After Yeltsin, Gorbachev?" *The New York Times*, November 22, 1987.

67. *News from Helsinki Watch*, No. 1, p. 2.

68. As *glasnost'* provides the light for restructuring, so democracy will the air. "Democracy is as essential as the air we breathe," Gorbachev insisted to the stubborn January 1987 Central Committee plenum. "Without a serious, profound democratization of Soviet society, we will not carry out the task of acceleration, will not assure restructuring . . . our policy will peter out, reconstruction will suffocate, comrades." Democratization is meant to help clinch *perestroika*, combat apathy and serve as a counterpoise to bureaucratism, by "directly involving wide masses of working people." *Pravda*, June 26 and 27, 1987.

69. *Pravda*, June 26, 1987.

70. *Pravda*, February 26, 1986.

71. *Pravda*, August 2, 1986.

72. Pyotr N. Demichev, Interview, Moscow Television Service, April 5, 1987, FBIS-SOV-87-066, pp. R1–R5; Yuri Korolev, Interview, TASS, April 1, 1987, FBIS-SOV-87-066, p. R5; results in *Pravda*, June 25, 1987.

73. P. Nikitin, "Misfire: Preelection meeting postponed in a Yaroslavl Oblast Rayon," *Sovetskaia rossiia*, April 26, 1987. FBIS-SOV-87-095, pp. R10–R11; V. Vasilyev, "Sovety i razvitie demokratii," *Pravda*, May 8, 1987.

74. Gorbachev, "Oktiabr' i Perestroika," *Pravda*, November 3, 1987.

75. Rosa Luxemburg, "The Russian Revolution," in *The Russian Revolution and Leninism or Marxism* (Ann Arbor, MI: The University of Michigan Press, 1961), p. 71.

76. Massimo Loche, "The Utopian Hill," *L'Espresso*, May 3, 1987, pp. 63–66, FBIS-SOV-87-094, pp. S3–S5.

77. *Pravda*, July 1, 1987.

78. L. Telen and L. Tsetkov, "Who to Elect and How," *Sotsialisticheskaia industriia*, February 17, 1987, FBIS-SOV-87-039, pp. S1–S6. "Can we expect cool dispassionateness from directors and their deputies and ministry employees whose interests are the first to be affected by the democratic innovations?" these reporters ask.

79. Ibid.; omitted portion of Gorbachev's speech to the Trade Union Congress, over TASS International Service, FBI-SOV-87, supplement (April 1987).

80. *Pravda,* June 26, 1987.

81. Walker, *Gorbachev's Russia,* p. 264.

82. *Pravda,* June 27 and July 1, 1987.

83. Iu. Korkhov, "Pautina prinuzhdeniia," *Novy mir* (May 1987), pp. 241–245; Gorbachev on the Party, *Pravda,* June 26, 1987.

84. Tat'iana Zaslavskaia, "Chelovecheskii faktor razvitiya ekonomiki i sotsial'naia spravedlivost'," *Kommunist,* No. 13 (1986), pp. 61–73.

85. *Pravda,* April 24, 1985, February 26, 1986.

86. *Pravda,* July 26, 1987.

87. *Pravda,* June 27, 1987.

88. Cindy Skrzycki, "The New Trend in the Workplace is Pay as You Go," *Washington Post National Weekly Edition,* June 6, 1987.

89. *Pravda,* February 26, 1987.

90. Burlatsky, interview in *La Repubblica.*

91. Nikolai Shmelev, "Avansy i dolgi," *Novy mir,* No. 6 (June 1987), pp. 142–157.

92. Zaslavskaia, "Chelovecheskii faktor razvitiia ekonomiki i sotsial-'naya spravedlivost'."

93. *Pravda,* June 27, 1987.

94. *Pravda,* November 20 and 21, 1986; Lev Barshevsky, "The Law is Coming into Force," Moscow Domestic Service April 30, 1987. FBIS-SOV-87-086, pp. S1–S4.

95. *Pravda,* June 26, 1987.

96. Shmelev, "Avansy i dolgi," p. 145.

97. S.I. Gusev, "Aktual'nye problemy bor'by pravokhranitel'nikh organov s netrudovymi dokhodami," *Sovetskoe gosudarstvo i pravo,* No. 2 (1987), pp. 58–63; Kennan Institute. *Meeting Report.* C.W. Patrick Murphey, Jr., "The Soviet Campaign against Unearned Income," October 1, 1986; Iu. N. Lyapunov, "Iuridicheskie aspekty bor'by s netrudovymi dokhodami," *Sovetskoe gosudarstvo i pravo,* No. 12 (1986), pp. 56–63.

98. "Cooperative Services," *Sovetskaia rossiia,* May 6, 1987, FBIS-SOV-87-092, pp. R4–R8.

99. *Pravda,* June 26, 1987.

100. Gorbachev gave the figure of 30% of farm communal produce freely marketable. *Pravda,* August 2, 1986.

101. Shmelev, "Avansy i dolgi," p. 143.

102. Korkhov, "Pautina prinuzhdeniia."

103. Andrew Rosenthal, "Glasnost tested in Victorian Setting," *The New York Times,* August 26, 1987.

Ideology and Reform

James P. Scanlan

The Soviet Union's radically new direction under Mikhail Sergeevich Gorbachev is defended, as all major turns have been defended in the USSR since the Bolshevik revolution, by appeals to the writings of Marx, Engels, and Lenin. Contrary to Western descriptions of a capitulation to capitalism and the victory of pragmatism over ideology in the USSR, the Soviet leaders steadfastly maintain their strongly ideological stance and insist that they remain devoted to the principles of Marxism, are seeking communism as an ultimate goal, and are working vigorously to perfect socialism as a stage in the attainment of that goal.

At the same time, Gorbachev has argued far more emphatically than any previous Soviet leader that new ways of understanding Marxism are needed. "New thinking" *(novoe myshlenie)* is required, he contends, in order to free Soviet Marxism from obsolete dogmas and from one-sided, oversimplified conceptions. Gorbachev has himself contributed to this new thinking in his public addresses, and his example is being widely followed in the society at large. Given the manifest importance Gorbachev attaches to the new thinking, wherever it is welcomed among his countrymen, we may speak not of the victory of pragmatism over ideology in the USSR but of the victory of new ideology over old ideology. There is a tendency to interpret the term ideology to mean *established* dogmas; but of course the system of concepts and principles that replaces established dogma, when change does come, is ideology, too—albeit fresher and less firmly rooted.

For decades now, most observers of the Soviet scene, in the West and in the USSR as well, have paid scant attention to the old Marxist–Leninist dogma, regarding it variously as a museum piece, a ritual dance, or a dialectical smokescreen for the dirty realities of power and privilege. But now that the leadership exhibits a firm resolve to change those realities and is seeking a new interpretation of Marxism–Leninism as part of the process, we can no longer comfortably ignore Soviet ideology. Marxism–Leninism, Gorbachev has stated, "teaches us to correctly understand the nature and interaction of economic and political forces";[1] philosophy, he said in a chatty interview with the editors of *L'Unita* on May 18, 1987, "is helping me now in theoretically cognizing the current stage of Soviet society's development, the problems and interconnections of the present-day world."[2] Perhaps he means it, in which case the new ideology is important as a determinant of Soviet policy. But even if his statements are mere window dressing, even if Marxism is not driving the current changes in the USSR, it appears to be at least a reflection of what is going on today—better still, a reflection, perhaps more revealing than what is actually visible in practice to date, of what the leadership *wants* to go on. It reflects the desired directions of what Gorbachev tirelessly calls "the restructuring [*perestroika*] of all aspects of Soviet society." In either case, Soviet ideology is interesting again, and following it may be one of the best ways we have of assessing the nature and the prospects of lasting change in the USSR.

What, then, are the transformations in Soviet society that the new ideology is promoting, or at least reflecting? It has become manifestly clear by now that what is going on in the USSR is a concerted attempt at a new socialist revolution—a revolution in the strict Marxian sense of a fundamental refashioning of the economic base of society, and correspondingly of its political and ideological superstructure as well. Both the need for and the anticipated character of this revolution are stated in terms so radical that major adjustments in ideology are required in order to explain and justify them, and it is just such major adjustments that Gorbachev has encouraged in his public presentations.

The rhetoric of revolutionary change in the USSR has emerged slowly over the past 3 years, in tandem with conceptual developments in Marxist–Leninist ideology. To understand the radical character of these developments it is instructive to contrast them with the ideology they replace—an ideology that was largely the invention of the Brezhnev leadership.

During the Brezhnev era, Soviet economic, social and political thinking was codified into a doctrine that was virtually immune to disconfirmation by future events and was capable of persisting unchanged for decades to come.[3] Attaining this condition was no mean feat, given Khruschchev's rash promise, written into the Third Program of the Communist Party adopted at its 22nd Congress in 1961, to the effect that full communism would be achieved in the USSR by the 1980's. "The present generation of Soviet people," that Program proclaimed, "shall live in communism!"[4]

During the Brezhnev years, this time bomb was defused by interposing a new and lengthy stage of socioeconomic evolution—called "developed socialism"—between the Khrushchev era and the millennium. The Soviet Union, it was said, became a fully mature or "developed" socialist society in the late 1960's, meaning that socialism was by then fully secure in the world and fully established on its own economic basis (that is, its "relations of production" were thoroughly and appropriately socialist). But the country was said to require many years yet—half a century or more—of slow, progressive growth on its "developed" foundation in order to reach its full potential and become capable of making the transition—international conditions permitting—from socialism (a society based on the principle, "From each according to his ability, to each according to his work") to full communism ("from each according to his ability, to each according to his needs)." Communism, in other words, was put off indefinitely, but at the same time the existing Soviet order was accepted as a great achievement and was said to be fundamentally and thoroughly sound, moving in just the right direction, though needing a long time to reach its goal. This was a comforting, undemanding outlook, which neatly combined self-satisfaction, optimism and caution.

Before he assumed the country's leadership, Gorbachev himself appeared to subscribe to the doctrine of developed socialism. In his major address at an ideological conference in December 1984, he spoke of the present task as that of "improving developed socialism"; "the conclusion," he stated, "that we are at the beginning of the historically long stage of developed socialism has received thorough substantiation."[5] Yet in rereading this speech with hindsight, we find many suggestions of a new approach. Despite his use of the terminology of developed socialism, Gorbachev called in the same breath for "profound transformation in the economy and in the entire system of social relations," transformation that would "raise socialist society to a new and higher level"[6]—odd statements from someone who was supposed to believe that Soviet socialism is already "mature" and "developed." Odder still was his call for "the restructuring of the forms and methods of economic management" so as to "create an economic mechanism that meets the requirements of developed socialism."[7] How, one might ask, could developed socialism even exist if it lacked an economic mechanism that met its requirements?

After the April 1985 plenary session of the Central Committee of the Communist Party of the Soviet Union (CPSU), Gorbachev's first as General Secretary, at which similarly mixed signals were given, Soviet concern with ideological questions was focused on the new Program of the Soviet Communist Party, then under preparation by a special commission. Although the new General Secretary was immediately named chairman of the commission, the Program itself, when it was approved at the 27th Party Congress in March 1986, did not at first glance seem to break radically with the past or proclaim a new line in ideology. For one thing, it was not called the Fourth Program (on a par with those adopted in 1903, 1919 and 1961), but simply a new version of the Third—a move that many attributed to an unwillingness to make thoroughgoing changes. Furthermore, the Program appeared to accept the ideology of developed socialism, proclaiming as it did that since the adoption of the 1961 Program the country had "entered the stage of developed socialism" and that its task was now "the systematic and comprehensive improvement of socialism," presumably on its "developed" basis.[8]

In fact, however, closer analysis sheds a different light on both these points. Calling the new Program a revised version of the Third was actually a more effective way of consigning the 1961 version to historical oblivion than calling the new Program the Fourth. It signified a virtual cancellation of the 1961 program—a return to the beginning to make a fresh start. In future compilations of "Programs of the CPSU," the 1986 Program will stand as the Third, with only a footnote or at best an appendix devoted to the 1961 version. Furthermore, the new Program's acknowledgment of "developed socialism" is minimal—two references in all, with none of the elaboration one might have expected, given the status of the concept as the key notion in Soviet ideology for years beforehand. The Program, far from suggesting contentment with the advanced level of socialism supposedly achieved in the USSR, speaks of the need for profound change—not change from socialism to communism, but change *within* socialism. Referring to the "mistakes of the 1970's and early 1980's" (the heyday of developed socialism), the Program calls not for steady growth but for faster growth—"the *acceleration* of the country's socioeconomic development"—looking to "the *qualitative* transformation of all aspects of the life of Soviet society."[9] Those familiar with Marxist-Leninist terminology would recognize a *qualitative* transformation as a fundamental or radical one—not simply a change but a shift from one *level* of change to another, the kind of transformation associated with revolution.

The revolutionary flavor of these statements was further enhanced by Gorbachev's main address at the 27th Party Congress, when he provided one of his clearest and most far-reaching statements to date of the theoretical underpinning of his new thinking. Admitting that there had been lively debate concerning the place of developed socialism in the new Program—some arguing for greater prominence, some for dropping the concept altogether—Gorbachev accepted the term but stated his own qualms about it: it had, he said, been used to justify complacency, "the registering of successes," while failures were overlooked. What is important now, he argued, is not recording what has been achieved but finding ways of moving forward more rapidly through "qualitative changes."[10] This was enough to indicate profound dissatisfaction at the highest level with the ideology of developed socialism, and after the Party Congress, despite the term's enshrinement in the new Program, it soon disappeared from the statements of Soviet leaders and theorists.

Besides indicating dissatisfaction with the concept of developed socialism, Gorbachev in his Congress speech presented the outlines of his own, revolutionary analysis of the Soviet Union's present situation— an analysis that is remarkable in its use of Marxist notions to criticize rather than defend the existing contours of Soviet society. For Gorbachev in effect applied to the USSR the fundamental Marxist conception of an economic system ripe for revolution—that is, an economic system in which the existing relations of production (the relations established among people in the society with respect to production, exchange and distribution) do not promote but impede, or (to use Marx's term) "fetter," the utilization and development of the productive forces—the labor power, tools, and technology available for the productive process.

According to Marx, it is just such a contradiction between productive forces and the relations of production that renders capitalism ultimately incapable of utilizing its means of production to its fullest advantage: by their nature, economic relations based on private ownership and free enterprise inevitably create chronic unemployment, the swings of the business cycle, the wastes of competition, and other bars to maximum productivity. Once socialist relations of production, based on public ownership and central planning, are established, on the other hand, these evils will be eliminated, the material productive forces will be given full scope to develop, and unparalleled productivity will result. This was the dogma stubbornly affirmed by generations of Soviet leaders, who looked confidently to "overtaking" the capitalist world economically in the near or not-so-near future, often in the face of a disappointing performance by the Soviet economy.

Gorbachev is the first Soviet leader in the history of the USSR to call into question this doctrine of the *inherent* superiority of socialism over capitalism. He did so in his address at the Party Congress by suggesting that under socialism, too, it is possible for relations of production to come into contradiction with productive forces in such a way as to hinder rather than foster the latter's use. He admitted, in other words, that there is no guarantee in the nature of socialism itself that it will promote economic growth more successfully than capitalism does. "Practice has shown," he stated, "the bankruptcy of notions according to which, in socialist conditions, *the conformity of production relations to the nature of productive forces* is ensured automatically, as it were. In life, everything is more complicated." Socialist production relations, he argued, must themselves change in order to keep pace with the growth of productive forces; but since they do not change "automatically," they must be altered deliberately by political action. If they are not altered, they will cease to be an effective framework for economic growth.[11] Indeed, Gorbachev conceded, in the Soviet Union just such a previously unthinkable situation has arisen: existing Soviet production relations, formed under earlier conditions, "have gradually grown obsolete, have begun to lose their incentive role, and in some respects have become an impediment."[12] Hense the need for restructuring, to "change the thrust of the economic mechanism" so as to "open up new scope for the development of productive forces."[13]

At the 27th Congress, the rhetoric of this impeccably Marxian description of a revolutionary situation in the USSR was still rather restrained. But it was not long before existing conditions were painted in darker hues and the needed change was openly called a revolution. Gorbachev first used the language of revolution in a speech in Khabarovsk on July 31, 1986—a speech in which he lamented that some comrades not only failed to embrace *perestroika* but even had difficulty pronouncing the word. Speaking of the need for fundamental restructuring, he stated: "I would equate the word restructuring with the word revolution," and he went on to describe the contemplated changes as "a genuine revolution in the entire system of relations in society, in the minds and hearts of people, in the psychology and understanding of the present period and, above all, in the tasks engendered by rapid scientific and technical progress."[14] That his statements were neither offhand nor idiosyncratic was shown by the simultaneous adoption of the vocabulary of revolution by other members of the Central Committee (including such reputed conservatives as Yegor Ligachev) and the Party press, both journalistic and theoretical. All these pronouncements on behalf of revolution, multiplying in the latter half of 1986 and continuing to the present day, also adhered to Gorbachev's Party Congress analysis of the situation as one marked by a contradiction between material productive forces and relations of production, with the consequent need to change the latter in order to develop the former.

This need was given significantly greater urgency by Gorbachev at the January 1987 plenary session of the Central Committee, at which he hoped, he said, to "end the discussion of whether or not restructuring is necessary."[15] He sought to do this by reciting the long litany of Soviet economic failures in the 1970's and early 1980's—surely the most damning assessment of the Soviet economy ever presented by a Soviet leader. Using the same conceptual apparatus of productive forces and relations of production, Gorbachev spoke, however, not simply of relations that had lost their incentive role and were "in some respects" an impediment, but of "mounting crisis phenomena" in the Soviet economy, which urgently require "a change of direction and measures of a revolutionary nature."[16] Referring to contemporary Soviet socialism not as "developed" *(razvityi)* but as "developing" *(razvivaiushchiisia)*—a usage now standard among Soviet writers—he argued that "the dialectics of its motive forces and contradictions" had not been properly understood. Existing relations of production, he said, were absolutized and regarded as essential to socialism. "The model of socialist production relations became set in stone, and the dialectical interaction between these relations and productive forces was underestimated."[17] The existing relations, then, became a "retardation mechanism" *(mekhanizm tormozheniia)*—another expression that is now part of the standard *perestroika* vocabulary of Soviet speakers and writers—weighing down the productive forces instead of encouraging their development.[18]

To say that existing relations of production are not simply imperfect and in need of improvement but form a retardation mechanism is to argue not for reforming them but for replacing them, and Gorbachev proceeded to that conclusion: restructuring, he stated, means "scrapping the mechanism of retardation, and creating a reliable and effective mechanism of accelerating the social and economic development of Soviet society."[19] The aim is to create a "new economic mechanism" (NEM—initials by which this period of Soviet history may one day be known). Essentially the same analysis and terminology were used by Gorbachev at the June 1987 plenum of the Central Committee, the difference being that there he described the present economic situation of the USSR in still bleaker terms, as a situation marked not simply by particular "crisis phenomena" but by a general precrisis condition.[20] It is true that at the June plenum the word reform was heard more often than the word revolution, but it was invariably characterized as *radical* reform, with the object of eliminating old, obstructive relations of production and replacing them with new, stimulative ones—that is, as a true socioeconomic revolution in the Marxian sense of that term.

The idea of a second socialist revolution is itself a revolution—a revolution in ideology which, like the concrete socioeconomic changes it proposes, will receive further elaboration and modification as it develops. The ideological revolution has already proceeded far enough, however, for its main outlines to be clearly discernible. Its novelty lies principally in two broad areas: in the very idea of a revolution *within* socialism (an idea without precedent in Soviet Marxism), and in the character of the socialist society envisaged as the result of that revolution.

Soviet writers admit that the idea of a revolution within socialism is a novel one, and they display some hesitancy in dealing with it: often, for example, they use qualifying phrases such as "transformations that are *in essence* revolutionary," "the revolutionary *nature* of restructuring," and the like. But they argue that the second socialist revolution has distinctive features that make it consistent with Marxism–Leninism. Four such features may be identified in the Soviet discussions.

First, it is not a revolution that destroys the fundamentally socialist character of the society. This is paradoxical, of course, for in traditional Marxist terms it would seem that for a socialist society to change *qualitatively*, its socialist base would have to be replaced by a base of a different order—by a fully communist or (retrogressively) a capitalist base. But Soviet theorists take pains to exclude these possibilities: the qualitative change in this case, they contend, is from one socialist base to another. This new thesis is grounded on the assumptions, first, that socialism is compatible with a *range* of different production relations— some better than others, some, perhaps, even worse than those of capitalism—and second, that deliberate *choices* must be made in a socialist society as to which relations to establish; proper relations do not arise "naturally" from the socialist situation. Even a long-established socialist society can be wrongly established, can exhibit stagnation and a retardation mechanism. The elimination of this mechanism is, then, a kind of *re-creation* of socialism, a form of starting over again from the beginning. Hence the strong Soviet interest currently in the NEP and in experiences of the 1920's generally.

This sense of a new socialist beginning is nicely reflected in the frequent appearance of two quotations—one from Marx and one from Lenin—in current Soviet speeches and publications. Marx, in "The Eighteenth Brumaire of Louis Napoleon," wrote that in proletarian revolutions it is necessary to "return to what would seem to have been accomplished already, in order to begin it over again."[21] Lenin, addressing the 11th Party Congress in 1922, spoke as follows in justification of the NEP: "We have not stopped being revolutionaries. . . . In a new and unusually difficult undertaking, one has to be able to begin from the beginning several times: You begin, you find yourself in a blind alley, you begin again. You'll achieve your goal, even if you have to redo something ten times." Recently one Soviet scholar, after citing this passage, added, "You will agree that this sounds as if it had been written today."[22]

Second, the revolution is not, of course, aimed at overthrowing the existing political order. Although it was made possible by changes in leadership and may eventually bring about still more important changes in the system of selecting leaders in the Soviet Union, the revolution itself does not call into question the supremacy of the Communist Party or its monopoly on power. Indeed, it is the Party that decides how socialism is to be re-created, that chooses the "proper" relations of production to establish. In that sense it is a thoroughly Bolshevik revolution, though taking place long after the victory of Bolshevism. For all the talk about a "revolution from below," this is again a revolution conceived, planned and directed by Party leaders. At times, and at the highest levels, it is defiantly Bolshevik: Gorbachev, at the end of his speech at the January 1987 plenary session of the Central Committee, sought to inspire his colleagues with these words: "We want to force even the skeptics to say: Yes, the Bolsheviks can do anything. Yes, the truth is on their side."[23] This is rhetoric, of course, but its character is symptomatic of an attitude.

Third, it is not a violent revolution or one directed against a clearly identified class enemy. The possibility of nonviolent revolution is not new in Marxist theory: it was accepted by no less an authority than Marx himself and it has long been an established tenet of Marxism–Leninism. The idea of a revolution without a class enemy, however, is more difficult to accommodate within a Marxist framework. Lenin argued that revolution is needed where the interests of opposing classes in a society are *irreconcilable*—that is, where class antagonisms cannot be overcome *within* the existing structure of relations of production. No such irreconcilable class interests are explicitly cited in the present situation by Soviet ideologists, who often seem to proceed as if the transformation were in the real interests of everyone. But if that were so, the existing structure of production relations would seem capable of accommodating change without revolution. No explicit treatment of this matter has yet appeared in the Soviet literature, though there is one obvious suggestion, hinted at by Gorbachev himself and developed obliquely by others: namely, that in the present social system of the USSR the interests of the *bureaucracy* are antagonistic to and irreconcilable with the interests of the public at large. If this suggestion were to be validated openly, it would legitimate the charge, made by observers of the Soviet scene from the time of Milovan Djilas to the present day, that classes with antagonistic interests exist in the USSR.

Fourth, it is not a revolution occurring all at once, but it is a protracted process, carried out over an indefinitely long period of time. Gorbachev has spoken of "separate stages" to be traversed in the advance toward the qualitatively new state of socialist society called for in the Party Program,[24] but he has also rejected requests for a timetable, noting that Lenin warned against promising too much. Gorbachev has been willing to say only that the process of reaching the new state would extend "into the next century."[25] It is interesting to note that in the original draft of the new Program, which was circulated for discussion in late 1985, the qualitatively new state was given a name, 'integral socialism'; but that expression was eliminated in the final text, no doubt as part of the effort to avoid specific commitments concerning the future.[26] In any event, full communism is now a still more indefinite prospect than before.

Fundamental changes in Soviet ideology concerned with the specific contours of the new form of socialism to be attained are too extensive to be examined here in any detail. But we may single out for brief attention a few of the articles of the new ideology that may appear to be in conflict with socialist principles.

One is the proposed change with respect to social ownership, directed against the assumption that *state* ownership is the only fully socialist form of ownership of the means of production. The new ideology, while certainly not abandoning the concept of state ownership, proposes that cooperative ownership is a perfectly legitimate and effective form of ownership in socialist society, and even argues that private enterprise is legitimate where it serves socialist ends—that is, where it provides socially valuable functions that cannot be carried out efficiently in other ways *and* is not used to exploit the labor of others. In his speeches Gorbachev has laid particular stress on the value of cooperatives.[27] In his litany of the failures of the Soviet economic system he cited as "incorrect" the attitude that cooperative property is " 'second-rate' and futureless"—an attitude that led, he lamented, to the elimination of producers' cooperatives in the USSR.[28] Accordingly, it is now argued by Soviet ideologists that a socialist order can appropriately combine state ownership with various forms of collective or cooperative ownership and (under specific conditions) with private enterprise. This is one of the things Gorbachev and his associates have in mind when they insist that restructuring is a way of fully utilizing the "advantages and possibilities" of socialism—for example, of combining different sorts of property relations for the most effective functioning of an economy that is governed overall by socialist principles.

Another controversial element of Gorbachev's revolutionary restructuring is the determination to move toward a reliance on exchange relations governed by market forces, or "commodity-money relations," as they are typically called in the Soviet literature. This is one of the provisions of *perestroika* that Gorbachev had in mind when he complained in his 27th Congress speech about the unfortunate tendency to perceive any change in the economic mechanism as "all but a retreat from the principles of socialism."[29] Here again, Gorbachev's simple answer to such misgivings is that socialism is not wedded to the administrative determination of all exchange relations. Market forces can be used *within* a system of socialist control, as a mechanism, the operation of which is subject to constraints set by fundamental socialist norms that include full employment, a living wage, adequate housing and medical care, and so on. Just how to structure this mechanism is, of course, a big question; but according to Gorbachev and his ideologists there is no obstacle in socialist theory to accepting the operation of market forces on what is called "a socialist basis."

The third and final provision of *perestroika* to be commented on in this chapter is paradoxically the easiest for which to provide a socialist defense, but potentially the most disruptive of orthodox Marxist–Leninist ideology. That is the strong emphasis on the human factor in the proposed transformations, and specifically the greatly increased reliance on material incentives—on tying remuneration to performance. The justification presented by Soviet writers is a familiar one: until full communism arrives, and it is possible to reward everyone according to needs, people must be rewarded on the basis of their work—that is, according to the quantity and quality of their social contribution. Though this principle has an impeccably socialist pedigree, the single-minded enthusiasm with which it is being implemented in the Gorbachev revolution raises certain ideological questions and suggests a long-term heretical trend in Marxist–Leninist ideology.

The immediate problem, of course, is the inconsistency between the psychology of personal gain now being promoted and the supposed future goal of an unselfish, unacquisitive, socially minded communist. Some Soviet spokesmen admit that in encouraging the quest for greater material rewards they run the risk of stimulating a "petit bourgeois," private ownership psychology.[30] But typically they pay no further attention to this danger, contending, for example, as Anatolii Butenko recently did, that if the use of material incentives should have undesirable consequences, "in a socialist state the necessary measures can always be taken."[31]

But this is not the main problem for Soviet ideology. The main problem, it could be argued, is that the *reason* Soviet ideologists are not disturbed by the paradox of promoting altruism through stimulating acquisitiveness is that they no longer really believe in the romantic Marxian ideal of the reborn, perfectly unselfish "new man" of communism. They have resolved at long last to take human beings as they are, rather than as they should be. The Soviet leaders have surrendered not to capitalism but to the power of personal interests, and, abandoning the effort to construct a new man, they have embarked on an enterprise of building society in such a way that present-day people can operate it productively. That is, they have decided to build society on the hoary principle that private vice is public virtue: the springs of personal interest, engaged by a properly contrived social mechanism, will operate to produce public benefit. Such springs will be the foundation of what Gorbachev called at the June 1987 plenum "a mighty system of motives and stimuli, prompting all workers to display their capabilities to the full, to labor productively, to utilize productive resources most effectively."[32] The residue of Marxism in this conception is that Gorbachev and his supporters believe the "mighty system" can best be contrived through the workings of an effective *socialist* mechanism, and that is what they are determined to set up.

The capitulation to personal interests, moreover, is a sign of a still broader heretical trend in Soviet ideology—a shift from its historical fixation on *class* interests to a greater concern for human interests of other sorts—personal interests, the interests of groups other than classes, even the common interests of all mankind. The diversity of human interests is making itself felt in Soviet Marxism–Leninism, and Soviet attention is shifting from the class as the unit of social analysis to the individual, and to the rich complexity of motives arising both from the individual's biological makeup and from his diverse social ties and affiliations.

This increased attention to human motives other than class interests may be seen in many current developments in Soviet thought. It is evident, for example, in the rapid expansion of sociological and psychological studies in the USSR. It is seen in the Soviet treatment of morality, in which class roles and values play a clearly diminishing part. It is apparent in the increased attention to the writings of the young Marx, whose criticism of capitalism was couched in humanistic rather than in class terms. It is abundantly evident in the campaign for democratization, an assumption of which appears to be the liberal principle that each individual is the best judge of his or her own interests (rather than the assumption that class interests, as judged by the class "vanguard"—the Communist Party—are of overriding importance).

Finally, one of the more intriguing manifestations of the diminishing weight of class interests in Soviet thinking may be seen in the sphere of international relations, where Gorbachev is now consistently stressing the priority of the common interests of all mankind over all other concerns, including class concerns. Recently, for example, he referred to a particular statement of Lenin's, saying that it contains "a thought of colossal profundity"—namely, "the priority of the interests of social development, of common human values, over the interests of this or that class."[33] The fact that, in the passage Gorbachev paraphrases, Lenin spoke only vaguely of "social development" and did not mention "common human values" at all[34] only serves to point out the seriousness of Gorbachev's own apparent commitment to the thought he attributes to Lenin.

In short, whereas the new thinking appears to concern material incentives, individual enterprise, cooperative property, revolution without a clear class enemy, democratization, and other aspects of *perestroika*, we are witnessing the metamorphosis of Marxism–Leninism from its original status as a class ideology into an ideology that recognizes the power and legitimacy of the personal, group and universal interests of individuals, regardless of class affiliation. And *that* is a revolution of truly massive proportions, which is bound to find further reflection in Soviet practice.

Notes

1. *Current Soviet Policies IX. The Documentary Record of the 27th Congress of the Communist Party of the Soviet Union* (Columbus, OH: The Current Digest of the Soviet Press, 1986), p. 41.

2. "Mikhail Gorbachev's Answers to Questions Put by 'L'Unita'," *Moscow News*, 1987, Supplement to issue No. 22 (3270), p. 2.

3. For an analysis of the doctrine as it was formulated in the Brezhnev era, see James P. Scanlan, *Marxism in the USSR: A Critical Survey of Current Soviet Thought* (Ithaca and London: Cornell University Press, 1985), pp. 224–260.

4. *The Road to Communism. Documents of the 22nd Congress of the Communist Party of the Soviet Union. October 17–31, 1961* (Moscow: Foreign Languages Publishing House, n.d.), p. 589.

5. "Gorbachev Keynotes Ideological Meeting," *The Current Digest of the Soviet Press*, Vol. XXXVI, No. 50 (Jan. 9, 1985), p. 2.

6. *Ibid.*, pp. 2, 27.

7. *Ibid.*, p. 4.

8. "PRAVDA Carries New Edition of CPSU Program," *FBIS Daily Reports*, March 10, 1986, p. 1.

9. *Ibid.*, p. 10 (italics added).

10. *Current Soviet Policies IX*, p. 44.

11. *Ibid.*, p. 23 (italics in original).

12. *Ibid.*, pp. 23–24.

13. *Ibid.*, p. 24.

14. "Gorbachev: Restructuring Equals Revolution," *The Current Digest of the Soviet Press*, Vol. XXXVIII, No. 31 (Sept. 3, 1986), p. 1.

15. "Gorbachev Addresses Party on Change—III," *The Current Digest of the Soviet Press*, Vol. XXXIX, No. 6 (Mar. 11, 1987), p. 14.

16. "Gorbachev Addresses Party on Change—I," *The Current Digest of the Soviet Press*, Vol. XXXIX, No. 4 (Feb. 25, 1987), pp. 3, 6.

17. *Ibid.*, p. 3.

18. *Ibid.*, pp. 3–4.

19. *Ibid.*, p. 6.

20. "O zadachakh partii po korennoi perestroike upravleniia ekonomikoi. Doklad General'nogo sekretaria TsK KPSS M. S. Gorbacheva na Plenume TsK KPSS 25 Iunia 1987 goda," *Pravda*, June 26, 1987.

21. Quoted by G. Smirnov in "Grounding Gorbachev's 'Renewal' in Theory," *The Current Digest of the Soviet Press*, Vol. XXXIX, No. 11 (Apr. 15, 1987), p. 24.

22. Quoted by S. V. Tiutiukin in "Honest Look at All Soviet History Asked," *The Current Digest of the Soviet Press*, Vol. XXXIX, No. 18 (June 3, 1987), p. 4.

23. "Gorbachev Addresses Party on Change—III," p. 14.

24. "Uchit' po-novomu myslit' i deistvovat'. Vsesoiuznoe soveshchanie zaveduiushchikh kafedrami obshchestvennykh nauk. Rech' General'nogo sekretaria TsK KPSS M. S. Gorbacheva," *Kommunist*, October 1986, No. 15, p. 3.

25. *Current Soviet Policies IX*, p. 45.

26. "The Draft Party Program (New Version)," *The Current Digest of the Soviet Press*, Vol. XXXVII, No. 44 (November 27, 1985), p. 8.

27. *Current Soviet Policies IX*, p. 24.

28. "Gorbachev Addresses Party on Change—I," p. 4.

29. *Current Soviet Policies IX*, p. 24.

30. "Ligachev Keynotes Nov. 7 Celebration," *The Current Digest of the Soviet Press*, Vol. XXXVIII, No. 45 (Dec. 10, 1986), p. 4; "Stalinism Linked to Restructuring's Foes," *The Current Digest of the Soviet Press*, Vol. XXXIX, No. 18 (June 3, 1987), p. 6.

31. "Stalinism Linked to Restructuring's Foes," p. 6.

32. "O zadachakh," p. 5.

33. "Vremia trebuet novogo myshleniia," *Kommunist*, November 1986, No. 16, p. 12.

34. V. I. Lenin, *Polnoe sobranie sochinenii*, 5th ed. (Moscow: Izdatel'stvo politicheskoi literatury, 1958–1965), Vol. 4, p. 220.

The Reform Movement: Power, Ideology, and Intellectuals

Nobuo Shimotomai

The reform program unfolding since Gorbachev's accession to power in March 1985 has, despite setbacks, exceeded most Sovietologists' expectations. Particularly after the January 1987 plenum, this tendency was accelerated to the extent that the blueprint for *perestroika* may properly be called radical reform. The January plenum decided to carry out a political reform, while the June plenum finally took the overdue course of fundamental economic reform, although its details are still vague and contradictory in some important respects.

Perestroika has reached beyond the economy to include foreign policy, cultural, and public affairs. Although it is too early for a conclusive estimate, *perestroika* can be compared with other historical turning points of the Soviet Union such as the year 1921, when the NEP (New Economic Policy) was introduced, or the period 1928–1930, when the Stalinist "Revolution from Above" changed Soviet society totally, abolishing the NEP. No wonder that Mikhail S. Gorbachev and his ideologues refer to the introduction of the NEP as an historical analogy. This analogy reflects their understanding that administrative management of the economy and society must be relaxed and basically altered, just as the NEP abolished "war communism." Unlike the NEP, *perestroika* originated not in sudden rethinking but in 30 years of episodic reform efforts, and in a reform movement that was emerging before Gorbachev assumed leadership.

This chapter will trace the origin and orientation of the reformist tendency or movement within the Soviet political establishment as well as the intellectual community; its implication for Gorbachev's *perestroika;* and the link between the reformist power and intellectuals. The word movement will basically refer to that of the official or semi-official groups, rather than to that of the dissidents. Details concerning particular issue areas, such as economic reform or foreign policy, are covered elsewhere in this volume.[1]

The Gorbachev Regime: Consolidation to "Reform"

Even before the advent of the Gorbachev regime, some movements for reform and calls for change existed. Particularly after the death of chief ideologue Mikhail Suslov in 1982, scientific journals began to discuss controversial problems such as "contradictions" of socialist society. Careful statements of General Secretary Yurii Andropov (November 1982 to February 1984) included new agendas for innovation and even reform, while his successor, Konstantin Chernenko, called for the sociological analysis of Soviet society, acknowledging the limit of the dogmatic approach. Scientific journals such as EKO (*The Economy and Organization of Industrial Production*, Novosibirsk), *Problems of Philosophy* (Moscow, Institute of Philosophy), MEMO (*World Economy and International Relations*, prepared by the Institute of the same name), and *Working Class and the Contemporary World* (Institute of the World Workers Movement) often published innovative articles or roundtable discussions. Even the historical journals were occupied with the essays of politicians and political scientists. Academician Tatyana Zaslavskaya's famous 1983 memorandum, which criticized the highly centralized economic system inherited from the 1930's, was read at the higher level and leaked to the West.

However, it was Mikhail S. Gorbachev's leadership that finally took the initiative of comprehensive reform. Many constraints (see this volume, Chapters 2 and 5) have forced Gorbachev into compromises. But some changes favored reform: the Brezhnevite older generation, born in 1900–1910, was leaving, and the next generation was damaged because of World War II; hence the new leadership team had to be composed of relatively young people by Soviet standards. They were born in the 1920's to 1930's, and naturally brought about fresh thinking. Also, the gradual shift of policy toward change after Brezhnev eventually widened the range of discussions, which diversified and even crystallized tendencies or nuances within the Soviet elites.

Gorbachev's policy statements after March 1985 often included important clues for drastic changes, even though they were printed with more cautious expressions.[2] Gorbachev's report at the 27th Party Congress in February 1986 as well as other addresses did include the term radical reform, and other portents of profound change. From the fall of 1986, Gorbachev began to push for political change and for criticism of "bureaucracy," heralding a new part of his strategy for the following years.[3]

The January plenum shows that the Gorbachev leadership acknowledged that piecemeal reform results in only partial success or none at all, and only a bold move forward produces significant change. The results of the "large scale economic experiment" inaugurated in 1984 and being applied on a national scale from 1987 seem moderate. This was revealed in an interview in late 1986 with the deputy chairman of the USSR Council of Ministers' Commission on Economic Mechanism chaired by Nikolai V. Talyzin.[4] The interview dropped public hints that the leadership was ready to go further and attempt change in the price mechanism and supply system.

By June 1987 the Central Committee plenum finally decided to introduce a "new economic mechanism" in place of the worn-out command economy that had been instituted in the Stalinist period and survived for 60 years. Even though this plenum approved only one law, leaving a related package of laws for future adoption, the general guideline for "fundamental reconstruction" was laid down.

Surprisingly, this plenum seemed to go smoothly, despite some tense moments, in comparison with the preceding January plenum, which was postponed three times.[5] Gorbachev's hopes for gains in party democratization and restaffing rested, in part, on the extraordinary Party Conference called for June 1988, the first such conference in 47 years, the first to be elected "by secret ballot."[6]

Personnel changes suggested that Gorbachev's position was strengthened at the highest echelon; from April 1985 to the time of the 27th Congress (February 1986), his personnel policy was mainly aimed at purging the appointees of the Brezhnev generation, such as Nikolai Tikhonov, Andrei Gromyko, Boris Ponomarev as well as his possible rivals or younger conservatives like Grigorii Romanov and Viktor Grishin. In their place, a new leadership team of technocratic background emerged. Premier Nikolai Ryzhkov and Secretary Yegor Ligachev were soon appointed as Politburo members, along with Viktor Chebrikov (KGB). The appointment of Foreign Minister Eduard Shevardnadze and Secretary Lev Zaikov followed. Grishin was replaced as Moscow party leader, as was Boris Yel'tsin, an apparently too outspoken candidate member of the Politburo. Nikolai Talyzin (Gosplan) and Yurii Solovyev (Leningrad Party Secretary) are of technocratic origin. Staffs, particularly at the Council of Ministers level, were dynamically renewed after the appointment of Ryzhkov as Chairman of the Council of Ministers.

A new generation was recruited particularly at the Secretariat level, at the 27th Congress. Anatolii Dobrynin, diplomat, replaced Ponomarev as head of the International Department and Vadim Medvedev replaced Konstantin Rusakov as head of the Department for Liaison with Communist Parties. Another new secretary, Georgii Razumovskii, is responsible for the Party organization, while a woman secretary, Aleksandra Biryukova, is responsible for social policy.

From January 1987, Gorbachev's own strategy on cadres became more apparent. He seemed to have chosen the Secretariat as the lever for *perestroika;* three important members in the Secretariat were advanced to the powerful post of member of the Politburo. Nikolai K. Slyun'kov, head of the Economics Department, was appointed as full member of the Politburo. Slyun'kov's promotion contrasts with Gorbachev's public reprimand (at the June 1987 plenum) of Talyzin, who was official chairman of the Committee for Radical Reform. The abrupt advancement of Viktor Nikonov, the secretary in charge of agriculture, seemed to contrast with the nonadvancement of Vsevolod Murakhovskii, who was responsible for agriculture in the government, even though Murakhovskii had close ties to Gorbachev in the Stavropol region. Anatolii Luk'yanov (General Department), a lawyer and once a fellow student of Gorbachev's, was also appointed as a Secretary in January 1987. The growing role of the Secretariat vis-à-vis the government and economic organization does not seem accidental.

These appointments suggest that Gorbachev chose the Secretariat as the motivating instrument to carry out the economic reform program in the face of reluctant implementation by and resistance of the bureaucracy. There remained a potentially strong brake on reform in the Politburo, especially in the persons of Ligachev, Party second-in-command, and Chebrikov, KGB head, as well as deep-seated resistance in the Party and government *apparat.* Boris Yel'tsin's removal on November 11, 1987, from the post of Moscow First Party Secretary, the humiliating denunciation of him and his abject apology for his "arrogance,"[7] apparently prompted by his direct criticism in October of leaders for the slow pace of reform, raised doubts about Gorbachev's power and his commitment to reform.

Intellectual Renewal under *Perestroika*

The June 1987 plenum suggested how influential the academics and intellectuals who were known as innovators on contemporary Soviet scenes had become. The most significant appointment was that of Aleksandr N. Yakovlev, reputedly personal adviser to Gorbachev, to membership in the Politburo. Yakovlev, an historian by discipline and a reformist-minded Party official, was sent to diplomatic service because of trouble with Russian nationalists.[8] In 1983, he was appointed director of the Institute of the World Economy and International Relations, the most prestigious center for international specialists *(mezhdunarodniki)*, after the death of former director, Inozemtsev. Yakovlev's tie with academic circles signifies the increasing role of academics in the Soviet decisionmaking process.

There was another indication of the rising role of innovative academics and ideologues in policy formation. Just prior to the plenum a meeting took place in the Central Committee where speeches of reformist academicians like Konstantin Popov, an economist at Moscow State University; Georgii Arbatov, director of the Institute on the United States and Canada; Oleg Bogomolov, director of the Institute on the Economics of the World Socialist System; and Leonid Abalkin, director of the Economics Institute, were welcomed by the General Secretary. Gorbachev even commented favorably on Nikolai Shmelev's radical criticism of Soviet economy, printed in the "Novyi Mir" No. 6 for 1987, though he rejected Shmelev's suggestion that some unemployment was inevitable and even desirable.[9] Shmelev, an economist, works in the Institute on the USA and Canada, but his article on his homeland has been his most widely discussed work—in fact, one of the most cited to come out of *glasnost'*.

Gorbachev appeared to count on the help of the Party apparatus coupled with social forces, including the intellectuals, to carry through economic and political reforms. A reform movement is not enough to start things going. Ideological changes also are essential to draw up the blueprints around which to rally the new forces for reform. That is the reason ideological *perestroika* precedes the actual reform (see also Chapter 4).

However, the ideological aspect of Soviet politics had been neglected. One of the reasons for this was that conservatives like the Party ideologues Suslov and Trapeznikov, the former head of the Science and Education Department of the Central Committee, played an important role during the Brezhnev period. No wonder that new leaders like Gorbachev and Yakovlev and others are now criticizing those whose theoretical views reflected the period of the 1930–1940's.[10]

Under new circumstances, however, things dramatically changed. An intellectual awakening resulted from debates on various levels that had been absent since the time of Khrushchev (three decades ago, and the NEP, 60 years ago). This had implications for policy, because, as has been noted, ideological innovation usually precedes real policy change. Also, those persons who advocated new ideas in the 1970's and 1980's play influential roles in *perestroika*, and some occupy important positions.

From this point of view, the new leadership team as a whole is being occupied by moderate or even radical reformists. At the Politburo level, Ligachev is often regarded as conservative, and with some reason, but one should not exaggerate this aspect. His speeches are not totally different from those of Gorbachev. Yakovlev is regarded as an architect of *glasnost'*. At the Secretariat level, Dobrynin, who may have some function as ideologue, is a supporter of "new thinking," while Medvedev is a moderate reformist, according to specialists.[11]

Below this level, the role of the Academy of Sciences may be the most important. In the social science sections, including history and philosophy, new persons were appointed and old reformists became more assertive. The elderly Pyotr Fedoseev, Vice President of the academy, who had a connection with Voznesensky, the first economic reformist, now plays an influential role in "the reform movement," particularly after his 1981 article detailing the contradictions possible under socialism. Abel Aganbegyan, who was appointed secretary of the economic section in 1987, had been an active advocate for reform in the 1970's or earlier. Georgii Smirnov, former aid to Gorbachev and new director of the Institute of Marxism–Leninism, now functions as a liaison between decisionmakers and academic circles. Smirnov's positive comments on Khrushchev's democratization efforts foreshadowed Gorbachev's praise of him (tempered by mention of his impulsive willfulness) for his critique of Stalin and "changes for the better in domestic and foreign policy."[12] Gorbachev's aides include reformists such as I. T. Frolov and A. S. Chernyaev; the latter's article in *Kommunist* on the important role of intellectuals was challenging by Soviet standards.[13] The head of the Cultural Department of the Party Secretariat is now a poet, Yurii P. Voronov.

The reform movement has brought changes in the editorial orientation of *Kommunist*, the theoretical journal of the Central Committee. Just after the 27th Party Congress, Richard Kosolapov, conservative editor-in-chief from the Brezhnev period, was dismissed.[14] Though Jerry Hough once depicted him as moderate, and he had been associated with Gorbachev's Komsomol (youth organization) activities at Moscow State University, his approach on topics such as "contradictions" or the national question was particularly antireformist. No wonder reformist thinkers like A. Butenko of the Institute of the Economy of the World Socialist System criticized him.[15] I. T. Frolov replaced him and soon became an aide to Gorbachev, after which Naily Bikkenin took over as *Kommunist* editor in June 1987. Among newcomers to the journal's editorial board was the Vice President of the USSR Academy of Sciences, Fedoseev, assigned soon after Frolov took over. Other new editorial board members included Otto Latsis, an economist specializing in economic reorganization, Edvard Arab-Ogly, a population specialist in the Party's Academy of Social Sciences, and Yurii Afanas'ev, a historian and champion of the truth about the Stalin era, later moved to head The Institute of the State Historical Archives. Frolov is a key figure bridging Party and academic circles in both natural and social sciences. He was an associate of Pyotr N. Demichev, still a Minister of Culture, and Alexei M. Rumiantsev, former liberal editor of *Pravda*, removed under Brezhnev in 1965 and elevated to a high post in the Academy of Sciences. Frolov also had good relations with the above-mentioned architect of *glasnost'*, Yakovlev.[16] After being appointed editor of *Problems of Philosophy* in 1967 under Brezhnev, Frolov recruited liberal natural scientists like Pyotr Kapitsa and Andrei Sakharov, part of a group opposed to Trofim Lysenko, a charlatan placed in charge of agricultural research by Stalin and Khrushchev. Frolov also launched a discussion on the "scientific and technological revolution," which drew in present proponents of reform like Vadim V. Zagladin (first deputy head of the International Department of the Party Secretariat under Gorbachev), and academics like Dzherman M. Gvshiani, an administrator and a leading specialist in systems analysis and management studies.[17]

Out of the reform movement have come ideological innovations such as the de-emphasis of "class," of the Marxist–Leninist view of the world as fundamentally polarized between capitalist–imperialist and socialist forces and interests, and an emphasis on "globalist" thinking. First appearing in the 1970's in academic circles, globalism places the interests of all mankind above class interests. Globalists perceive humankind as threatened by the nuclear and ecological crisis. They see the world economy as one of interdependence rather than divided along ideological lines.

Frolov is, along with Zagladin, a proponent of globalism. Another globalist is Georgii Shakhnazarov. A lawyer by training and political scientist by vocation, Shakhnazarov, like some of the other members of Gorbachev's circle, brings an academic background to Party activity. An advocate of "new thinking" *(novoe myshlenie,)* he was elevated under Gorbachev to first deputy head of the Department for Liaison with Communist and Workers' Parties of the Socialist Countries. New thinking is strongly represented among scholars of IMEMO, the Institute of World Economics and International Relations, beginning with its director, Evgenli Primakov, and the above-mentioned Arab-Ogly, also a member of the editorial board of *Kommunist*.[18] The web of reformist connections and thinking stretches over time and space. It was not something improvised in 1985, and it crosses the line between Party work and academia.

In sum, the old Stalinist generation with its neo-Stalinistic dogma is now leaving the leadership ranks, and new (though not necessarily younger) people who had a connection with the Academy of Sciences, including natural scientists, are coming to the foreground. Academician Sakharov's return from exile is interesting in this context. Second, innovative social scientists and philosophers have been more visible in the discussion. Third, even in the party apparatus, new thinkers like Zagladin, Medvedev and Shakhnazarov are gaining influence.

Another important indicator of ideological change is the fact that Gorbachev and Ligachev have adopted the term "developing socialism" instead of "developed socialism." Though the reason is unclear, no serious article on developing socialism has appeared so far, compared with the spate of treatises on developed socialism in the late 1920's and early 1970's. Soviet leaders now seem less prone to dogmatic, "diamat" type of thinking. In addition, they are more critical of the real situation of the Soviet economy. Anyway, they do not want to jump ahead of history. This surely implies that they hold a sober view of socialism in the developing world.[19]

Political Implications of Intellectual Renewal

The difficult issue for the new leadership remains how to change, not whether to change. There are no ready-made answers. The *Kommunist* discussions on social justice constitute an attempt to define the new objectives. Under the new circumstances, corporatist integration of the important social groups and institutions that existed in the Brezhnev period no longer works. Economic reform surely produces winners as well as losers, and social cleavages are unavoidable. A new alignment of social forces is inevitable.

Reformist sociologist Zaslavskaya's *Kommunist* article pointed out two important things: first, Soviet society should be viewed as a pluralistic one, which contradicts the orthodox image of a harmonious socialist society. More importantly, she argues that a producer's incentive to work is more critical than the problem of distribution. The present policy of leveling distribution coupled with the shortage of basic goods has resulted in speculation and black market activity and de facto inequality. She therefore supports a cut in state subsidies and eventually higher prices for housing and food.[20]

The conservatives have their own arguments for social justice. In fact, several are against the differentiation of incomes. Conservatives see "Shabashniki" (illegal migrant contract workers) and individual labor activity as paving the way to a differentiation of the social strata that will endanger the Soviet social system. Recent discussion on privilege, particularly on the "spetsshkola" (special school), reveals this dilemma: justice, on the one hand, productivity, on the other, although reformists favor emphasizing both.[21]

What, then, is new in the approach of the new Soviet elites? We can identify three aspects of it: sociological, ecological and economic, and last, limited destatization. These aspects emerged because of the limitations of the traditional ideological frame of reference.

The first new dimension is the sociological one. Although the institutionalization of sociology is not new, sociology in the 1970's suffered a serious setback. This discipline was regarded as a second-rate science, and able sociologists were discouraged, as Zaslavskaya wrote recently.[22] But Andropov and Chernenko acknowledged the necessity of an empirical survey of Soviet society. Sociological research is needed to analyze social interests and changes involved in the economic reforms. Economic restructuring entails the reorganization of Soviet society, in which class, strata and groups are distinguished, and "human factors" must be understood and mobilized as tools to carry out the reforms. The June 1983 plenum under Andropov decreed the use of sociology and, particularly, of the opinion poll, which had been introduced in such advanced regions as Stavropol and Georgia in the 1970's.[23]

Second, the ecological approach is now in vogue because the super-industrialization drive and vast investment policy resulted in the deterioration of the environment. A response to this problem began in the 1970's. Then Gorbachev was a member of the Supreme Soviet Commission on Conservation. The Party's cancellation of the diversion program of the Siberian and other rivers (in August 1986) marked a turning point in this respect; and campaigns against the pollution of Lake Raduga, Lake Baikal, and Yasnaya Polyana are underway, involving novelists, ecologists, journalists and others. Frolov argues that the ecological situation is the number two global problem, following nuclear survival.[24]

Third, in the economic sphere, a movement for limited privatization is underway. The long-standing identification of state ownership as the highest stage of socialism is being questioned, and the idea of self-management is emerging, although on a limited scale. A bold critic has identified Soviet socialism as "state socialism."[25] The first step in privatization is the revival of cooperative enterprises and the official endorsement of individual enterprise. This, in turn, implies that the *kolkhoz* (farm cooperative) system should not be underestimated, and the movement to reorganize *kolkhozes* into *sovkhozes* (state farms, run like factories, and with smaller private plots than on the kolkhozes) should be stopped.

Also relevant to this discussion is the problem of the decentralization of enterprises, which leads to the problem of the bankruptcy of enterprises as *khozrashchet* (self-financing) units. Actually, a Leningrad enterprise has been bankrupted.

The speed of the public debate on decentralization and its practice is astonishing. In the fall of 1986 Hungarian bankruptcy was discussed.[26] The next January, Dr. Latsis only referred to the legal problem;[27] a draft law on the state enterprise appeared in February and was passed in June, to go into effect January 1, 1988 and to be implemented within 2 years.

Sources of Reformists' Ideas

The ideas for economic reforms relate to two areas: first, the process of the economic reform and its implementation, or, more concretely, the lessons of economic experiments; and second, the lessons from fraternal countries.

It ought to be kept in mind that various kinds of experiments preceded economic reform, aside from the 1965 or 1979 decrees. Several reform experiments proceeded in the beginning of the 1980's, first in Georgia and the Baltic republics. Here a large-scale economic experiment was introduced selectively in 1984 and spread to all enterprises by 1987. The extent of the reform is limited and was never called economic reform. Also, the 1983 decree on workers' collectives introduced some collective principles as well as some kind of social contract with management. From 1987 on seven ministries and their enterprises operated under the principle of full *khozrashchet*.

The point is that the tempo of the experiment-results cycle is swift and the process is open. Academic journals such as *Sociological Research* (on workers collective) and *Soviet State and Law* often discuss the interim results. The shift toward radical reform is now necessitated by the recognition that lukewarm measures provide no substantial results.[28]

A second source of ideas, the input from the fraternal countries, has had an international impact, posing a serious problem for the Soviet Union, which had monopolized the orthodoxy of socialist states on reform. In 1985, just after Gorbachev was appointed, a harsh attitude toward small socialist countries was revealed in a *Pravda* article by Vladimirov (pseudonym for O. Rakhmanin, first deputy head of the

Department for Liaison with Communist and Workers Parties of the Socialist Countries). But articles in *Kommunist* and elsewhere encouraged moderation and respect for reform.[29] The Institute of Economics of the World Socialist System under its director, Oleg Bogomolov, is a base for reformist-minded scholars. Soviet scholars pay close attention to reforms by socialist countries including China.[30]

This readiness to consider the Chinese experience as legitimate and instructive has had an impact on Chinese–Soviet relations. Fedor Burlatskii's objective and somewhat favorable article on Chinese reform in *Literaturnaia gazeta* in May 1986, as well as his TV program, was reportedly a shock for Soviet audiences. Burlatskii, a lawyer by training, member of the Academy of Social Sciences of the Central Committee, correspondent of *Literaturnaia gazeta,* and once a speech writer for Khrushchev, had been a harsh critic of Chinese reforms before the Soviet Union undertook a similar program. The coverage of China in *Problems of the Far East (Problemy dal'nego vostoka)* is positive. Even after the fall of General Secretary Hu Yaobang in January 1987, *Izvestiia* ran a lengthy article on Chinese reform.

Changing Frame of Reference: Lessons of History

The movement for *perestroika* is closely related to the revival of NEP ideas and to strong criticism of the Stalinist system. This aspect of ideological innovation is necessitated by the introduction of radical reform, which goes beyond the technological modernization of the system. After the 27th Party Congress where Gorbachev referred to Lenin's 1921 *prodnalog,* a tax-in-kind on produce (an incentive to grow more), which actually brought about the NEP, some writers, most notably Burlatskii, again advanced the idea of a tax-in-kind on produce.[32]

This new tendency of ideology directly affects the work of the Commission on Economic Reform by encouraging a radical reform program for decentralization. Although the NEP itself is not directly applicable to the present Soviet economy, as economists like Abalkin and others emphasize, the necessity for both drastic change as well as "normal" management of the economy put the reevaluation of the NEP on the agenda.[33] This, in turn, involves the negation of the highly centralized command economy built during the Stalinist period of the first and second 5-year plans.

It was natural that by the end of 1986, neo-NEP ideologues began to criticize the Stalinist system. Ambartsumov and Loginov (a pseudonym for Afanas'ev) identified the Stalinist system with "war communism," which implied that the Stalinist period was a deviation from socialism, thus abandoning long-standing dogma of Stalinist-type industrialization as the sole method of socialism.[34] The Stalinist period was untouchable in the 1970's, partly because the contemporary Soviet institutions—and political careers—were rooted in this period; institutions remained basically the same, though the coercion mechanism was criticized and curtailed by Khrushchev in the 1950's.

Questioning the Stalinist system opened a Pandora's box of new issues. Above all, new research on this topic had to be allowed for specialists as well as for novelists and intellectuals. Second, those people who criticized Stalinism and/or fell victim to it merited rehabilitation. Third, a new mechanism to prevent its recurrence had to be built into the system; that is, democratization of the system had to be allowed.

In the first place, this move resulted in the intellectual revival that had been frozen during the Brezhnev period. This *glasnost'* campaign in particular is related to free discussion of the past. Gorbachev and others mentioned that there should be no forgotten name in history. Gorbachev eventually explicitly endorsed reconsideration of Stalin and his era.[35] Historians like Afanas'ev and I. Mints argue that historical research was hindered under Brezhnev by the official historians. Afanas'ev, already identified as Rector of the Institute of Historical Archives, started an open seminar series where progressive historians and writers gave lectures on forbidden themes, such as the origins of Stalinism, collectivization and the Soviet bureaucracy.

This provoked a reaction by some conservative historians, and public protest on their behalf.[36] But on the whole, progressive historians are gaining power. Dr. Viktor Danilov, whose work on collectivization was repressed in the 1960's by conservative historians, is publishing again.[37]

As far as the social scientists are concerned, political scientists and reformist economists generally favor the idea of the NEP. Academician Bogomolov and his colleagues, Ambartsumov, Butenko, Latsis, and Novopashin, are supporters of the type of economic reform instituted in Hungary or Poland. They favor cooperatives or individual initiative in the agrarian sector and decentralization of economic management.

Novelists like Boris Mozhaev and Anatolii Rybakov exposed more assertively than did historians the dark sides of collectivization and Stalinism.[38] Tengiz Abuladze's film "Repentence" as well as Rybakov's novel *Children of the Arbat* re-create the terror of the Stalinist period. It was novelist M. F. Shatrov (a relative of Mikhail Rykov, second chairman of the Council of the People's Commissariats Soviet premier), whose film and play on Lenin first showed how Lenin's government, including Trotsky, argued problems such as the 1918 Brest–Litovsk peace Treaty.[39]

This movement paved the way for the rehabilitation of the anti-Stalinist Party leader Nicolai Bukharin and for the possible rehabilitation of such politicians as Grigorii Zinoviev and Lev Kamenov, had been Lenin's comrades and Politburo members during the 1920's, and who were purged in the second half of the 1930's. Zinoviev and Kamenev were discussed in full pages of *Sovetskaia Rossiia*, though their behavior in 1917 was criticized. The name of Trotsky and "Trotskyites" such as Rakovsky, Muralov and Smilga appeared in print.[40]

In the case of Smilga and Serebryakov, party level rehabilitation was already in process.[41] N. I. Bukharin, famous ideologue of the NEP period who was sentenced to death in 1938, received a partial rehabilitation, with qualifications, in Gorbachev's 70th Anniversary speech,[42] after years of petitioning by his widow that the Party honor the request in Bukharin's testament for rehabilitation.[43] Gorbachev's oral rehabilitation of Bukharin was not unexpected. Yurii Afanas'ev asserted that Bukharin would be reinstated. This was followed by an article by Burlatskii in which Lenin's testament was referred to citing more or less favorable references to Bukharin among Lenin's last words to the Party.[44] Party theorists are now editing the writings of Bukharin, though the works written during his leftist communist period are still under discussion.

This move toward rehabilitation is not limited to the party level. Chayanov, Kondrat'ev and thirteen other noncommunist economists who were purged in the early 1930's are also rehabilitated.[45]

"Demokratizatsiia": A New Soviet Union?

Reformists are also critical of the Stalinist model of a socialist system. B. Kurashvili, a specialist on administration, the economist Shmelev, and others regard the Stalinist system as a kind of military or abnormal way of managing society, which has nothing in common with socialism. Gorbachev himself is more cautious, though he openly condemned the great purge and later, Stalin too.[47]

The movement for de-Stalinization surely is part of a wider campaign for democratization. From the fall of 1986 onward, Gorbachev criticized the bureaucracy and lack of democracy in Soviet society. This was followed by the introduction of the multiple-candidate system for Soviets and enterprises at the January 1987 plenum.[48]

Democratization is closely related to the campaign for economic reform. A loosening of the centralized hierarchical structure cannot occur without democratization. Economic reformers also advocate political reforms. Boris Kurashvili, one of the leading scholars for decentralization, is advocating the building of a kind of countervailing power within the bureaucracy; actually he is one of the active supporters for the democratization of the Academy of Sciences.[49] His colleagues, such as Mikhail I. Piskotin in the Institute of State and Law, have criticized the centralized system. An effort continues to enliven local soviets (government councils) and give them effective authority over enterprises on community matters.[50]

One of the salient new developments is the emergence of autonomous "informal" organizations of various kinds, from ecologists to nationalists like Pamyat. Indeed, various small ad hoc groups including writers like Valentin Rasputin, are discussing and acting effectively on the need to protect Siberian rivers, architectural monuments and lakes.[51]

In 1987, novelists are assertive and bold enough to criticize the military establishment. Thus the well-known novelist Ales' Adamovich criticized some military thinkers because they were still sticking to the nuclear deterrence strategy with which Gorbachev already had found fault.[52] This was countered by Dmitrii Volkogonov, deputy head of the Main Political Directorate of the army, who said novelists' conscience is one thing but military responsibility is another, suggesting that Adamovich was a "vegetarian pacifist."[53] Another novelist, Chingdis Aitmatov, also criticized the military burden on the economy, along with Academician Evgenii Primakov.[54]

It ought to be noted that this type of social movement, coupled with political control from above, can easily be applicable to economic reform. No wonder that the role of political initiative is a topic for scholarly discussion.[55] It is a means of bringing reformist pressure on the reluctant economic administration to change its ways. The political reform program for democratization advocated at the January plenum was a sign that Gorbachev's was prepared to modify the political system to guarantee radical change and to rally social forces, to the support of *perestroika.*

The *perestroika* policy will be larger in scale, *if it succeeds,* than was the de-Stalinization campaign carried out by Khrushchev. This is because Gorbachev has begun to change completely the foundations of the Soviet social system, parts of which were established in the 1930's and have remained almost untouched.

Of course, changing ideology and political control over the intellectual is one thing, implementing the ideas of intellectuals is quite another, even when they are included in the party documents. The future of radical reform is not easy to predict. The reformist leadership must secure the cooperation of various social forces to enforce and carry out reforms, unless they abandon the objective of reform. Soviet society under Brezhnev had stagnated enough to compel his successors to try radical reform, and to prompt intellectuals years before that to develop the new ways of thinking and ideological changes necessary to give at least some direction to reform.

Notes

1. I am thankful to the other participants of the Conference for their insights.
2. M. S. Gorbachev, *Korennoi vopros ekenomicheskoi politiki* (Moscow: Politizdat, 1985). This pamphlet differs slightly from his speech, broadcast by Moscow TV at that time. His clear TV statement on the necessity of price reform was printed as "perfection of the price system" in the text.
3. *Pravda*, September 20, 1986.
4. *Pravda*, December 22, 1986.
5. The political and particularly the administrative agendas of the Gorbachev government are already suggested 'on the plan of the drafting legislative acts for the completion of legislation for 1986–1990,' published in *Sobranie postanovlenii pravitel'stva*, No. 31 (1986). This list of 39 decrees is more or less related to the reforms, although more concrete laws of radical reforms are not mentioned.
6. Thane Gustafson and Dawn Mann, "Gorbachev's Next Gamble," *Problems of Communism*, 36, No. 4 (July–August 1987), pp. 1–20.
7. *Pravda*, November 13, 1987.
8. Alexander Yanov, *The Russian Challenge and the Year 2000* (Oxford, NY: Basil Blackwell, 1987), pp. 120–23.
9. *Pravda*, June 13, 1987; N. Shmelev in *Novyi mir*, No. 6 (1987); *International Herald Tribune*, July 4–5, 1987.
10. *Pravda*, January 29, 1987.
11. S. Fortesque, *The Communist Party and Soviet Science* (London: Macmillan, 1986), p. 77.
12. *Pravda*, March 13, 1987; November 3, 1987.
13. A. Chernyaev, "Postoianno rastuiuschii i razvivaiushchiisia klass-gegemon," *Kommunist*, No. 11 (1972).
14. N. Shimotomai, "Controversy on contradictions under Socialism (in Japanese)," *Kokusaiseizi (International Politics)*, Vol. 81 (Tokyo), 1986.
15. A. Butenko, "Teoreticheskie problemy sovershenstvovaniia novogo stroia," *Voprosy filosofii*, No. 2 (1987).
16. A. Nekrich, *Otrekshis' ot strakha* (London: Overseas Publication, 1979), p. 265.

17. W. G. Hahn, *Post War Soviet Politics* (New York: Cornell Univ. Press, 1982), pp. 169–181.

18. N. Shimotomai, "G. Orwel wa ikani yomaretaka," *Sekai*, No. 2 (1986).

19. See, Jerry Hough, *The Struggle for the Third World* (Washington: Brookings, 1986), and others. Incidentally, the idea of "developed socialism" was originally proposed in the 1960's and early 1970's by Burlatskii and Butenko, who had been reformists even at that time, and they included democratization and economic reform, though L. Brezhnev's idea was not identical to theirs. *Voprosy filosofii*, No. 10 (1984), p. 23; A. Zimin, *Sotsializm i neostalinizm* (New York: Chaldize Publications, 1981), Chap. 7.

20. T. Zaslavskaia, "Chelovecheskii faktor razvitiia ekonomiki i sotsial'naia spravedlivost', *Kommunist*, No. 13 (1986), pp. 61–73.

21. *Sovetskaia rossiia*, February 22, 1987.

22. *Pravda*, February 6, 1987.

23. Incidentally, Mrs. Raisa M. Gorbacheva was a sociologist by training and specialized in rural sociology.

24. Moscow TV (vtoraia programma) on June 8, 1987.

25. *Literaturnaia gazeta*, June 3, 1987 (A. Zlobin).

26. *Literaturnaia gazeta*, November 26, 1986.

27. *Moskovskie novosti*, No. 3 (1987).

28. "Krupnomasshtabnyi ekonomicheskii eksperiment," *Sovetskoe gosudarstvo i pravo*, No. 7 (1985), pp. 44–68; "Obsuzhdaem proekt zakona SSSR 'o gosudarstvennom predpriiatii," *Sovetskoe gosudarstvo i pravo*, No. 5 (1987), pp. 3–10.

29. O. Bogomolov, "Soglasovanie ekonomicheskikh interesov i politiki pri sotsializme," *Kommunist*, No. 10 (1985), p. 91; *Pravda*, March 17, 1986; June 21, 1985.

30. A. A. Goryachev, S. Yu. Shchavleev, "Metodologicheskie voprosy sravnitel'nogo analiza khozyiaistvennikh mekhanizmov sotsialisticheskikh stran," *Vorposy filosofii*, No. 2 (1986).

31. *Literaturnaia gazeta*, June 11, 1986.

32. *Literaturnaia gazeta*, April 23, 1986.

33. *Sovetskaya Rossiya*, July 19, 1987.

34. *Moskovskie novosti*, Nov. 9, 1986.

35. *Pravda*, February 14, 1987; November 3, 1987.

36. *Moskovskie novosti*, May 10, 1987; *Sovetskaia kul'tura*, July 4, 1987.

37. *Pravda*, August 9, 1987.

38. B. Mozhaev, "Muzhiki i babi," *Don*, No. 1 (1987); A. Rybakov, "Deti Arbata," *Druzhbi narodov*, Nos. 4, 5, 6 (1987).

39. Moscow TV, January 19–21, 1987; *Novyi mir*, No. 4 (1987).

40. *Yomiuri Shinburn*, August 26, 1987.

41. *Sovetkaia industrializatsiia*, July 5, 1987.

42. *Pravda*, November 3, 1987.

43. N. Shimotomai, "Buhharin fukken undo no imi," *Ashi Journal,* November 24, 1978.

44. *Literaturnaia gazeta,* July 22, 1987.

45. *Moskovskie novosti,* August 16, 1987.

46. *Ivestiia Sibirskogo otdeleniia AN SSSR. Seriia ekonomiki i prikladnoi sotsiologiia,* No. 7, vyp. 2 (1985), pp. 12–23.

47. *Pravda,* July 15, 1987; November 3, 1987.

48. *Pravda,* January 29, 1987.

49. B. Kurashvili, *Ocherki teorii gosudarstvennogo upravleniia* (Moskva: Nauka, 1987), pp. 203–205.

50. *Nash sovremennik,* No. 1, 1987, pp. 160–62.

51. N. Shimotomai, Gorbachev no seizi, *Gendai no riron,* No. 1, 1987; S. P. Zalygin, *Povorot* (Moscow, MYSL'), 1987, and Personal information in Moscow in June 1987.

52. *Moskovskie novosti,* March 8, 1987.

53. *Literaturnaia gazeta,* May 6, 1987.

54. *Ogonek,* No. 28 (1987).

55. V. P. Mushinskii, "Politicheskaia sistema i politicheskaia initsiativa," *Sovetskoe gosudarstvo i pravo,* No. 5 (1987), pp. 3–10.

Gorbachev's Economic Reforms

Tatsuo Kaneda

Few people would question Gorbachev's intense desire for change. His statements introducing reforms have conveyed his sense of a severe crisis looming in the present trend of the Soviet economy. The fall of the economic growth rate clearly makes it increasingly difficult to find sufficient resources for investment, military needs and consumption. No less apparent is the loss of prestige of the Soviet system both inside and outside the country, and the erosion of the Party's authority over the citizenry.

Soviet leaders face the wastefulness of their entire economy; a decrease in the Soviet capacity for technological development; dependency on the technological progress of the West; a drop in international competitiveness; chronic shortages of basic necessities; the existence of black markets; widespread bribery and corruption; growing debt; feelings of alienation and habitual drinking among the people, who avoid work and whose rates of illness and mortality are increasing. An immediate solution is needed. Under the circumstances, it is natural that reform to revitalize the economy is the current Soviet administration's top priority.

The first of the immediate goals of economic recovery is to achieve a rate of economic growth that makes it possible to simultaneously expand investments, meet military needs, and provide for adquate consumption.

Curing economic maladies would close the gap between ideology and reality, restore the authority of the government and Party, and ensure the Soviet Union's position as a superpower.

There is no accurate measure of the extent to which Gorbachev's sense of danger and his willingness to restructure the economy are shared by Party officials and by the general citizenry. There is evidence that a circle of Party leaders and specialists share his views, but there are also signs of widespread resistance to all or parts of *perestroika*, as well as indifference, a sense that *perestroika* is just another one of those caprices Soviet leaders have indulged in over and over again. (See Chapters 1, 2, 4.)

Ambitious development goals have much to do with Gorbachev's willingness to discard conventional Soviet economic models and to construct a radically new economic system.[1] The officially pronounced aim is to renovate the technical base in the 1980's, and thereby to increase economic growth rates dramatically in the 1990's. The percentage of internationally competitive industrial goods produced is to be raised from only 29% of the total production today (it may actually be far less than that) to 85 to 90% by 1990. This is too ambitious a goal given the state of the Soviet economy.

Shortcomings in the Soviet Economic System

Much of Gorbachev's critique of the Soviet economic system showed a debt to expert analysis already developed by the early 1960's. Arguments for reform proliferated then, supported by the rapid blossoming of mathematical economics and by Khrushchev's encouragement of economic experiments, though reform efforts under Khrushchev such as the regional economic councils failed. Recognition of the structural problems of the Soviet economic system was almost as fully developed as it is today. Then as now the critics drew attention to excessive centralization of planning, pricing and allocation of production inputs; the predominance of command methods in administering the lower levels of organization; the lack of rational standards for decisions on economic policy; autocratic styles of management neglecting the human factor, and so on. Urgent calls for systematic reform came from economists like Nemchinov, Novzhilov, Venzher, Birman, Malyshev, Fedorenko and Lisitsyn.[2] Academician Novozhilov led the arguments for reform. Along with his critique, he submitted a general model of a new mechanism to replace the old one. Nemchinov died in 1964, before the 1965 attempt at reform by Premier Alexei Kosygin, who served under Brezhnev. His penetrating analysis of defects in the Soviet economic system and proposals for reform left an influential legacy.

Andropov's brief term in office following Brezhnev brought a spurt in reformist thinking, typified by the 1983 Novosibirsk economic report to a closed seminar, said to be written by Tatiana Zaslavskaia, an economic sociologist and one of the leading influences on Gorbachev. The report points out that the centralized Soviet economy grew out of the unusual drive for heavy industrialization in the 1930's. Since the completion of that drive, the structure of industry has changed extensively, the citizens' level of education has risen, and the old system has become obsolete and an obstacle to economic development. It cramps individual initiative, sustains a superfluous middle level of administrators who will not be removed without "social conflict," and breeds a dispirited labor force lacking in discipline and incentive.[3]

The shortcomings of the Soviet economy described in the Novosibirsk report and elsewhere can be found in analyses by Western researchers of the Soviet "command economy," as they called it. The diagnoses of Soviet and Western economists almost completely converged.[4]

Gorbachev's diagnosis of the current situation and his prescriptions for its remedy follow the points of argument in the Novosibirsk report. Furthermore, he followed the logic of the reformists of the 1960's in his program for all-out economic reconstruction.[5] In fact, he quoted from Nemchinov's essay, published in 1964, on the fossilization of the Soviet economic system and its eventual collapse therefrom, to the June 1987 Central Committee plenum.[6]

Gorbachev's serious view of the economic situation can be appreciated from his measured and partially acquiescent response to Nikolai Shmelev's merciless impeachment of the economy in an article that had Moscow buzzing in June 1987.

Shmelev depicted an economy both overcentralized and out of control under conflicting bureaucratic interests, an economy of the producer's monopoly in a situation of goods scarcity, an economy characterized by indifference among enterprises to technological upgrading, an economy producing, in other than "patriotic" estimates, only 7 to 8% of output meeting world standards of quality, an economy in which agricultural production will soon be hopelessly inadequate if the official stranglehold on the farms is not eased. Shmelev suggested that the present centralized system of economic administration is not the only possible form of socialism, but one which wrongly turned its back on the economy of the New Economic Policy (NEP period 1921–1928) and grew out of the war communism preceding NEP and a ruinous collectivization and forced industrialization after NEP, historical accidents that have outlived their time.[7]

Assertions like this have been common among Western researchers for quite a while. For the Soviet reader indoctrinated to believe that the present system is sacred and inviolable, Shmelev's article smashed many idols. Gorbachev, in his limited comment on the piece based on references to Shmelev's "dubious remedies" by a voter, called Shmelev's depiction "close to what exists in actual fact." At the same time, however, Gorbachev put a limit on any move toward the market in rejecting Shmelev's prescription of unemployment to remedy shirking and indiscipline as "inappropriate" in light of socialism's valued gift of individual security in the form of the right to work.[8]

Reform Measures During the First Two Years

Gorbachev began his reform program with a series of sociopolitical measures that include: an antialcoholism drive, tightening of labor discipline, *glasnost'*, democratization, new legislative curbs on "unearned income" as part of a drive against corruption, retirements and reshuffling of high-ranking officials, and the rechanneling of investments from construction to retooling aimed at increasing productivity.

The government also turned to piecemeal economic restructuring, often in line with recommendations of the 1983 Novosibirsk report. One group of measures brought about reorganization within the central economic administration. Five agricultural ministries were integrated into one super-ministry, the State Committee for Agroindustry, and a functional bureau was set up in the Council of Ministers to oversee the work of ministries in matters of energy, machine building, and social problems. Construction ministries were shifted from functional to regional subdivisions, creating a Scientific and Industrial Complex to speed up research and development, and a State Committee for External Economic Relations was established to coordinate foreign economic transactions.

A second group of measures was aimed at freeing up enterprise and local initiative. Among them, a large-scale reform experiment started in 1984, along with self-financing and economic accountability (rewards linked to profit and loss) for some enterprises. A *prodnalog*, or tax in kind system, which harked back to NEP, was initiated based on the idea that farms could dispose of all production as they wished on the open market after a stated level of delivery to the state. Farmers were encouraged, at least in principle, to operate in groups or as families on the contract system, which tied returns directly to the group's results. Some twenty-five enterprises and ministries received the right to engage directly in foreign trade on a profit and loss basis. Work went ahead on the State Enterprise Law (see below).

A third group of measures diversified forms of ownership. Private individual and cooperative undertakings received legal sanction (see Chapter 2), as did the contract system already mentioned. The door opened to joint ventures with foreign capitalist enterprises.

At the same time a state quality control system *(gospriemka)* began that must be deemed regressive, inhibiting liberation of the enterprise through increasing government intervention.

Western opinion concluded that such measures yielded no significant change.[9] The Soviets concurred. Gorbachev warned the Party that it would be impssible to overcome the crisis facing the Soviet economy with only such incomplete measures, and that the time was ripe for a genuine sweeping reconstruction.

There must have been some members of the Central Committee who felt secretly that the direction of the reform policy was wrong from the beginning. However, at its meeting of June 25 and 26, 1987, the Party Central Committee affirmed the judgment passed by Gorbachev on the current situation. The plenum depicted the results of reform to that date as "partial and trivial," leaving a system still overcentralized, wasteful, inefficient, and guided by obsolete planning and administrative mechanisms. The Party called for "radical reform" to bring about an "efficient, flexible system of economic management," one which would "demonstrate the superiority of socialism to the maximum,"[10] and adopted in broad outline a schedule for "radical economic reform."[11]

Principles of the "Radical Economic Restructuring"

The Central Committee was not prepared to elaborate a complete blueprint for change. The five basic principles of reform included only one that the Central Committee deemed ready for legislation, and that was the establishment of enterprise autonomy (see below). The other four principles remained just that.

First, central economic administrative agencies were to shift from detailed administration to making strategic decisions on priorities and balance of development, and to desist from interfering in the day-to-day operations of enterprises.

Second, there was to be a shift from a mechanism driven by detailed planning and administrative orders to one propelled by economic levers, meaning a change in price formation and the system of financing. The supply of producer goods was to be based on the wholesale market, not central allocation. *Perestroika* in retail trade meant going from fixed contracts to a retail market and consumer primacy, and there were to be reforms in the field of foreign trade, labor, and social affairs.

Third, the new economic structure must be built so as to promote a direct link between science and production, thereby upgrading product quality to world standards.

Fourth, excessive central controls should be replaced by democratic and autonomous production relations in order to revitalize the human factor.

Blocked on inner-Party democratization once again (see Chapter 2), Gorbachev had to be content with the unusual measure of calling a Party conference for 1988 (its delegates to be elected by secret ballot, a new departure) to consider that subject, along with Party work and economic plan results. The process of economic *perestroika* was not scheduled for completion for 4 or 5 years, by 1991–1992—actually a short time for such far-reaching changes.

Enterprise Autonomy

Without waiting for these changes, the State Enterprise Law[12] decrees that the center of decisionmaking shift from the ministries and planners to the enterprises, as the 1983 Novosibirsk report had recommended. Enterprises are, in principle, to prepare their own economic plans, choose their suppliers and compete for customers. This market-type behavior will be impossible until old habits of dependency are broken and the contextual reforms anticipated in the remaining four basic principles of reconstruction translate into a market environment. Only such an environment will give both space and need for enterprise choices and risktaking.

Introduction of Complete Profit–loss system

Enterprise self-financing and economic accountability enter the law as essential accompaniments of management autonomy. Self-financing means enterprise income and profit will be the sole source of the remunerations of the workers of funds for investment and of expenditures on social welfare (nurseries, canteens, housing, clubs, etc.). If and when the law is fully carried out, an enterprise with chronic deficits in its balance sheet (requiring the state's assistance for a considerable period of time) would merge with other enterprises or close down. Economic accountability means that the remuneration of management and workers will follow a strict merit system, and reflect their enterprises' profits and losses.

Wholesale Market Role in Production Inputs

The central allocation of production components has been the hard core of the Soviet economic system. Numerous kinds of detrimental effects are ascribed to this supply mechanism. Now, according to the

Basic Provisions, this mechanism will be converted to a wholesale trade system in 4 or 5 years, that is by 1991 or 1992. This, supposedly, will enable an enterprise to procure machinery, materials, fuel and other necessary production items of the types and at the times its production schedule requires. The Novosibirsk report did not mention specifically the meaning of removing this mainstay of the centrally planned economy. It is, however, comparable in importance to the decreeing of enterprises' operative autonomy.

Democratization of Enterprise Management

Although the law left the traditional one-man management system untouched, it calls for the participation of workers in the preparation of management plans and in the appointment and dismissal of the director and managerial staff. To the extent that this occurs, it will bring a revision of the long-standing principle of vertical management.

All told, from a legal point of view, the new Soviet economic mechanism is a big departure from the one inherited from the Stalin era. The problem is to implement the law and to realize operatively the broad ideals of reform.

The ideal state of the reformed economy sought by Gorbachev will be a harmonious combination of intelligent central planning and creatively producing units. The center concentrates on formulating long-term development strategy, on targeting the direction of scientific and technological progress, and on means of accumulating investment resources. State requests to reorganize production will coincide with the economic interests of the enterprises as they calculate them.

Legally, it makes no difference whether the contracting customer be the government or another enterprise. Enterprises do not have to undertake production for unfavorable prices. Although the government will continue to be a huge consumer, it does not have any surpassing privilege in comparison with individual enterprises.

Economic indicators *(normativi)* include only those government parameters fiscally necessary in capitalist systems too, such as the enterprise income tax rate. Myriads of regulations and restrictions that hindered the creativity and initiatives of the enterprises were slated for elimination. At the same time, the sustenance and expansion of enterprises and the welfare of their members have become completely their own responsibilities. The government is not supposed to intervene in the enterprises, but it does not guarantee their survival either. The existence and rewards of the enterprises and their employees are to depend on the success of their efforts to produce high-quality outputs, to lower production costs, to increase production efficiency, and to achieve technological advances. No longer will such efforts come about reluctantly after urging from higher organizations. Without such efforts, the enterprise will be ruined.

Ideally the economic reconstruction will enable the Soviets to realize the potential superiority of Soviet socialism. They maintain that the Soviet economy will differ from the capitalist market systems in that it will not give capitalists' profits priority over the welfare of citizens. Such countries, the Soviets argue, cannot have a long-term program since private business people cannot be directed systematically. Soviet planners, on the contrary, can project the future of the nation rationally for the long run. The government can promote new fields of technology and continually improve on industrial administration. A wise combination of central planning and enterprise autonomy, the Soviets assert, will reveal the genuine advantages of the socialist economy.

As a result, the reformed Soviet economic mechanism will enable Soviet industry eventually to perform more efficiently even than capitalist economies, to accelerate technological progress, and to radically improve the quality of manufactured goods.

The Prospects for Reform

Until the June 1987 measures came to light, many Westerners shared the pessimism of Seweryn Bialer, because prior measures had left the economic mechanism basically intact. At most, Bialer forecast, the piecemeal reforms preceding the 1987 measures would add one quarter or one half of a point to the country's gross national product, which had been growing at a rate of 2% a year. "Those who think of a Hungarian reform or a Chinese revolution are mistaken."[13]

Despite the 1987 measures, grounds exist for skepticism that the Soviet reforms will soon complete even the limited adoption of the market as economic determinant undertaken by the Hungarian New Economic Mechanism of 1968, despite apparent intentions to do so. The troubled Hungarian economy signals the problems that arise with inflation, and with the grant of subsidies to unprofitable enterprises that the government will not close for fear of unemployment. The largest Hungarian enterprises remained under central directives and without autonomy. They continued, therefore, to function in the absence of "the three fundamental conditions necessary for entrepreneurship: the choice of economic activities based on profit, the capacity to endure failure as a result of unsuccessful economic activities, and the clarification of the borders and limits of responsibility for failures, for both individuals and policies."[14]

In the Soviet conception of the new economic mechanism, too, regulatory devices remain, such as control figures and state orders, which formally do not exist in much of the Hungarian system. Moreover, the basic principle of economic planning has as yet not been changed so as to entrust the current adjustment of demand and consumption to the play of prices, and to confine the central organization only to long-term planning. Hence, it is too much to expect the Soviet reform to leap forward at once to emulate the Hungarian model.

It appears unlikely that the reform program will be completely implemented or that the reform mechanism will evolve close to the ideal that has been envisioned. This does not mean that the reform effort at economic *perestroika* will yield nothing in terms of systems improvement. Even the aborted reform of the 1960's succeeded in removing some extreme irrationalities then prevalent. Moreover, the current reform has many advantages over those of the past. The economy has slipped into a critical situation. The general secretary, unlike the indifferent Brezhnev, was determined this time around to make these changes work. Past experiences have left their mark. Reforms in other socialist countries provide a more favorable environment for change in the Soviet Union than existed in the 1960's.

In concert with a change of investment policy (less construction, more research and development, and modernization of existing facilities) and other nonsystemic measures, the reform efforts will bring some improvement in the performance of the Soviet economy. The tempo of economic growth will rise over the recent low level. Some increase in the supply of consumer goods will occur.

On the other hand, attitudinal and systemic holdovers will tend to bar the way toward achievement of original reform ideals; only incremental benefits will accrue.

The long-standing tradition of centralized command economy has deeply affected the psychology of the Soviet people. Passive acceptance of commands from above, a wait-and-see attitude, double standards of value prevail among citizens, officials and enterprise workers. In this situation, for reform to be successful, a revolutionary *perestroika* of all phases of society and social outlooks is sorely needed, as Gorbachev recognized and advocated. His relentless urging of democratization as a sine qua non of economic reform should be taken at face value, not as a political maneuver.

Disagreement over reform strategy still divides high officials of the Party and the government. Some spokespersons for reform, like Party

Secretary Ligachev, seem to advocate a slower pace than originally projected, especially in the ancillary processes of *glasnost'* and democratization. Other officials wish to stick only to the piecemeal measures described earlier, those touching discipline, investments, technological upgrading, and devices for improving consumer goods and services. Such conservatives may attempt to preserve tight control over businesses utilizing methods of enterprise guidance listed in the Sate Enterprise Law. There is more to this than a mere counterattack by conservatives standing firmly for their "vested interests." Even without their excessive intervention, the question of how to combine central control and enterprise autonomy would remain.

F. Klothuvog, a department head of the Economic Research Institute attached to Gosplan, said on June 22, 1987, that the allocation of production inputs by the state will remain for about 80% of supplies, and the figure for the wholesale sector is only 20%. He published an article arguing that the allocation of production inputs should be shifted from Gossnab, the State Committee for Supply, to the pertinent ministries.[15] Gosplan closely examined the article and finally agreed with its contention.

Considering that divergent opinions continue even among reformist scholars on how reforms should be implemented, it is questionable that any comprehensive and practical blueprints for the economic mechanism after the abolition of the command mechanism actually exist.

Economic realities challenge the new system's adaptability. As the Party leadership acknowledges, and as Shmelev and others have vividly described, imbalances are spreading throughout the Soviet economy. Glaring examples are the imbalance between consumer goods and money in circulation, an inflationary situation, and the constant undersupply of consumer goods. Gorbachev reported at the June 1987 plenum that even though circulation of money increased 3.1 times from 1971 through 1985, the production of consumer goods increased a mere two times.[16]

As long as such imbalance is dominant in the economy, it is hard to believe that the behavior of the workers and the enterprises will effectively change, as it is expected to do under the new mechanism. Reforms depend for their success in part on the stimulus of pay rewarding merit. Under conditions of goods scarcity and chronic inflation, it is doubtful that workers will feel such incentives, or that enterprises can believe that the quality of their goods and the technological level of their enterprises are the important indicators that will fatally influence their profits.

The imbalance between money and consumer goods has been produced in part by excessive military spending, which generates income without producing consumer necessities. Moreover, heavily subsidized retail prices have been untouched in order to display apparent price stability to people inside and outside the Soviet Union. Such things are based on a historically shaped policy propensity of the Soviet system. Therefore, they are not transitional economic problems but long-term constraints.

Aside from economic imbalances, the coexistence of new and old systems presents a special transition problem. The State Enterprise Law was to apply to 60 percent of all enterprises by 1988, and to the rest by the beginning of 1990. As the enterprises shift to a position of greater legal autonomy, they do so in a system that is only beginning to change into the partial market environment needed for that new-found autonomy to be exercised. Central supply was to continue into 1991–1992. Prices reflecting true costs or consumer demand, a prerequisite for meaningful enterprise decisions, will only begin to appear during the enterprises' ostensible transition to autonomy. Irrational prices will continue, meanwhile, to affect enterprise incomes more than any state indicators. Moreover, well conceived long-term indicators of performance are yet to be calculated. During the transition period, only short-term, temporary indicators will be provided to the enterprises.

For the first years of reform, at least, enterprise autonomy will be more fiction than reality. The new "state orders" are stipulated to be optional. Actually, act as a means of continued central control. A specialist at the Central Institute of Mathematical Economics estimated that in the 5-Year Plan period, through 1990, there will be no difference between state orders and the old, previously binding production directives. His opinion has been confirmed by the economist, Gavril Popov. Despite reformers' efforts to limit state orders, Popov has stated about two thirds of enterprise products were to be sold on state orders during the first years of reform, the remainder on contract with other enterprises. State orders have replaced the old strict production quotas as a means of ministerial meddling in enterprises. Moscow's annual plans, though theoretically not binding, will be treated as such because of the power retained by the ministries.[17]

For state orders to be actually optional as stipulated, there must be plural suppliers for each product the state wishes to order, and there must be a choice of accepting, declining or renegotiating the orders. Given permanent shortages and the high targets of the twelfth 5-Year Plan (1986–1990), it was unthinkable that a redundant productive capacity would be allowed. Hence, the prospects for enterprise autonomy during the implementation of reforms were dim from the start.

Systemic Constraints

Perestroika's purpose is to realize simultaneously a high level of economic growth, a rapid advance in technology, and a higher quality of manufactured goods through rationalization of the economic mechanism. The main underlying thrust is the reinvigoration of autonomous activity. This prerequisite for reform runs up against certain long-standing systemic principles that will not vanish overnight, including the highest possible growth and utilization of productive capacity, the superiority of socialism over capitalism, and the Communist Party's control over all aspects of Soviet life.

Despite the definition of enterprises under the law as producers of socialist commodities, items produced and sold competitively for the market, the function of enterprises is primarily to produce goods and services to meet national goals. In that sense they are fundamentally different from their counterparts in the capitalist market economies. There, private persons and companies use capital to serve their individual purposes. In the Soviet economy, the profits have been, and will remain, secondary measurements of the enterprises' usefulness to the state. As long as the Party pursues high growth levels through full utilization of productive capacity, the profits and losses of each enterprise cannot be the basis of determining whether or not the enterprise will be continued or closed down. It is doubtful whether the postulate of maximum growth and early retirement of unprofitable plants are compatible, as long as political profit intrudes on goals of economic profitability.

To the extent that the government keeps its older goals in mind and goes after maximum capacity at the expense of efficiency, it will set long-term economic indicators at different levels for more and less profitable enterprises. To the extent that the government differentiates indicators on the basis of each enterprise's earning ability, it will undercut incentives for inferior enterprises to catch up to superior ones. Uniform indicators, however, would run contrary to prereform ideas of boosting production and of social justice, especially the right to work.

To the extent, moreover, that national goals hold top priority, they will conflict with enterprise self-management. Internal democratization will tend to turn each enterprise into an interest group pursuing aims at variance with the national goals already mentioned. Additionally, the principle of workers' participation will have to be reconciled with the system of *nomenklatura*, or posts requiring Party approval. While trade unions would be a natural way to democratize enterprise management, there is no sign that the stultified unions will be allowed independent status as representatives of workers' interests.

Remnants of antagonism and distrust toward the capitalist system indicate that, even in a reformed economy, the domestic market will not open up to foreign goods, and Soviet organizations will be allowed to trade directly abroad only insofar as this promotes exports. There is no possibility as yet apparent that Soviet producers will be exposed to true competition by foreign companies. Enterprises will long remain monopolistic producers.

The leading national economic purpose has been to underpin Soviet military might and security. Over the long run, needs of investment for efficiency and development will clash with immediate military demands for resources. If the ideal of reform completely materializes it is inconceivable that the present priority given to armaments would be allowed to continue. Such a pace of military buildup would run counter to the need to produce a balance between productive investment and nonproductive military expenditures.

Whether the Soviet leadership will be able to reconcile an acceptable arms policy with reform will depend on its ability to mobilize public support (a problem already touched on), as well as on political and social developments both within the country and abroad. There is recognition within the military that a breakdown in the economy and technological inferiority will negatively affect the reinforcement of military power from the long-range point of view. There is no definitive answer to the question of the military stand on reform. For now, they are cautiously watching.[18] But the military are divided on this issue and cannot as yet be considered a unified interest group (see Chapter 7). Nor for that matter can the Party, divided as its leadership and cadres are on issues of reform. Nevertheless, Party officials appear to unite around the idea that the Soviet economic system, as well as all Soviet public life, will continue to be dominated and guided by the Communist Party. Reformist Leonid Abalkin wrote that both central planning and enterprise autonomy are just instruments of the policy of the Party, nothing more or less.[19]

The Communist Party of the Soviet Union responds more actively than do parties in capitalist countries to the vicissitudes of the economy. It has a long-range program to pursue, an ambition to surpass capitalist economies, the status of a superpower to maintain at the cost of enormous resources, and overall responsibility to guarantee the people's living standards. Fulfilling these purposes provides the ideological and economic basis of the Party's legitimacy. As long as this imperative remains, it rules out a passive role for the Party.

This dynamic has another consequence counterproductive to reform. When things go wrong, the Party passes blame on to government organizations. Everything from slow growth to poor quality output and consumer goods deficits are ascribed to government ministries and agencies. Even the slow progress of *perestroika*, a process supposedly dependent on the spontaneity of the people, is being attributed to the central organs and ministries. All in all the central economic organizations still hold final responsibility for the conduct of enterprises subordinated to them. The pressure on them is great to intervene day to day in violation of the new law.

Conclusions

There seems to be no doubt that the USSR has experienced a serious economic decline and that its leaders know it, and want to stop and reverse that decline. The decline shows not only in slowing rates of growth but in growing imbalances.

The economy's defects have long been recognized among economists. Leaders, too, perceived needs for reform. Andropov and then Gorbachev were the first leaders to listen seriously to their economists and to perceive a crisis looming. Gorbachev was the first leader to turn his specialists' proposals into a full-fledged program of economic reconstruction.

In pursuit of that reconstruction, the Soviet Union has entered the phase of implementing large-scale reform after an initial period of piecemeal policy changes. Some benefits are to be expected. But realities already appear to be far from original ideals for many reasons.

Reform means initially operating a new system despite old attitudes of dependency and old interests. Genuine disagreements over the pace and scope of reforms remain among high Party officials. The constraints of established commitments are making themselves felt.

The economy still is closely tied to national goals of military power and security. There seems to be an ambivalence, a conflict between old concepts of security through maximizing production and military allocations, and new concepts of efficiency as the ultimate way to security—a conflict that is still unresolved. The logic of *perestroika* and the new thinking is not yet internalized throughout the Soviet elites. Antagonism toward capitalist forms of ownership intrude on reforms and tend to hold the door to international commerce less open than might be optimal for Soviet development.

Centrally, the Party's concept of its own mission and the present activist basis of its legitimacy and power appear to contradict principles of autonomy underlying the vision of full-fledged reform.

Notes

1. *Pravda*, February 26 and March 4, 1986, and June 26–27, 1987.
2. On the various reformists' views see Moshe Levin, *Political Undercurrents in Soviet Economic Debates* (Princeton, NJ: Princeton University Press, 1975), pp. 158–188.
3. "Die Studie von Novosibirsk," *Osteuropa*, No. 1 (January 1984), p. A5.
4. See, for example, Paul R. Gregory and Robert C. Stuart, *Soviet Economic Structure and Performance* (New York: Harper and Row, 1981), pp. 111–407; Joseph S. Berliner, "The Prospects for Technological Progress," in Morris Bornstein, ed., *The Soviet Economy: Continuity and Change* (Boulder, CO: Westview Press, 1981), pp. 293–331, and analyses by Gregory Grossman, James Millar and Holland Hunter in the same volume.
5. See, e.g., *Pravda*, January 28, 1987.
6. Gorbachev's speech, *Pravda*, June 26, 1987; V.S. Nemchinov, *Izbrannye proizvedeniia*, Vol. 5 (Moscow: Nauka, 1968), p. 88.
7. Nikolai Shmelev, "Avansy i dolgi," *Novyi mir*, No. 6 (June 1987), pp. 142–157.
8. Gorbachev in conversation with voters, *Pravda*, June 22, 1987.
9. Gertrude E. Schroeder, "Gorbachev: Radically Implementing Brezhnev's Reform," *Soviet Economy* (October–December 1986), p. 300.
10. *Pravda*, June 27, 1987.
11. *Pravda*, June 26 and 27, 1987.
12. *Pravda*, July 1, 1987.
13. Seweryn Bialer, "The Soviet Union in a Changing World," in Kinya Niiseki, ed., *The Soviet Union in Transition* (Boulder, CO: Westview Press, 1987), p. 14.
14. Terez Laky, "Elozlott mitozok—tetova szandedok<" *Volosag*, Vol. 7 (1987), pp. 44–46, quoted in Ivan Volgyes, "Hungary: Before the Storm Breaks," *Current History*, No. 523 (November 1987), p. 374.
15. *Pravda*, June 3, 1987.
16. *Pravda*, June 26, 1987.
17. Bill Keller, "A Gorbachev Ally Calls Latest Changes 'Fiction,'" *The New York Times*, January 6, 1988.
18. G.G. Weickhardt, "The Soviet Military-Industrial Complex and Economic Reform," *Soviet Economy*, Vol. 2 (July–September 1986), pp. 193–220.
19. L. Abalkin, "Perestroika sistemy i metodov planovogo upravleniia," *Planovoe khoziastvo* (May 1987), p. 11.

Gorbachev's Foreign Policy and the "New Political Thinking" in the Soviet Union

Alexander Dallin

CHAPTER 6

I

The accession of Mikhail Gorbachev in 1985 provided the occasion for the formulation of a new Soviet political agenda. Advertised by its architects and advocates as amounting to a set of "revolutionary" reforms, it proposed to deal with a wide range of issues that had been neglected in the preceding years, or that had recently crystallized as serious and troublesome, from the slowdown in economic growth to pervasive alienation.

As has characteristically been true in Soviet history, the primary attention of the leadership was on the domestic scene—first, on economic and social conditions, and later, on political and cultural affairs—rather than on foreign relations. By comparison with the ambitious plans for domestic "restructuring" and the discussion of other changes—from multiple candidate elections to a comprehensive price reform—the sphere of Soviet foreign policy appeared, at first sight, to have been relatively neglected and seemed to have been altered more in form and appearance than in substance.

This impression turned out to be both true and false. Insofar as it was correct, there were reasons for the prevalence of continuity in foreign affairs. A programmatic shift in foreign policy had (to the best of our knowledge) not been part of the new leadership's advance commitments; nor was it clear that most of its protagonists (perhaps with the exception of Aleksandr Yakovlev, a newcomer to the top echelon) had spent much time thinking about it. By comparison with Gorbachev's determination to make a clean break with his predecessors' domestic policies and ethos, the attack on what came before in foreign policy was less obvious and less sweeping.

This, it is true, has been the custom, going back to Khrushchev's attack on Stalin in 1956 (which scarcely assailed Stalin's foreign policy, though in fact it was significantly modified). Moreover, there is, especially for a major power, a presumption of unchanging national

97

interest and strategic posture that implies continuity. No new leadership would wish to be perceived, either by the rival superpower or by its domestic critics, as unduly soft or easy to push around. Finally, Soviet foreign policy in the 1970's seemed to score successes that contrasted with the decisionmakers' concerns at home and thus—despite the Afghan venture—did not invite similar alarm.

In other regards, however, such an image of continuity was misleading. Though less salient than the symbolism of domestic *glasnost'*, what soon came to be labeled the "new political thinking" represented some significant new departures—in concept and approach, if not necessarily in political practice. In its most effective expressions it produced statements of considerable power and persuasion, much in contrast with earlier Soviet rhetoric on such subjects.

II

Amid the doubts and questions concerning the meaning and significance of this new thinking, the clearest changes occur in institutions and personnel. Among the latter the foremost was the nominal elevation to Chief of State of Andrei Gromyko, who had been in charge of Soviet diplomacy for a generation. While he retained his vote in the Politburo, his transfer effectively removed him from the conduct of foreign policy. His successor as foreign minister, Eduard Shevardnadze, though a novice in diplomacy, represents a younger generation. He is a loyal ally of Gorbachev and has shown an instinct for flexibility, dynamism, and rapid learning. The replacement of some fifty ambassadors abroad and many more officials in the foreign ministry since March 1985 is indicative of the housecleaning he has undertaken, with the full support of the General Secretary. By and large the promotions have gone to more creative, less ideological, and less bureaucratic individuals.

No less significant have been the changes in the staff of the Party Central Committee. The retirement of the octogenarian Stalinist, Boris Ponomarev, as head of its International Department opened the door to the appointment of Anatoli Dobrynin, the veteran Soviet ambassador to the United States, as a Secretary of the Central Committee and head of the International Department—a most unusual case of "lateral entry" of an expert from outside the Party hierarchy. In addition to its traditional concerns with foreign communist parties, that department now also appears to function as a foreign policy planning staff, bringing within the parameter of the Central Committee the one area—diplomacy—that in the Gromyko days had effectively remained beyond its direct purview.

There are also ample indications that many of the new ideas and new formulations—in foreign affairs, in culture, and in ideology—are either the work of Aleksandr Yakovlev, former ambassador to Canada (and incidentally a former exchange student in the United States), close associate of Gorbachev, and now both a Secretary of the Central Committee and a powerful member of the Politburo, or else are transmitted by him to the General Secretary.

Finally, it would appear that more expert advice in foreign affairs— from a special "group of consultations" and from the staffs of various internationally oriented institutes in the Academy of Sciences—is being solicited and taken more seriously by those assigned to structure the options placed before the top decisionmakers.

All this has helped spark new Soviet diplomatic initiatives; it has replaced the previous spirit of political rigidity with a sense of inventiveness and zest. Many of the new Soviet officials dealing with foreigners are better trained, know foreign languages, and exhibit sophistication that their predecessors had lacked.

And yet none of this proves that there has been a fundamental change in the substance of Soviet foreign policy objectives, or a change in outlook among the policymakers. Moreover, not all the old-timers have yet been removed. As in Soviet domestic affairs, there have been zigzags, and apparently some political deals and compromises had to be struck; some efforts to clean out veteran practitioners seem to have failed, and in other instances "old style" and "new style" officials function side by side. By mid 1987 something of a backlash was setting in against the whole reform effort, domestic and foreign, of the Gorbachev team.

In this regard, as in many others, future policy will be shaped by the general political balance and climate at the apex of the Soviet Party and government. Over time, if only for reasons of biology, the odds favor the younger generation, but it would be unwise to assume any political homogeneity among them. Nor are the principal cleavages in outlook and policy any longer defined by generational differences.

III

Even before replacing Chernenko, Mikhail Gorbachev had used the new phrase. On his visit to Britain in December 1984 he stressed the implications of nuclear weapons for the survival of mankind. "The nuclear age [he concluded] inescapably dictates a new political thinking."[1] He again called for new thinking in his sweeping arms control proposal of January 15, 1986. "What is required [he declared] are new and bold approaches, fresh political thinking and a heightened sense of responsibility for the destinies of the peoples."[2] Thereafter the term and the argument would recur with some frequency—at the Twenty-Seventh Party Congress and on many occasions thereafter.

It is unusual, in Moscow or elsewhere, to prescribe fresh thinking on command, but this occasion is also notable for its break with Soviet traditions of stressing continuity in outlook and policy, a custom presumably calculated to maximize legitimacy and reassure the audience. On the contrary, Gorbachev and his interpreters, though persisting in identifying their own outlook and values as truly Leninist, began to stress the unprecedented complexity and contradictory nature of the contemporary world scene. As one of the leader's most authoritative academic advisers, Evgenii Primakov, director of the Academy of Sciences' Institute of World Economy and International Relations (IMEMO, in its Russian acronym), put it in a major article in *Pravda*, ". . . at present qualitatively new conditions, as M.S. Gorbachev, General Secretary of the CPSU Central Committee, has repeatedly emphasized, make it necessary—perhaps more insistently necessary than at any earlier time in our history—to treat a whole series of key problems of international life in an innovative way." Referring in particular to "the accumulation of weapons of mass destruction in such quantities and of such high quality," he concludes, "Isn't it natural for such a situation to insistently demand not only new methods of carrying out foreign policy, especially for the great powers, but also a fundamentally new philosophy of approaching international problems?"[3]

Primakov exaggerates in labeling the new thinking a "new philosophy." And yet, taken at face value, it does include a number of novel and important propositions. What then does it amount to, as far as it concerns foreign affairs? Despite its repeated reindorsement by leading figures in the Gorbachev team, there is no formal Soviet summation of its defining features. The following, therefore, is based in part on explicit Soviet statements, in part on private comments by Soviet academics and practitioners, and in part on inferences drawn from a comparison of recent Soviet writings and pronouncements on the subject with earlier ones. It is confirmed in all essentials, without being significantly modified or advanced, by Gorbachev's book, *Perestroika*, apparently produced in the summer and released in English just prior to the Washington summit in December 1987.[4]

The most explicit linkage of the new foreign policy orientation with

domestic priorities is Gorbachev's own assertion, in various formulations, that at a time of essential, stressful and far-reaching domestic
reforms the Soviet Union needs an international environment that is
unthreatening and predictable, permitting Moscow to avoid both potentially dangerous crises and additional demands on scarce resources.[5]
There is a plausibility to this argument that is hard to question. Whether
this proposition can in fact be consistently implemented by the makers
of Soviet foreign policy remains to be seen. Nor does it, in any event,
imply any abdication of Soviet involvement abroad; on the contrary, the
ruling generation fully takes for granted a global presence that presumably befits either superpower.

What then is new here? The current linkage of Soviet domestic
priorities to the foreign policy calculus may be seen as part of the more
pervasive shift away from the erstwhile preference for chaos in the
noncommunist world to the novel quest for international stability. Not
that it leads to a celebration of the status quo: far from it. But the notion
that Moscow must welcome what used to be perceived as disruptions in
the enemy's camp and as evidence of the workings of the inevitable laws
of history has remarkably vanished; it has been replaced by an abiding
worry about the dangers of superpower confrontation in the nuclear
age.[6]

Thus a weakening of general optimism—of faith in the benign
consequences of the passage of time, of belief in the desirability of all
"revolutions," in their inevitability and their concomitant benefits for
the Soviet Union[7]—goes hand in hand with a weakening perception of
the utility of "class analysis" (which in fact has often provided a ritual
jargon rather than a tool for the understanding of social and international phenomena).

It should be understood that these are subtle processes that touch on
deeply ingrained and endlessly reiterated concepts. Some of the sacred
old formulae cannot be attacked frontally; some Soviet politicians resist
the novel ideas and rally to the defense of the time-honored outlook; and
many, no doubt, are split between the reaffirmation of something familiar
but tired and the attraction of something new and unknown. Tactically
many of the advocates of a new and different outlook feel compelled to
protect themselves by massive references to orthodox Leninist formulations. Moreover, as controls over publications have been relaxed, one
can detect—here as in other subject areas—a far greater variety of expression suggesting the existence of substantial diversity among Soviet
establishment observers in regard to assumptions underlying foreign
policy preferences. The new political thinking is thus best regarded as
part doctrine and part lobby, at times in uncertain proportions.

Another, related instance of fundamental conceptual revisionism is the gradual abandonment of the zero-sum game perspective on world affairs. The dichotomous Leninist approach to class warfare and national politics was logically extended to world affairs—the globalization of *kto kovo?* The underlying approach survived even when, in fact, Soviet coexistence with the "hostile environment" (and a Soviet commitment to coexistence) illustrated the presence of at least some shared values, such as survival, that belied the facile notion that what was good for one side was bound to be bad for the other. Once again, in the age of ICBMs and Chernobyl, Moscow has come to stress (for instance, in Gorbachev's appeals to foreign leaders) the shared priorities of human survival, international and mutual security, global welfare, joint exploration of outer space and protection of the environment.[8]

Aside from the public relations aspects of such implied sentiments of global fraternity, they seem to reflect a genuine shift in the world view of their Soviet sponsors. A sense that this shift runs below the surface comes from extensive private conversations of at least some foreign observers with Soviet officials and academics. Attitudes and values stressing world interdependence are now widely (though by no means universally) shared among the second level of Soviet experts, consultants, and advisers.

The same orientation finds expression in the notion of "interdependence" in Gorbachev's speeches—and, once thus sanctioned, in the writings of Soviet international affairs experts. For a long time the term and its implications (so alien to the belief in the victory of one world system over the other) had been rebuffed in Moscow; indeed, at one point it had been denounced as a subversive Western import. Now, on the contrary, it too serves to underscore the shared priorities that (quite explicitly, in some Soviet writings) are said to come before the class struggle, class interests or the class approach. Conveniently, a forgotten quote from an early (1899) Lenin draft of a Party program has come to the rescue: it is good Marxism, he wrote, that the common interests of mankind are higher than the class interests of the proletariat. . . . Accordingly Genrikh Trofimenko, a senior Soviet commentator on international affairs, has reminded his readers that Gorbachev (in October 1986) cited Lenin's "thought of colossal depth, concerning the priority of the interests of social development, the priority of the values of all mankind ahead of the interests of this or that class."[9] The scope and operational meaning of the new terminology remain a bit vague, but they are clearly meant to encompass not only the strategic universe but also ecology and resources, economics as well as science and technology.

One other important area, which deserves separate analysis, concerns the changed Soviet view of national and international security. The change becomes dramatically apparent in light of Stalin's notion that Soviet security was in substance a function of the insecurity of all other states. Compare this with the remark of Gorbachev that there can be no security for the Soviet Union without security for the United States.[10] American insecurity, others have added, would only generate a lack of confidence and promote international instability. In the new thinking the mutuality of security thus emerges as an essential new element.[11]

The most obvious and the most urgent aspect of all these conceptual and terminological revisions and reformulations is the nuclear view. This issue indeed seems to be both a major cause and consequence of the new revisionism. Authoritative Soviet analysts (such as Trofimenko) condemn earlier strategic planners—Soviet as well as American—who believed in the possibility, and planned for the achievement, of victory in nuclear war. This does not question or suspend Soviet planning, training and preparations for the use of nuclear weapons as a technical military task. The arguments are presumably addressed to political analysts and decisionmakers. They explicitly condemn the notion that the arms race can provide greater security for any of the international players. One distinct implication of this argument is that military and technical means—offensive or defensive—cannot assure any country's security: in this new formulation, as Gorbachev has asserted more than once, security becomes increasingly a political task.[12]

The operational expression of these generalities has been, first and foremost, the various arms control proposals offered by the Soviet government since January 1986. They have included the abolition of nuclear weapons by the year 2000, with a step-by-step destruction of strategic (intercontinental) missiles, preceded by the elimination of intermediate-range missiles from Europe as well as Asia, a comprehensive ban on nuclear testing, perhaps on chemical weapons, and a variety of other proposals.

It is virtually certain that many of these propoals, which were far more forthcoming and imaginative than earlier ones, have scored public-relations victories for Moscow. The proposals have reflected, at the same time, a genuine Soviet interest in negotiating at least some of the proposed agreements (or agreements based on these proposals). The line dividing these two sets of objectives remains unclear: on the Soviet side, it is at times unnecessary to make a clear distinction between them; on the American side, the best way to discover it is to engage in earnest negotiations about them, rather than dismissing them a priori as grandstanding or mere propaganda.

The Soviet arms control proposals have been widely analyzed elsewhere. Whether or not there is considerable opposition to their implementation within the Soviet elite, it is clear that they are considerably more constructive, far-reaching and innovative than previous ones. The new willingness not only to place a cap on weapons acquisitions but to proceed to significantly destroy existing stockpiles is unprecedented; and the proposed policy on verification, including on-site inspections, appropriately translated into international agreements, removes a major hurdle and source of American objections to proposed arms control agreements.

None of this challenges the assumption that the Soviet proposals are self-serving. What they do, however, is reflect the changing conception of security that the new thinking implies. While the INF agreement concluded in Washington in December 1987 shows an attractive new flexibility on the part of Moscow, it goes without saying that (unless there is a palpable trade-off) Gorbachev will not consent to accords and behavior that are perceived as worsening the strategic position of the Soviet Union. By the same token, the fact that the Soviet leadership believes in the desirability of a given proposal tells us nothing about its possible effects on Russia's treaty partners abroad.

Perhaps as significant as any of the specific planks is the gradual, still very timid entry of national security issues into the arena of legitimate public debate in the Soviet Union. This is indeed a new phenomenon. If some manifestations of it are apparently "grass roots" initiatives,[13] others would seem to have sanction and support from within the leadership. Given Kremlin approval of "reasonable sufficiency" as a formula for Soviet (and Soviet bloc) military procurement,[14] the implication for possible cuts in the defense budget is stated in unprecedented fashion by E. Primakov (see footnote 3). In his circuitous but unmistakable words, "The need for optimizing the ratio between productive expenditures and military expenditures necessary for the country's reliable security has [become] manifest as never before."[15]

IV

We need scarcely review the course of recent Soviet relations with the United States. Surely the summit meetings—Geneva, Reykjavik, and Washington—reflect something of the new Soviet calculus and behavior. If the Soviet–American relationship has begun to improve, albeit without producing a fundamental breakthrough, the success of recent

Soviet efforts in the direction of the Third World, Western Europe and the Far East has been more questionable.

Moscow has recently refrained from picking up new clients among national liberation movements in the Third World. It is perhaps premature to decide whether this has been due primarily to a lack of suitable opportunity or to a sense of restraint. But more broadly, Russia has clearly trimmed its expectations in regard to the Third World.[16] It has begun to pursue a course of what might be labeled universal positive engagement. It has sought membership or observer status in international organizations, from Association of Southeast Asian Nations (ASEAN) to General Agreement on Tariffs and Trade (GATT), and has labored to enhance its role in the United Nations. It also has striven to establish its presence in regions to which it had previously paid relatively little attention. This has included, on the one hand, countries such as Brazil and Mexico, and, on the other, the new states of the South Pacific region, at times leading Moscow to couple cheap promises with an effort to capitalize on antinuclear (and anti-American) sentiments.

Whereas the general outlook has been remarkably fresh, Moscow has not been willing to pay a substantial price for the attainment of its foreign policy objectives anywhere. This has imposed distinct limits on what Soviet diplomacy has been able to achieve other than in such reasonably symmetrical issue areas as arms control.

With regard to Afghanistan, China, Vietnam, and Japan, efforts have been even more complex and results more ambiguous. One may accept the assertions of Soviet leaders that they would like to disengage from the fighting in Afghanistan, but the terms on which Soviet intervention can be terminated have eluded identification. While efforts are underway to find a formula acceptable to all parties, clearly Moscow has not yet been prepared to pay a heavy price in influence and prestige for its withdrawal. Substantially the same is true of Kampuchea, though here it may be easier to find a formula for Vietnamese withdrawal at a lower cost to Moscow.

Nor is there any doubt of the desire of the Gorbachev leadership to bring about a substantial normalization with China. Indeed, relations have improved a good deal, even if mutual suspicions remain intense. Gorbachev signaled a modest willingness to make a symbolic concession to China in defining the Sino-Soviet border on the Amur River in accordance with Chinese claims rather than in accordance with previous Soviet allegations, but this was scarcely a costly move. There may be room for mutual Soviet and Chinese troop withdrawals from the border (and perhaps of more Soviet troops from Mongolia), but on a relatively modest scale. While Sino-Soviet talks continue at various levels, and while trade, cultural, academic and sports contacts have been restored, the fundamental political conditions for normal relations set by the Chinese side (notably, concerning Afghanistan and Kampuchea/ Vietnam) remain unmet by Moscow. If, indeed, the Soviet leadership wants to bring about a full normalization with China, it will need to decide to pay a price. In any event, a return to the alliance relationship of the early 1950's is not in the cards.

On an even more modest scale, the same has been true of Soviet-Japanese relations. Given the protracted ineptitude in Soviet policy toward Japan, the new style—symbolized by Shevardnadze's visit to Tokyo—has been a welcome change. However, the rumored Gorbachev visit has been indefinitely put off, since there is no palpable agenda of possible agreements for such an occasion: the old conundrum of the Northern Territories remains virtually unaltered, and no serious effort seems to have been made to find a new compromise. Again, Moscow has not been willing to pay a price for improved relations.

By a combination of fairly conventional political, maritime and military means, Moscow has sought to reinsert itself in the Middle East, an area where it rejects the status quo. At the same time, though it has moved significantly toward resumption of contacts with Israel, there is little indication that it will be prepared to pay a price for the reestablishment of diplomatic relations, presumably in permitting Jewish emigration in more substantial numbers and inevitably worsening its relations with the Arab world. But in any event it would appear that Moscow is now prepared to give the Middle East a lower priority on its foreign policy agenda.

Gorbachev's greatest foreign policy success, it may be suggested, has been the remarkable change in public opinion, dramatically visible in Western Europe and even in the United States. Whatever Europeans may think of the Soviet reforms or of the Soviet system, they have overwhelmingly come to believe that the Gorbachev regime has made a far more substantial contribution to "peace" than has the United States during the last several years; after the Washington summit many Americans came to see the Soviet leader as someone the United States could do business with.

Though by no means negligible, however, despite the INF treaty, this accomplishment has been difficult for Moscow to translate into tangible new agreements, be it in trade or security, especially with the countries of Western Europe. Meanwhile, Soviet commitments of economic and military assistance to a number of countries seems to continue without significant reductions.

And in regard to Eastern Europe—the chronic problem area—Soviet policy has vacillated between greater discipline and greater tolerance, but again without seriously reducing Moscow's role. Interestingly, there is scarcely any revisionism in Soviet "theoretical" pronouncements with regard to the Soviet bloc.

Thus it may be argued that the tangible effects of the new thinking have been modest or uneven. And yet, partly because it is too early to take stock of Gorbachev's foreign policy record, it would be a serious error to dismiss the new thinking as irrelevant window dressing.

V

Several arguments have been made against taking the new Soviet thinking seriously. They deserve a brief review.

A serious case can be made that, in one form or another, most of the elements now identified as new political thinking had in fact been in existence or in circulation well before Gorbachev came to power. Indeed, the linkage of domestic to foreign policy dates back a long time, and so does the specific avoidance of international conflict and adventures at times of domestic stress.[17] Disillusionment with the Third World and with national liberation movements had been growing well before Brezhnev's death. The abandonment of the Leninst–Clausewitzian view of war and the conclusion that there could be no victor in a nuclear exchange had both made considerable headway in Moscow for perhaps 15 years.[18] The search for normalization with China began soon after Mao's death, prior to the Soviet invasion of Afghanistan. The redefinition of "peaceful coexistence" goes back to Khrushchev. And arms control has been the centerpiece of Soviet-American diplomacy for a generation.

Still, it remained to put the pieces together, to draw the more general and theoretical inferences from them, and above all, to come up with a new, more overt and more coherent formulation sanctioned from the top of the Soviet machine. While some of the notions found in the new thinking previously were smuggled piecemeal into the arsenal of Leninism, now the protagonists of the new thinking glory in insisting that the novel, qualitatively different nature of our age requires their novel, qualitatively different thought and behavior.

No new belief system is ever born fully grown from a politician's head. The policies of Franklin Roosevelt or the ideology of Karl Marx— to cite two examples at random—had their clear roots and forerunners elsewhere. This does not diminish their contribution or importance. The same may well be true with the (as yet less epochal) reconceptualizations of the Gorbachev era.

Another line of criticism would build on the tenable observation that the Soviet–American adversary relationship has structural and geopolitical causes and is not due to—nor can it be wished away by—personalities or their rationalizations. This is partly a level-of-analysis problem, partly an underestimation of the extent to which at certain junctures—such as the present, in Soviet–American relations in particular—individuals and ideas can play a critical role in change. It is not too much to say that in 1985–1988 the coincidence of a Ronald Reagan and a Mikhail Gorbachev in office *has* made a significant difference.

A related argument maintains that traditional Russian political culture is more tenacious and recalcitrant than the trendy notions of a handful of clever intellectuals. In the end, this determinist point of view insists, all new thinking will collapse under the overwhelming weight of familiar, traditional attitudes and perspectives. Ultimately this may or may not prove to be the case. But the argument cannot predict the outcome; it extrapolates (correctly or not) from the past to the future; it ignores the possibility and the reality of changes in political culture, assuming its necessary dominance, and it dismisses the evidence of learning by the Soviet leadership. Time will show whether or not this is too facile—and too stubborn—an approach.

To be sure, there is a profound and pervasive skepticism in the West concerning change in Russia. There is a record of bitter earlier disappointments when Soviet facades turned out to be deceptive, when Soviet words were shown to have been used precisely to deceive foreign observers, and when seeming efforts at change—from the NEP in the 1920's to the "Basic Principles" signed by Brezhnev and Nixon in 1972—were aborted or reversed. Even George Kennan, in his "X" article entitled "The Sources of Soviet Conduct," 40 years ago intoned, caveat emptor.

> When there is something the Russians want from us, one or the other of these [disturbing] features of their policy may be thrust temporarily into the background; and when that happens there will always be Americans who will leap forward with gleeful announcements that 'the Russians have changed,' and some who will even try to take credit for having brought about such 'changes.' But we should not be misled by tactical maneuvers. These characteristics of Soviet policy, like the postulate from which they flow, are basic to the internal nature of Soviet power and will be with us . . . until the internal nature of Soviet power is changed.[19]

While such skepticism is understandable, it fails to deal with the particular changes under investigation at the present time, under particular and unprecedented conditions. Indeed, it fails to ask precisely whether there are changes taking place in "the internal nature of Soviet power."

In fact, there is a school that argues that the whole body of new thinking is but another Soviet tissue of deception and disinformation, intended to dupe the naive citizen abroad. In its more complex formulation, this argument maintains that the new thinking is but the latest Soviet device intended to couple the avoidance of nuclear war with the continued struggle against the West, as the following summation suggests:

> New thinking thus has the operative function of exerting influence on Western opinion to help reduce NATO's deterrent capability and thereby achieve by other means what in Moscow is termed reliable security: the possibility of waging war without running a nuclear risk.[20]

While by its very nature this kind of argument cannot be disproved to everyone's satisfaction, many observers (this author included) are persuaded that this is a thoroughly mistaken view. One reason is that the new thinking on international and security questions is part and parcel of the broader reconsideration taking place within the Soviet elite, covering a wide range of intellectual, political and cultural questions. We can observe the payoff of the domestic debates; the international aspects of the new thinking and the debates over it are fully congruent with their domestic counterparts.

Moreover, differences among Soviet observers today are not orchestrated to confuse the outside world. Private conversations with well-informed Soviet analysts and journalists, against a background of prolonged experience in reading Soviet materials, help establish beyond any reasonable doubt that the new thinking is being taken seriously—and is therefore seriously debated and contested—among influential members of the Soviet establishment. And for good reason.

Perhaps the most serious question raised is the continuing gap between the new thinking and Soviet foreign policy behavior. This does indeed present a challenge to the analyst. But it is by no means a surprising or unfamiliar one. The conduct of policy often bears but scant resemblance to the blueprint by which it was designed, and its result, even less.

Soviet foreign policy is being made within a complex parallelogram of forces. No one can tell as yet how seriously the new thinking will shape

Soviet behavior. It is honed in the context of both domestic and external pressures and constraints, and the objectives that would seem to flow from the new thinking—or any other mind-set in international affairs—may be frustrated or modified or only partly pursued in practice. It is far easier to propound generalities than to persuade decisionmakers of the need to make unilateral concessions or to pay a price for uncertain goals.

What will come of the implementation of the new thinking is an open question. But the body of beliefs and concepts, though in some part as yet inchoate and untidy, deserves to be taken seriously and to be carefully traced and examined in its various manifestations. This should be seen as not only a matter of academic curiosity but also as a matter of U.S. self-interest.

Notes

1. Gorbachev's address to British parliamentarians, December 18, 1984, in M. S. Gorbachev, *Izbrannye rechi i stat'i* (Moscow: Izd. politicheskoi literatury, 1987), II, 112.

2. Gorbachev statement of January 15, 1986; English trans. in Mikhail Gorbachev, *For a Nuclear-Free World: Speeches and Statements* (Moscow: Novosti, 1987), p. 15.

For general discussions of the new thinking, see the excellent paper (with which I was regrettably not acquainted when producing mine) by Tsuyoshi Hasegawa, "The New Thinking and Gorbachev's Foreign-Military Policy" (Tokyo: May 1987); and Charles Glickham, "New Directions in Soviet Foreign Policy," Radio Liberty Research Bulletin, Supplement 2/86 (Munich: September 6, 1986).

In the Central Committee Report delivered to the 27th CPSU Congress on February 25, 1986, the General Secretary identified several of the principal propositions of the new thinking, clearly the result of extensive prior discussion within the Soviet leadership. These themes were echoed, later that year, in articles by other leading foreign-policy makers in Moscow, including Anatoli Dobrynin and Aleksandr Yakovlev (see e.g., *Kommunist*, 1986, nos. 9, 16, 17).

3. E. Primakov, "Novaia filosofiia vneshnei politiki," *Pravda*, July 10, 1987; English trans. in *Current Digest of the Soviet Press*, XXXIX: 9, pp. 1–4.

4. Mikhail Gorbachev, *Perestroika: New Thinking for Our Country and the World* (New York: Harper & Row, 1987).

5. On the eve of the Geneva summit, Gorbachev remarked in an interview with *Time* magazine, "I don't remember who, but somebody said that foreign policy is a continuation of domestic policy. If that is so,

then I ask you to ponder one thing: If we in the Soviet Union are setting ourselves such truly grandiose plans in the domestic sphere, then what are the external conditions that we need to be able to fulfill these domestic plans? I leave the answer to that question with you." (*Time*, September 9, 1985.)

At the world peace forum in Moscow Gorbachev declared that only if one understands the "revolutionary transformations" being undertaken within the Soviet Union can one correctly judge Soviet foreign policy. "Our international policy is, more than ever, determined by our internal policy, by our interest in concentrating on creative work to make our country more perfect. Precisely for this reason we need stable peace, predictability, and a constructive orientation in international relations." (*Pravda*, February 17, 1987.)

Primakov remarks (op.cit.) that "perhaps the organic link between our country's domestic policy and its foreign policy has never before been as manifest as it is today."

6. This theme recurs countless times in Gorbachev's remarks.

7. One of those developing these themes with novel candor is Aleksandr Bovin. On the one hand, "the ability of capitalism to adapt to new historical conditions has surpassed our expectations. The prospect of socialist transformations in developed capitalist countries has receded indefinitely." On the other hand, "in a number of countries of socialist orientation, the situation remains unstable, fraught with the possibility of retrogression." He goes on to describe the failure of most communist parties in the developed countries and in the Third World to become mass parties or even "to win for themselves the support of the bulk of the working class." One of the reasons for this, he declares, has been "the reversals, contradictions, crises, and stagnation" in the Soviet Union. (*Izvestiia*, July 11, 1987.)

8. While this theme is apparent in the 27th Congress report, it becomes more prominent in Gorbachev's Vladivostok speech on July 28, 1986, his statements during his trip to India in November 1986, and his speech to the International Peace Forum in Moscow in February 1987.

9. G. A. Trofimenko, "Novye real'nosti i novoe myshlenie," *SShA*, 1987, no. 2, p. 15.

A leading economist who is an adviser to the leadership, Oleg Bogomolov, in an interview linked the zero-sum and the interdependence themes:

> Previously we reasoned: the worse for the adversary, the better for us, and vice versa. But today this is no longer true; this cannot be the rule anymore. Now countries are so interdependent on each other for their development that we have quite a different image of the solution to international questions. The worsening of the situation in [Western] Europe will not at all help the development of

the socialist part of Europe; on the contrary, the better things are going in the European world economy, the higher the stability and the better the propsects for our development.

(Czechoslovak TV, transl. in Foreign Broadcasting Information Service, *Daily Report: USSR*, April 16, 1987, p. F2.)

10. *Pravda*, February 8, 1986.

11. For a popular but effective exposition of the notion of "mutual security," see Alexander Bovin, *The Imperative of the Nuclear Age* (Moscow: Novosti, 1986).

12. This too is a persistent theme, from Gorbachev's 27th Congress report to commentaries such as Primakov's July 1987 article.

13. Ales Adamovich, a well-known Byelorussian writer, in an article that attracted a good deal of attention (in *Moskovskie Novosti*, March 8, 1987), challenged the notion of a nuclear second strike as suicidal. "We don't want to take part in the destruction of mankind," he wrote, "not with a first, nor with a second, nor with any further strike. . . . We will not hold on to the status of a nuclear power. . . . For me there are no military men more courageous and worthy than those who . . . give their military expertise to the antiwar movement." His remarks promptly drew fire from Colonel General Dmitri Volkogonov, a deputy chief of the Main Political Administration, who warned that "pacifism and the battle for peace are not the same thing." Adamovich retorted, in Gorbachevian terms, that "in nuclear war there can be no winners. . . . The truth of the new thinking is obligatory even for military thought." But Volkogonov and other military writers came back to attack "not only naive but harmful" notions that reject the possibility of victory in nuclear war. (See *Literaturnaia* 15; also Stephen Foye, "Intellectuals Attack the Military," CSIS *Soviet News*, III: 9 [July 30, 1987], and Tom Nichols, "Volkogonov and Nuclear Victory," ibid., III:10 [September 8, 1987]).

Meanwhile Adamovich has produced another blunt essay on "Problems with the New Way of Thinking" (in *Breakthrough: Emerging New Thinking* [New York: Walker Publ., 1988]).

14. For the first public statement legitimizing the notion of military "sufficiency," see "O voennoi doktrine gosudarstv-uchastnikov varshavskogo dogovora," *Pravda*, May 30, 1987. The concept implies that there is no need for the Soviet Union and its allies to keep up with the U.S. or NATO either in defense budgets or in the procurement and deployment of weapon systems, so long as even short of such a copycat policy, their reliable security is assured. The concept is explicitly supported by Defense Minister Dmitri Yazov (*Pravda*, July 27, 1987).

15. *Pravda*, July 10, 1987. Soviet participants in the Chappaqua, New York, discussions in August 1987 acknowledged with refreshing and unusual candor that actual defense budget figures differed from pub-

lished ones but argued, with some validity, that it would take a major price reform in the Soviet Union to be able realistically to compute actual costs for the various elements in the Soviet defense picture.

16. See, e.g., in Francis Fukuyama, *Moscow's Post-Brezhnev Reassessment of the Third World* (Santa Monica: Rand Corp., 1986); and Elizabeth Valkenier, "Revolutionary Change in the Third World: Recent Soviet Reassessments," *World Politics*, April 1986.

17. See Alexander Dallin, "Domestic Sources of Soviet Foreign Policy," in Seweryn Bialer, ed., *The Domestic Context of Soviet Foreign Policy* (Boulder, CO: Westview Press, 1981).

18. See, for instance, Tsuyoshi Hasegawa, "The Soviets on Nuclear War-Fighting," *Problems of Communism*, July–August 1986; Coit D. Blacker, *Under the Gun* (Stanford: The Portable Stanford, 1986); or Michael McGwire, *Military Objectives in Soviet Foreign Policy* (Washington, D.C.: Brookings Institution, 1987).

19. "X" [George F. Kennan], "The Sources of Soviet Conduct," *Foreign Affairs*, July 1947, reprinted in A. Dallin, ed., *Soviet Conduct in World Affairs* (New York: Columbia University Press, 1959), p. 251.

20. Gerhard Wettig, "Gorbachev and 'New Thinking' in the Kremlin's Foreign Policy," *Aussenpolitik* [English ed.], 38 (1987): 2, p. 144. The same applies to the argument—equally impossible to falsify—that the new foreign policy outlook is intended as a temporary device—either as a defensive tactic while Gorbachev has domestic difficulties (see, e.g., Boris Meissner, "Gorbachev's *Perestroika:* Reform or Revolution?" in *Aussenpolitik*, 38 [1987] :3) or as a new instance of Leninist *peredyshka*—a breathing spell, presumably to permit the Soviet Union to gather strength before reverting to a more aggressive foreign policy. In fact, Primakov (op. cit.) explicitly distances the current thinking from the "breathing spell" tradition, which he declares inadequate and obsolete under current conditions.

CHAPTER 7

Gorbachev, The New Thinking of Soviet Foreign-Security Policy and the Military: Recent Trends and Implications

Tsuyoshi Hasegawa

The emergence of the "new thinking" in Soviet foreign policy is posing challenging questions to the West. Does it represent a fundamental departure in Soviet foreign policy, or is it merely a tactical ploy to camouflage Russia's unchanged goal of expansionism? Should Gorbachev's arms control initiatives be interpreted as a manifestation of the new thinking, or viewed as having resulted from the cold calculations of political and strategic correlation of forces? Will it significantly change the traditional approach to foreign policy that was characterized by the primacy of the military factor? The answers will have significant practical implications concerning U.S. policy toward the new Soviet foreign policy initiatives.

This chapter is an attempt to examine the significance of the new thinking and its implications for actual Soviet foreign-military policy. Specifically, it is divided into four parts: (1) characteristics of the new thinking; (2) significance of the new thinking and its implications; (3) the new thinking and Soviet military doctrine; and (4) the military's attitude toward the new thinking.

The New Thinking

Key Concepts

The new thinking can be reduced to two interrelated but separate concepts: interdependence and mutual security.[1] The concept of interdependence has resulted from an increasing awareness that the contemporary world is characterized by a mutuality of needs that transcends national barriers and social systems. Interdependence is increasing not only in science and technology, information and communications, but also in economics and politics. It is integrating certain areas of human activities beyond national barriers, and in the process has created global problems that transcend the differences between the social systems, and that are threatening the existence of civilization itself. "Interdependence" and "global problems" indicate that in the contemporary world there have emerged areas of human activities to which the traditional Marxist–Leninist principles can be no longer applied. A new approach is required to secure further development of science and technology and further integration of economic activities, and at the same time to solve global problems.

The concept of mutual security has a different origin. It was borne out of the acutely felt sense of urgency of the threat of nuclear war, and the realization that in the nuclear age security cannot be attained unilaterally even for superpowers such as the United States and the Soviet Union. Therefore, security can only be mutual.

Although they have different origins, the two concepts are interrelated in the sense that in the nuclear age interdependence takes the form of "interdependence of survival." Given that nuclear weapons threaten the survival of mankind itself, the concepts of national and international security have become indivisible. Thus, the issue of nuclear weapons has become recognized as one of the most important global problems.

Background of the New Thinking

The new thinking is not really new. Its key concepts had appeared during the détente period under Brezhnev, although they remained basically outside the orthodoxy accepted by the leadership.[2] According to Charles Glickham, Gorbachev used the term new political thinking for the first time in his comprehensive arms control proposal in January 1986.[3] It was at the 27th Party Congress in February, however, that Gorbachev introduced the new thinking as a comprehensive part of the basic framework of Soviet foreign policy. Nevertheless, its significance was obscured by a stark contrast between the first part of his speech that dealt with the ideological sphere, and the operational aspect of the foreign policy section.[4] The first part of Gorbachev's speech was studded with the traditional Marxist–Leninist verbiage reflecting the traditional bipolar vision of conflict between capitalist and socialist systems. In sharp contrast, all the elements in the new thinking were introduced in the foreign policy section of his speech.[5]

It soon became clear that Gorbachev's sympathy rested with the new thinking, as various commentaries began to appear and Gorbachev himself began speaking more openly in its support. The first important article that indicated the importance of the new thinking was Anatolii Dobrynin's article in *Kommunist* in June 1986, which supported what Gorbachev said about the new thinking in his political report to the 27th

Party Congress.[6] Since Dobrynin is a secretary of the Central Committee and head of its International Department, his endorsement indicated that the new thinking was being accepted at least in part by those who were engaged in policy formulation, rather than merely discussed as an academic subject divorced from reality, or remaining a harebrained scheme of the general secretary. Expression of the new political thinking also found its way in a diplomatic document in the form of the Delhi Declaration in November 1986, which was signed by Gorbachev and Rajiv Gandhi.[7]

Nevertheless, as Glickham explained in his article in September 1986, there were some grounds to believe that the new thinking did not gain full citizenship as the basis of Soviet foreign policy. Concepts such as mutual security, interdependence, and global problems cannot be ideologically acceptable for the purest theologians of Marxism–Leninism. The concept of mutual security was developed, but there seemed to exist an ideological resistance to acknowledging nuclear rivalry as one of the global problems, along with issues such as ecology and natural resources. Gorbachev's political report to the 27th Party Congress, for instance, excluded nuclear weapons from the list of global issues.[8] National security seemed to touch the raw nerves of Marxist–Leninist orthodoxy, which appeared to resist the proliferation of such non-Marxist concepts as global problems into its sanctum sanctorum.

Gorbachev's Speech at the Moscow Forum

Gorbachev's speech at the Moscow Peace Forum in February 1987 represented a new stage in the evolution of the new thinking. There are striking similarities between Gorbachev's political report to the 27th Party Congress and this speech. But in three important respects he went farther than his other previous statements.[9]

First, he discussed the question of security in the nuclear age in the context of global problems, thus removing a major obstacle that was blocking the new thinking from acquiring full legitimacy. Gorbachev stated: "Our world is united not only by the internationalization of economic life and by powerful information and communications media, but also in facing the common danger of nuclear death, ecological catastrophe and global explosion of the contradictions between its poor and wealthy regions."

Second, Clausewitz's axiom that had been the pillar of the Marxist–Leninist approach to war was rejected. Gorbachev declared that the axiom that world war is an extension of politics by violent means is no longer applicable in the nuclear age. The question, however, remained whether this rejection applied to all wars or to world war only.

Third, Gorbachev maintained that regional conflicts should not be viewed through the geostrategic vision of East–West conflict. This indicated a new departure from the traditional approach to the Third World conflict that was interpreted in the context of the zero-sum game, where both sides cannot gain together—one's win is the other's loss.

Primakov's Pravda *Article*

Soviet ideology is somewhat akin to Catholic doctrine. Dogmas enunciated by the General Secretary and the Party Congresses often become clearer in commentaries written by their trusted advisers. Evgenii Primakov, Director of the Institute of World Economy and International Relations, reputed to be a close adviser to Gorbachev, is one such commentator. His article, published in *Pravda* on July 19, 1987, is an authoritative interpretation on the new thinking, accentuating its significance and elaborating on what previously remained ambiguous.[10]

Primakov emphasizes that the new thinking is not a reformulation of previous principles, but that it represents a totally innovative way of approaching the new reality of international situations. He defends the previous Soviet policy that stressed readiness to wage nuclear war by unleashing a crushing retaliatory blow at imperialists as a necessary evil at the time when Soviet military power was inferior to that of its adversary. But the Soviet Union has now acquired sufficient military power, and the quantity as well as the quality of weapons of mass destruction have reached such a level that the survival of mankind has become an urgent question. The situation requires a new philosophy, a different approach.

Primakov also underscores the importance of Gorbachev's speech at the 27th Party Congress as an attempt to reject the previously held distorted view that saw world competition between capitalism and socialism without interdependence. Here, he not only clearly includes the nuclear issue in his list of global problems, but also identifies it as the most serious one of all. Another point made by Primakov is the "organic" connection between domestic reform and the new thinking. He argues that the new concepts are an outgrowth of larger, more fundamental changes that are taking place in the domestic front.

Finally, he advances the argument developed by Gorbachev on Soviet policy toward the Third World a little farther. Social change has to happen in the Third World, but such transformation has to be carried out according to the objective social circumstances of each country.

Thus, export of revolution to other countries is an anathema in the nuclear age, although Primakov hastens to add that stability of the international situation also excludes imposition of the social status quo from outside, that is, the export of counterrevolution to countries seeking change.

Gorbachev Steps Up His Rhetoric

In the fall of 1987 Gorbachev stepped up his rhetoric in support of the new thinking. It was first seen in his message to the United Nations in mid September, which signaled the Soviet willingness to use the United Nations as a vehicle to solve international conflicts.[11] Toward the end of September, in his conversation with the French delegation, he stated that where the threat of nuclear war is real, "Clausewitz's formula that war is an extension of politics by different means is no longer applicable."[12]

The publication of his book, *Perestroika and the New Thinking*, in the middle of October represented another radical step by Gorbachev. In the chapter dealing with the new thinking, he identifies "nuclear weapons, ecology, scientific-technical revolution, and information" as factors that connect the world. He argues that difference in social choice, ideological, and religious convictions, and way of life must be overcome "for the sake of all-human values," thus making his preference between all-human values and class values clear.[13] As for Clausewitz's formula, he rejects it as follows: "Clausewitz's classical formula has become hopelessly obsolete. It belongs to libraries. To place all-human, moral-ethical norms in the foundation of international politics and to humanize interstate relations has for the first time in history become a vital requirement."[14] As if to anticipate conservative criticisms, he hints that the military-industrial complex may not be an unchangeable attribute of capitalism.[15]

More important is Gorbachev's speech on the occasion of the 70th anniversary of the October Revolution. This speech, delivered in the midst of the Yel'tsin affair, the first serious political crisis under Gorbachev, is a good indicator of the nature of the internal debate that might be taking place within the leadership with regard to the new thinking.

The West primarily has focused on the historical part of his speech. The general conclusion is that Gorbachev did not go far enough to insist on a thorough reexamination of the past, although he began to move in the right direction. His hesitation to revise radically the party's official view on the sensitive issues of the past has been attributed to the strength of the conservative opposition, which surfaced in the Yel'tsin affair. Too much attention is given, however, to the historical part of this speech. The most important portion was the last part, which dealt with foreign policy.

The possibility that Gorbachev was responding to conservative criticisms can be surmised by some peculiarities in this part. The usual extolling of new thinking's high-sounding ideals are absent, and the speech is characterized by a tone of defensiveness. The major part is devoted to the relationship between the nature of imperialism and the new thinking. In defending the latter, he had to make some concessions by resurrecting the old themes of the revolutionary nature of the working class and the need to maintain the defense capability "to the level that would exclude military superiority of imperialism over socialism, as long as the danger of war exists, and as long as the social reprisal is the pivotal strategy of military programs of the West."[16]

At the same time, however, the speech is Gorbachev's counteroffensive. Since he and his supporters had thus far avoided confronting the crucial question of the relationship between the new thinking and the fundamental nature of imperialism, it is natural that his critics attacked him on this vulnerable point. In response, however, he raised three basic questions. First, given the nature of imperialism, is it possible, at the new level of interdependence and wholeness of the world, to influence the nature of imperialism in such a way as to prevent its most dangerous aspects? Second, can capitalism exist without militarism? Third, can capitalism survive without neocolonialism? A detailed analysis cannot be given here, but it suffices to state that Gorbachev gives an affirmative answer to all these questions.[17]

The significance of his speech becomes immediately apparent if it is compared with the first part of his political report to the 27th Party Congress. There, the major theme was the irreconcilable nature of competition between socialism and capitalism. The nature of imperialism was said to result in an aggressive, reckless policy that stemmed from the existence of the military-industrial complex, the monopoly-capitalist pursuit for profit, and fear by the bourgeoisie of social change.[18] The difference between this assessment and Gorbachev's speech on the 70th anniversary of the October Revolution is striking. It may be said that the new thinking has completed its final process by challenging the very basis of the traditional Soviet approach to the contemporary world. Thus, the nature of imperialism has become the focal point between the new thinking and traditional Marxism–Leninism.

Significance of the New Thinking in Soviet Foreign Policy

Fundamental Change in Ideology

How should the new thinking be interpreted? There are skeptics who dismiss it as nothing but propaganda, or cosmetic change without much substance in the actual implementation of Soviet foreign policy. However, we might be better advised to take the new thinking seriously.[19]

Despite the fact that the role of ideology as a guide for actual policy has declined in recent years, the Marxist–Leninist ideology continues to give the Soviet elite a general framework in which to view their society and the outside world. To that extent, ideology is taken very seriously in the Soviet Union, and the leadership does not dare change its basic postulates even for foreign propaganda purposes without preparing to accept far-reaching domestic political consequences. This is the reason the Marxist–Leninist ideology has clung with amazing, often quixotic tenacity to the obsolete but self-contained abstract logical consistency that has little relevance to the real world. This does not mean that Marxism–Leninism has not changed. During the last 70 years of Soviet history the sacred letters of Marxism–Leninism have been chipped away by reality. The importance of ideology also explains why significant changes in policies began in the past with highly esoteric theoretical debates that seemed irrelevant. The following paradox in the socialist states that adopt the Marxist ideology as its official religion must be understood: the relationship between the super-structure of ideas and the economic basis is turned completely on its head. What the Soviets say cannot be dismissed as propaganda; on the contrary, by analyzing what they say, we can discern important signs of change in Soviet policy.[20]

The new thinking represents a departure from the traditional way of approaching the world. As Primakov states and Gorbachev's October Revolution speech clearly affirms, the new thinking rejects the traditional bipolar vision that views the world through the competition between capitalism and socialism. Instead, it emphasizes the interdependent nature of the contemporary world that transcends the differences in the social systems. This new philosophy fundamentally differs from that of peaceful coexistence under Khrushchev and détente under Brezhnev, which saw the world basically as an arena where the two irreconcilable systems competed with each other. The new thinking presupposes the existence of the world community that exists beyond the two systems. It also accepts capitalism as a system whose interests are not necessarily incompatible with those of socialism, and with whom socialism has to work to ensure its survival and to build its future progress. It also rejects the zero-sum vision through which to view Third World conflicts.

The question is whether the new thinking will solidly take root as the framework of Soviet foreign policy. Marxist–Leninist ideologues have good reason to worry, because ultimately the new thinking will lead to the destruction of the central core of Marxism based on the conflictive model of society, class analysis, and historical inevitability of progress from capitalism to socialism. Thus, it would be naive to think that the internal debate on the new thinking was solved once and for all by Gorbachev's October Revolution speech.

Reorganizations and Personnel Changes

Another reason the new thinking represents more than propaganda is that at the level of both the Foreign Ministry and the International Department of the Central Committee, drastic organizational changes are taking place. Moreover, those who support the new thinking are advancing rapidly in these areas. The new thinking, therefore, is acquiring its own organizational basis.

The changes at the Foreign Ministry and the International Department have occurred on at least three levels. First, a far-reaching organization of the Foreign Ministry was carried out.[21] Second, academics and foreign policy experts outside the government have been more closely brought into the decisionmaking process. For instance, a new advisory organization consisting of academics and foreign policy experts was established directly under the Minister of Foreign Affairs.[22] Third, a new section dealing with arms control has been established both in the Foreign Ministry and in the International Department, thus consolidating the locus of arms control policy more solidly into the party.[23] The pattern of personnel changes also clearly indicates that those who are putting forward ideas for the new thinking are in ascendancy.[24]

It does not mean, however, that actual implementation of the new thinking in foreign policy is a foregone conclusion. In this respect, it is interesting to note that Dobrynin himself indicates that the formulation and implementation of new thinking is a difficult task and that there arise "bitter clashes, acute discussions, and painful divergences."[25] Such clashes might already be taking place. As the fundamental debate on the nature of imperialism is becoming the issue, the conflict will likely be sharpened in the future.

Domestic Roots of the New Thinking

As Primakov says, the new thinking is also "organically" connected with domestic reform. The connection between domestic reform and foreign policy, however, should not be narrowly confined to the issue of tactics designed only to build an international environment suited for domestic reform. The new thinking has deeper roots related to a broader intellectual ferment that can be properly called a revolution in consciousness.[26]

Behind this revolution there is a recognition of the crisis of socialism—the painful awareness that the Soviet system has reached a blind alley and that it has lost its economic, social, political, and spiritual vitality. The need for economic reform was the first to be recognized, but it soon became apparent that economic reform narrowly focused on economy alone would not be possible; hence, there emerged *perestroika, glasnost'* and democratization. There was wide recognition that the Stalinist system had outlived its historical usefulness, and that society could restore its vitality only by overhauling the Stalinist legacy. Once the Stalinist fetters were removed by *glasnost'*, all ideas that had smoldered under Brezhnev—mostly suppressed by orthodoxy and confined in their own narrow specialties, cut off from other similar ideas in other fields—were suddenly coalesced into a single intellectual movement. But this movement is remarkable precisely because it does not pretend to present the only correct point of view to replace the old, but allows a diversity of opinions and the possibility of genuine debate. A fundamental reexamination of foreign policy is only part of this broader intellectual ferment, and the development of the new thinking has closely paralleled the radical development of the process of *perestroika*.

There are basically three factors connecting domestic reform directly with foreign policy. Most importantly, foreign policy is integrally related to economic reform, which is decisively moving to accept and facilitate global interdependence. Second, in the process of mapping out strategies for economic reform under *glasnost'*, the question of the rational allocation of resources between military and civilian sectors is inevitable.[27] This is bound to lead to a debate on national security. Third, the impact of the Chernobyl incident on the consciousness of the nuclear issue cannot be dismissed. Chernobyl served to alert the world of nuclear power's potential for catastrophe when it gets out of human control. The nuclear issue is no longer exclusively one for the political and military leadership.[28]

Criticism of Brezhnev's Foreign Policy

The last and most important reason the new thinking should be taken seriously is that it represents a fundamental criticism of Brezhnev's foreign policy. Détente was based on the mistaken assumption that the "correlation of forces" in international relations was moving inexorably in favor of the Soviet Union. Furthermore, the growth of Soviet military power that finally succeeded in the attainment of strategic parity with the United States was recognized as one of the most important factors in the changing correlation of forces. In fact, Brezhnev's policy can be said to have elevated the military factor to the core of Soviet foreign policy, partly because military power was an undeniable accomplishment that the Soviet state could be proud of, and partly because there were no other foreign policy instruments available to them. Another consequence of this appraisal of the correlation of forces was that the Soviet leadership came to believe that it could pursue its activist foreign policy in the Third World without affecting U.S.–Soviet relations.

Until recently, Soviet commentators never acknowledged their country's responsibility for the failures of détente, conveniently shifting all the blame to the American side. The new thinking indicates that for the first time the Soviet leadership and foreign policy elites are engaging in a thorough self-criticism of their own détente policy.

It should be noted that in the general background of the new thinking there is a recognition that the correlation of forces is no longer moving in favor of the Soviet Union. On the contrary, the Soviet Union is on the defensive, challenged by the rapid modernization of U.S. military power and activist foreign policy hostile to the Soviet Union. In the Third World, despite its expansionism in the 1970s, it finds itself isolated and limited in influence. There is a sense of crisis, a sense that if this situation is allowed to continue, the Soviet Union will lose its international prestige and ultimately its status as a superpower.[29] This urgent sense of crisis lay at the heart of Gorbachev's reforms and the new thinking.

A fundamental criticism of the Brezhnevite notion of détente, the new thinking thus contains some important elements, which, if allowed to develop, might effect a significant departure from traditional Soviet foreign policy. First, the exclusive reliance on the military factor as the primary foreign policy instrument is criticized. Both Gorbachev and Dobrynin emphasize the importance of a multifaceted foreign policy approach, including military, political, economic, and humanitarian factors. Second, the need for a qualitatively higher level of flexibility in foreign policy and a readiness to move toward reasonable compromises is emphasized. Third, there seems to be a recognition that the Soviet Union cannot pursue an activist policy in the Third World without affecting the relations between the superpowers, which occupy the central place in Soviet foreign policy. Fourth, by emphasizing interdependence, the Soviet Union is expressing a greater willingness than it has hitherto shown to participate in international cooperative activities and organizations. Finally, there is a significant change in their notion of national security, a recognition that the unilateral military buildup in the Brezhnev period did not buy a commensurate guarantee of national security; on the contrary, it brought the Soviet Union closer to the danger of nuclear confrontation. This last point is important enough to be examined in more detail.

The New Thinking and Soviet Military Policy

Key Concepts

On the basis of official pronouncements and commentaries written by various foreign policy advisers, the following can be singled out as key concepts of the new thinking with regard to military policy:[30]

Mutual security: In the nuclear age security can only be mutual in bilateral relations; on the global scale, it can only be universal and comprehensive.

No victory in nuclear war: It would be suicidal to start a nuclear war.

Impossibility of achieving military superiority: It is impossible to achieve military superiority in the strategic relations between the USSR and the U.S. and between East and West.

Insufficiency of military-technical capability: National security cannot be achieved by military-technical means alone. An increasingly important role should be played by politics in the attainment of arms control and disarmament.

Rejection of deterrence: Deterrence cannot provide the basis for solid peace. It perpetuates the arms race and increases the chance of military confrontations.

Rejection of parity: Parity can no longer guarantee peace. The level of nuclear capability of both sides must be lowered, and eventually such weapons must be completely eliminated.

Strategic stability: The transition from the present stage to a nonnuclear world must be guided by the principle of strategic stability.

Reasonable sufficiency: Goals concerning the level of military strength and force should be based on the principle of reasonable sufficiency rather than on parity.

Defensive military doctrine: Both sides should adopt a defensive posture in
   formulating operational strategy.
Glasnost' in the military sphere: Excessive military secrecy will contribute
   to mistrust. *Glasnost'* should be applied to the military sphere.
Rejection of military means to solve international conflicts: In the nuclear age
   any local conflicts have the potential to escalate to a major superpower confrontation. Thus, all conflicts should be solved through
   peaceful means.
Rejection of Clausewitz's formula: The axiom that war is an extension of
   politics by violent means is no longer applicable in the nuclear age.

Evolution of Soviet Military Doctrine

Although this is not the place to describe Soviet military doctrine in
detail,[31] it must be looked at within the context of its basic evolution in
order to understand the significance of the new thinking.

It is possible to view the history of Soviet military doctrine as one in
which the Soviet leadership has struggled to integrate nuclear weapons
into the operational system of foreign-military policy, and at the same
time to maintain the ideologically consistent system of Marxism–
Leninism.

Nuclear weapons have undergone various stages of evaluations.
Stalin underestimated their value, which reflected the decisive inferiority of the Soviet Union in strategic relations with the United States.
Under Khrushchev a complete turnaround called a "nuclear revolution"
in military doctrine took place, and nuclear weapons were deemed the
most decisive element for the purpose of deterring imperialists' attacks
on the Soviet Union. Under Brezhnev nuclear weapons were the
decisive factor that propelled the Soviet Union into superpower status.

As nuclear weapons became integrated into Soviet foreign-military
policy, however, the leadership had to face basic contradictions between
the fundamental postulates of Marxism–Leninism and the implications
of the nuclear-inclusive operational system of foreign-military policy.
Specifically, nuclear weapons touched the following raw nerves of
Marxism–Leninism: (1) Is war inevitable, even in the nuclear age, as
long as imperialism exists? (2) If the transition from capitalism to
socialism is an inevitable historical process, will socialism win in a
nuclear war?[32] And (3) even in a nuclear age, is war an extension of
politics by violent means?

The first Marxist–Leninist dogma to be thrown out the window was
the inevitability of war. As soon as Stalin was dead, Malenkov declared
that in a nuclear age war no longer became inevitable. But it was

Khrushchev who had the rejection of the inevitability of war accepted at the 20th Party Congress in 1956. Nevertheless, the two other dogmas remained in effect. Khrushchev stated that the reason war no longer was inevitable was that the Soviet Union possessed nuclear weapons, and that even the imperialists were soberminded enough to realize that their attack on the Soviet Union would mean the end of capitalism. Had this referred to mutual suicide, Khrushchev's military doctrine would have been close to mutual assured destruction (MAD). But in two respects it was different. First, true to the Marxist–Leninist postulate of the historical inevitability of the transition from capitalism to socialism, Khrushchev hastened to state that if imperialists decided to wage war against the Soviet Union and its allies, the Soviet Union would emerge victorious even after nuclear devastation, while imperialism would perish. Thus, the belief in victory in nuclear war was one of the cornerstones of Khrushchev's military doctrine. Second, it was believed that the best way to deter a nuclear attack by imperialists was by the Soviet Union's possession of superior military power. The intention to seek military superiority was, therefore, the second cornerstone of Khrushchev's military doctrine.

In the late 1960's and the beginning of the 1970's, a significant reappraisal of the military doctrine took place. In 1972, the Soviet Union concluded SALT I with the United States, which meant, first of all, that the Soviet Union accepted the concept of mutual vulnerability inherent in the ABM Treaty. Second, "parity and equal security" was accepted as the foundation on which to create the framework of strategic relations with the West. From 1977 on, Brezhnev and other Soviet leaders openly declared that the Soviet Union would not seek military superiority, and that the parity that existed between the United States and the Soviet Union and between the NATO nations and the Warsaw Pact Treaty nations was the guarantee for world peace. From at least 1981, Brezhnev began to state that "only a madman who decides to commit suicide can start a nuclear war," implying the rejection of victory in nuclear conflict.[33]

It is, therefore, possible to say that during the 1970's and in the beginning of the 1980's, there was an important shift in Soviet military doctrine. It was moving away from the previous thinking that centered around the concept of victory in nuclear war and military superiority, toward a position that basically accepted mutual deterrence as its foundation. Brezhnev's arms control policy, however, seemed to contradict this movement in one important respect; the Soviet Union never agreed to reduce its stock of its most destabilizing big missiles, particularly the SS-18s, even if such concessions would have contributed greatly to strategic stability. This attitude led many in the West to conclude that despite what Brezhnev and other Soviet leaders repeatedly stated, they actually never abandoned their old doctrine centered on first strike capability in a nuclear war.[34]

It is important to note that the military, notably represented by Marshal Nikolai Ogarkov, resisted accepting the political leadership's notion that there would be no victory in nuclear war. Perhaps for ideological reasons or perhaps to boost the morale of the soldiers, Ogarkov clearly insisted on the need to prepare for victory even in nuclear war, refusing to endorse the notion that there would be no such victory.[35] This conflict also may have been connected with the serious struggle between the military and the party leadership concerning allocation of scarce national resources.[36]

There was a common thread that ran from Khrushchev to Brezhnev. Under both leaders the Soviet Union basically viewed the world in terms of the conflict of the two irreconcilable systems, in which imperialists were determined to destroy socialists. The logical conclusion was that there was no choice but for the Soviet Union to rely primarily on military means, particularly nuclear weapons, to deter the imperialists' aggression. Although Brezhnev's military doctrine moved toward acceptance of mutual deterrence, it contained in itself the inevitable logic to further the spiral of the arms race, and ultimately contradicted the concept of strategic stability.

Change in the Analytical Framework

Until the end of the Brezhnev era the Soviet approach to national security was guided by the principle of absolute security, which meant that the Soviet Union would not feel secure until its adversaries became completely insecure. The principle of mutual security thus represents a departure from this tradition. The important point, however, is to recognize that the change has resulted from a fundamental alteration in the basic analytical framework within which Soviets view the world.

Behind the concept of mutual security there is an acutely felt sense of the danger of nuclear war. Mutual security is derived from the reality of mutual insecurity, wherein mankind as a whole, whether living under capitalism or socialism, is in danger of extinction from nuclear conflict. A number of important factors coalesced to bring this sense of crisis to the forefront of foreign-military policy. First, there was a military challenge from the U.S., which virtually nullified the strategic gains made by the Soviets in the 1970's and forced the Soviet Union to reexamine seriously what responses would be best suited to ensure national security. They must have concluded that responding to the U.S. challenge with a reciprocal arms buildup and emulative military programs would not increase their security; on the contrary, this would reduce the security of both sides, since a new arms race would inevitably lead to qualitatively different strategic instability, thus bringing the world closer to the brink of nuclear war.[37]

Coincidentally, the Chernobyl accident must have had a profound effect on the nuclear issue.[38] It injected into Soviet consciousness a sense of the reality of nuclear catastrophe. Nuclear strategy could no longer be treated as an esoteric abstract intellectual exercise or as the exclusive prerogative of a handful of military officers.

Moreover, the reexamination of the security policy coincided with the debate on domestic reform. While it might be possible to respond to the U.S. challenge militarily, such response would make it difficult for the Soviet Union to carry out economic reforms to which the first and foremost priority is given. More profoundly, the critical examination of the past, necessary to advance domestic transformation, inevitably led to critical reappraisal of foreign-military policy as well. It was no longer adequate to place all the blame for the arms race on the other side, as the "presumption of infallibility" was rejected. This led to an admission that past Soviet military policy, while objectively defensible in its time, also contributed to the momentum of the arms race.[39] Particularly, criticism was directed at the attempt to seek security by exclusive reliance on military–technical means.

Mutual security, however, is based on a more fundamental change in the approach to international relations than a recognition of the danger of nuclear war. Mutual security presupposes that one's national security depends on the understanding and good intention of the other side. The reason past Soviet security policy relied exclusively on military–technical means lies in their understanding of the nature of imperialism. As long as imperialism is thought to conceal within itself a momentum of militarism with which to attempt to crush socialism, it is inevitable to conclude that only military strength can guarantee Soviet security, and thus the interests of the two systems are in a fundamental sense mutually exclusive. The new thinking rejects this view. It takes the position that nuclear war threatens socialism and capitalism alike, and to that extent the fate of both systems are bound together by the danger of mutual extinction. Neither side can remove this danger unilaterally by military–technical means alone; unilateral attempts are bound to increase the danger. Risking one's security on the understanding and intention of the other side is not a matter of choice, but of necessity.[40] In his speech at the 70th anniversary of the October Revolution, Gorbachev clearly formulated the revised approach to imperialism: in this new stage of world interdependence, the most dangerous aspects of imperialism can be suppressed, and imperialism can exist without militarism. When the world was threatened by fascism, the Soviet Union and the U.S. were united in a grand alliance against a common enemy; there is no reason such an alliance cannot be formed to combat the common threat of nuclear war.[41] The idea of a world community that encompasses the different social systems may well be one of the most important notions of the new thinking.

Rejection of Clausewitz's axiom that war is an extension of politics by violent means can be understood in this context. This thesis was previously recognized as the foundation of the Marxist–Leninist approach to war, as cited by Ogarkov in his pamphlet, *History Teaches Vigilance*, published in 1985.[42] Criticism appeared as early as 1986 in an article by Aleksandr Bovin.[43] But it was in Gorbachev's speech at the Moscow Forum that the general secretary rejected the thesis for the first time. Although he initially said that this axiom was no longer applicable to "world war," he later removed this qualification and stated that war in general could not be an extension of politics in the nuclear age.[44] This is tantamount to removing the question of war and peace from Marxist–Leninist class analysis. The process of dismemberment of the Marxist–Leninist approach to war that began with the rejection of the inevitability of war has been completed.

The New Thinking and Mutual Deterrence

The new thinking contains two contradictory elements. The first is the acceptance of mutual deterrence by means of strengthened strategic stability. The second is the rejection of deterrence itself.

While in the Brezhnev era arms control functioned only in a supplementary sense, to buttress the military means of acquiring national security, Gorbachev's new thinking elevates arms control to a central place in security policy. His initiatives indicate that the Soviet Union is decisively accepting the concept of mutual deterrence as the basis of strategic relations with the U.S. and the West. Unlike Brezhnev, Gorbachev's guiding principle in pursuing arms control seems to be strategic stability. This is shown by his willingness to reduce drastically the stock of big missiles Brezhnev had jealously guarded, even at the expense of strategic stability, as well as by his numerous concessions on INF negotiations. It seems that the Soviet Union's primary concern is to assure the survivability of a second-strike deterrent capability. The attempt to increase survivability of their new missiles—SS-24 and

SS-25—in the mobile mode may be part of this overall objective. In their global and theater warfighting strategy they are emphasizing the conventional option, while nuclear weapons are losing operational significance, relegated more and more to the deterrent role.[45]

Gorbachev's arms control initiatives are not the only evidence that the Soviet Union is moving to accept mutual deterrence through strengthened strategic stability. Another important concept that they have entertained is "reasonable sufficiency." This concept resulted from the critical examination of Brezhnev's policy, which maintained that parity would guarantee peace. According to the new thinking, parity is no longer a guarantee of peace, since it has provided both sides with an excuse to increase their nuclear arsenals. The adoption of the concept of reasonable sufficiency will break the vicious cycle of the arms race. Previously, the Party's commitment to the armed forces was guaranteed in the promise to provide "everything necessary to defend" the Soviet homeland. At the 27th Party Congress, however, both Gorbachev's political report and the final resolution said that "armed forces are maintained at the level sufficient to insure peaceful labor and peaceful life of Soviet people." In the new edition of the Party program, it is declared that the armed forces are maintained "at the level that excludes strategic superiority by the forces of imperialism."[46] This change is important, since it may mean that Soviet military doctrine might be moving to accept the concept of sufficiency inherent in mutual deterrence.

Furthermore, it is possible that the Soviet leadership is revising the notion of parity and equal security, which lay at the foundation of Brezhnev's military doctrine.[47] This concept contains an inherent logical contradiction. If the Soviet Union insists on equal security, parity cannot be realized either at the global level or at the regional level, because pursuance of equal security—the notion that the Soviet Union has to possess military power equal to the aggregate military power of all its opponents—will inevitably lead to Soviet superiority.[48] Glickham notes that Gorbachev avoids the phrase equal security.[49]

Another important concept that has developed under the new thinking is that of defensive military doctrine. Previously, it was maintained that although Soviet military doctrine was defensive in nature, "to create conditions for seizing the strategic initiative to begin offensive" was considered the best means of assuring effective defense.[50] The new thinking, however, is beginning to explore the possibility of rewriting Soviet military doctrine so as to incorporate the policy of no-first use of nuclear weapons, the adoption of defensive strategy by removing offensive actions, and the implementation of reasonable sufficiency into force planning.[51] The document on military doctrine adopted by the Political Consultative Committee of the Warsaw Treaty Organization in Berlin in May 1987 was the first step in this direction, although what such a defensive doctrine really means in the force posture, strategy and arms control policy is unclear at this point.[52] This document, incidentally, proposes the exchange of information between NATO and WTO, allowing them to compare their respective strategies. This, too, is meant to increase strategic stability by removing fears and mistrust that exist between two military alliances.

Another means that has been proposed under the new thinking to increase strategic stability is the extension of *glasnost'* to the military sphere, which was hitherto protected in impenetrable secrecy. The Soviets have made concessions on verification, allowing the inspection of military installations deep in their territory, unthinkable only a few years ago. Moreover, they have opened the controversial Krasnoyarsk radar site and a chemical weapons factory to Western observers. *Glasnost'* has been extended to military expenditures as well. Deputy Foreign Minister Vladimir Petrovskii admitted for the first time that the military outlay for R & D was not included in the Soviet military budget.[53] This admission was followed by Chief of the General Staff Sergei Akhromeev's statement that the official military expenditure in the budget did not include military R & D or weapons procurement.[54] In his message to the United Nations in September 1987, Gorbachev promised that the Soviet Union would publish its real military expenditures in such a way as to allow comparison with expenditures in the West.[55]

Rejection of Deterrence

The new thinking, adopted by Gorbachev, contains not only the acceptance of mutual deterrance, as just demonstrated, but also, contradictorily, its repudiation. The clearest formulation of this position is given in Gorbachev's speech at the Moscow Forum, in which he gives four reasons deterrence should be rejected.

First, deterrence is amoral because it is based on the balance of terror, which takes the world as a hostage. He states: "In the nuclear age no one, neither the Soviet Union nor the United States, has the right to pronounce a death sentence on mankind. . . . Neither are we judges, nor billions of people criminals who have to be punished."

Second, as long as nuclear weapons exist, mankind will always be threatened by the possibility of a nuclear war that might occur because of the inability of man to control these weapons. The nature of the nuclear weapon is such that there will be less chance to "train [personnel] to follow obedient behaviors." In Gorbachev's words, "proliferation, increasingly sophisticated nuclear weapons systems, the greater scale of delivery systems, and the constant risk of technical error, human error or malice are all accidental factors on which the survival of mankind depends."

Third, the policy of deterrence is based on intimidation. In his opinion, when threats become a political resource they must be taken seriously by the other side, and in order for threats to be taken seriously, they must always be backed by definite actions. Thus, "the policy of deterrence, if examined in historical context, has not reduced the risk of military conflict. In fact it has increased that risk."

Fourth, on philosophical grounds Gorbachev rejects the notion that man is violent by nature and that war is but a manifestation of human instinct, because this idea would lead to the logical consequence that "ever more sophisticated weapons of mass destruction will continue to be developed."

Hence, his goal is not merely to accomplish complete elimination of nuclear weapons, but to abolish war itself. "We believe that it is possible to build such a world," he declared, "and we shall do everything to ensure the accomplishment of what is perhaps the most ambitious social goal ever."[56]

Gorbachev's True Intention

How can the contradiction in Gorbachev's stand on military doctrine be reconciled? There are basically four hypotheses to explain it. First, his real intention is to achieve military superiority by denuclearization, and the new thinking is nothing but propaganda to serve this purpose. Second, Gorbachev's renunciation of deterrence is real, and he accepts mutual deterrence only as a transitional stage to achieve his final goal of a nonnuclear world. Third, his goal is to achieve mutual deterrence, but either for propaganda purposes (to gain support in the West) or for the purpose of reaching an arms control agreement with the U.S., he renounces deterrence. Fourth, Gorbachev believes in both, accepting contradictory opinions and choosing the most expedient alternative to fit the circumstances. These four hypotheses and their implications have been reviewed already.[57] It suffices to say here that although all four hypotheses have merit, the second emerges as the best candidate for explaining Gorbachev's true intention, to move to a nuclear-free world.

For one thing, Gorbachev's aversion to deterrence is persistent. He succeeded in including the rejection of deterrence in the document on military doctrine of the WTO in May. He repeated his attack on deterrence in his interview with the French delegation in September as well as in his speech on the anniversary of the October Revolution. His persistence is striking in view of the increasing irritations expressed by the military on this point. But he is realistic enough to see that his goal of total elimination of nuclear weapons cannot be achieved immediately. Mutual deterrence through maintenance of strategic stability seems to be the best instrument in the transitional stage to reduce the level of the nuclear arsenal of both sides. Rejection of deterrence also underscores Gorbachev's determination to break the vicious cycle of the spiraling arms race, which he believes will continue as long as deterrence persists.

The New Thinking and the Military

Potential Sources of the Military's Dissatisfaction

The new thinking is in one sense an assault on the military, attacking the traditional privilege given to them in allocation of resources. As civilian advisers and commentators are beginning to voice their opinions on national security issues, the dominance of military–technical affairs has eroded. Clausewitz's formula, which the military held to be central to the Marxist–Leninist approach to war, is rejected with a stroke of pen. In the long-coveted sanctuary once held in strictest secrecy, foreign observers now are allowed to inspect a nuclear test site, a chemical weapons factory and a radar site. The situation will worsen once the verification clause on the INF agreement of December 7, 1987 is implemented. There is strong pressure to extend *glasnost'* to military expenditures, which will inevitably lead to tougher competition in the battle for resource allocations.

In terms of the relative weight of the military in decisionmaking, the defense minister remains only a candidate member of the Politburo, in comparison with the KGB chief, who enjoys full membership. When Defense Minister Sokolov was unceremoniously sacked for the laxity of discipline that allowed a West German youth to have violated the vital Soviet airspace and land his Cessna plane on Red Square, General Yazov was selected as his successor over several senior officers in line for promotion. Most importantly, the new thinking has downgraded the role of the military in foreign policy, inevitably leading to a declining role of the military in the decisionmaking process and in society generally. Seweryn Bialer once remarked that one must make a distinction between the military factor in Soviet policy and the military sector in Soviet decisionmaking. While the military sector has always subordi-nated itself to the authority of the Party in the decisionmaking process, the military factor has always been dominant in determining the nature of Soviet policy throughout Soviet history.[58] The emergence of the new thinking indicates that for the first time the military factor is relegated to a secondary position.

Despite this impressive list of potential conflicts, Western analyses on the relationship between Gorbachev and the military overwhelmingly portray harmony rather than conflict.[59] Dale Herspring, for instance, states: "Though Gorbachev lacks Brezhnev's strong attachment to the military, he does not appear to be particularly antimilitary."[60] Never-theless, it is difficult to subscribe to this opinion. Some signs of opposition to the new thinking can actually be gleaned between the lines of articles written by military officers. Although they are not openly critical, subtle nuances of differences emerge on issues such as deterrence, Clausewitz's formula, and reasonable sufficiency.

Deterrence

In Gorbachev's mind there may not be a contradiction between his opposition to deterrence and the necessity of seeking mutual deterrence in the real world. But in terms of practical policy, the rejection of deterrence itself may undermine the efficacy of mutual deterrence.

This question became a central issue of the debate between Ales' Adamovich, a Belorussian writer, and Colonel General Volkogonov, deputy chief of the Main Political Administration of the Soviet Army and Navy. What sparked the debate was Adamovich's article in *Moskovskie novosti*, in which he recounted his interview with a commander of a nuclear submarine. In a hypothetical case where the Soviet Union received a first nuclear strike, the commander was asked, would he push the button to release a retaliatory second strike. The commander responded: "I'll remain silent regardless; nobody, most of all they, must know how I will act." Adamovich, though understanding the com-mander's need for silence, felt no inhibition in expressing this own refusal to push the button:

> No, we don't want to participate in the murder of mankind, either in the first or second, or any kind of strike, because we are for the complete elimination of nuclear weapons; we are ready to part with the nuclear "might" with relief; we do not rejoice at all at these cancerous pseudobicepts; we do not hold on to the status of a nuclear power. . . .

> In nuclear war there cannot be a victor. This is the absolute truth
> of our time—the very foundation of all real politics.[61]

It should be pointed out that the above argument reflects what Gorbachev has been advocating in the name of the new thinking.

Volkogonov sharply attacked Adamovich's article on two occasions;
first at the conference of the Writers' Union, and then in his own
Krasnaia zvezda article. He began by qualifying the significance of the
new thinking, which in his opinion is not a new world view, but merely
"a new facet that enriches our understanding of commanding imperatives (objective requirements) of the nuclear age." He insisted that the
new thinking does not contradict Leninist teaching.[62] Thus, Volkogonov
resurrected Leninist orthodoxy in the name of the new thinking, thereby
skillfully disguising the latter's true meaning.

He went on to argue that the possibility of nuclear war exists, but
there are some who see this reality only through "the prism of
apocalypse."[63] Volkogonov accepted the view that to start a nuclear war
would be suicidal under contemporary conditions, but by no means has
it become impossible, as long as imperialists insist on irrational, crimi-
nal, adventuristic policies, believing that they could achieve decisive
strategic superiority against socialism. Adamovich claims that to have
the bomb is no less shameful today than Auschwitz's existence was to
Germany. This is to ignore the political context in which the problem of
war and peace is posed in the contemporary world, Volkogonov argues.
Socialism stands for peace, while imperialism seeks war. Ignoring this
dialectic, Adamovich falls into the mistake of moral relativism, where he
asserts that in order to achieve, peace both sides must get rid of "illusory
ideas." This means that the possibility of maintaining peace is predi-
cated on the rejection of one's own ideals and spiritual values. The
unacceptability of such an approach is obvious, with nuclear capability,
at present, threatening contemporary existence; the Soviet Union could
not create a nonnuclear world unilaterally. The world view of the two
systems will continue to be different.

Imperatives of the nuclear age are powerful, imposing their imprint
on a correlation of forces, contemporary strategy, priorities of resources,
and perspective for the future. One cannot ignore the militaristic nature
of U.S. policy. The U.S. nuclear strategy, military program, pronouncements of leaders responsible for military policy—all indicate that it
intends to wage and survive nuclear war. Soviet military doctrine is, on
the contrary, completely defensive, aiming at the prevention of war as
its goal. In fact, Soviet defensive capability is the only guarantee for
peace. Volkogonov states:

For us the phenomenon of nuclear competition is what is especially imposed on us as an answer to threatening challenges. . . . For the other side, nuclear deterrence is the conceptual, strategic objective. Therefore, it is hardly correct, as many authors do, to view this process without discrimination. It has indeed dual characters: for the one side, it is imposed, and for the other it is purposeful *(tselopolagaiushchii)*. . . .

In other words, deterrence advocated by the West should be denounced, but deterrence pursued by the Soviet Union is the only guarantee of peace. Thus, Volkogonov denounces both rejection of deterrence and acceptance of mutual deterrence, which amounts to the total attack on Gorbachev's position.

By condemning the second strike, according to Volkogonov, Adamovich leads readers to the logical conclusion that it is not necessary to prepare for it. This view is not original; it is widely held by "nuclear pacifists," who believe that the use of nuclear weapons even for self-defense or retaliation is amoral. Such a view is dangerous, because it jeopardizes the efficacy of Soviet soldiers to fulfill their military duty. He labels this position "vegetarian pacifism."

Every day thousands of Soviet soldiers take up their duty at the missile complexes. They are directly joined to a task of strategic, or I might call, fateful significance. We all hope and believe that no one of them would have to execute commands to fire at real targets. But to *prepare for it* (Volkogonov's italics) as the highest expression of his military duty and as a duty of a citizen continues to remain a threatening, deterring factor. And as long as no political mechanism to prevent war is established, only one indisputable truth exists for the Soviet military men in the form of an axiom: the higher our military preparedness is, the less likelihood there is of our potential aggressor deciding on a nuclear adventure.[64]

This is the most classical Soviet formulation of deterrence one could think of, a mirror image of that evoked by the American advocates. It is based on the bipolar vision, the total mistrust of the other side, and the belief in a unilateral means of security. In this sense, Volkogonov's view is in total opposition to the new thinking, but, importantly, it is shared by other military authors.[65] Comparing Volkogonov's argument with the key concepts of the new thinking supported by Gorbachev, it is difficult to support Herspring's opinion: "The doctrinal trend observed under Gorbachev . . . has long been visible within the Soviet military establishment. Gorbachev is following the military's lead in this area."[66]

Clausewitz's Formula

In his speech at the Moscow Forum, Gorbachev first rejected Clausewitz's formula. It was obvious that he intended to extend the rejection to all wars, not merely to "world war" involving both superpowers.[67] Whether the rejection is applied only to world war or to all wars has profound practical significance on the approach to armed conflict, the role of the military factor in foreign policy, and the role of the military in society.

Marshal S. L. Sokolov, then defense minister, in what turned out to be his last article before his dismissal, stated: "*World war* (italics by author) in the nuclear-cosmic era has outlived itself, and ceased to be a means to achieve political aims."[68] It should be noted that Sokolov did not mention anything about Clausewitz's formula; he presumably intended to disassociate this disclaimer with the frontal attack on Clausewitz's axiom. If this disclaimer were limited to world war, then what became impossible would be confined only to war that might involve both superpowers. But there are other wars that do not necessarily develop into world war. Sokolov implies that Clausewitz's axiom is still applicable to them.

A similar attempt can also be found in Volkogonov's article. He explains that "in the contemporary epoch, nuclear war cannot be a reasonable, rational means of politics, if one refers to its functional aspect."[69] Volkogonov concedes that nuclear war is no longer a realistic means of pursuing political objectives, but by stating that this applies only to its operational aspect, he reaffirms that nuclear war continues to have significance. What he means by this is already clear. He takes the deterrent role of nuclear weapons seriously; he believes that the more the Soviet Union prepares for nuclear war, the greater the likelihood it would be able to prevent it. Furthermore, Volkogonov, like Sokolov, refuses to associate the rejection of operational utility of nuclear war with Clausewitz's axiom. His reference to Gorbachev's Moscow Forum speech without mentioning Gorbachev's rejection of Clausewitz's formula, which was the most notable part of this speech, underscores his intention to ignore Gorbachev's innovation.

While Gorbachev himself stepped up his tone by applying the rejection of Clausewitz's formula to all wars, it is important to note that no military men have so far openly endorsed this view. Thus, it is possible to surmise that the rejection of Clausewitz's axiom is far from being accepted in the military.

Reasonable Sufficiency versus Parity

The concept of reasonable sufficiency [*razumnaia dostatochnost*] is, like many other Soviet strategic concepts, American in its intellectual origin. It was first formulated in 1956 by Secretary of the Air Force Donald W. Quarles in his article, "How Much Is Enough?" Its central notion was that once a sufficient level of nuclear deterrence was achieved, any increase to match the other side's buildup would be meaningless.[70] Thus, reasonable sufficiency is fundamentally in contradiction with parity and equality.

In his last article Sokolov defends the maintenance of Soviet military preparedness "at the level that will guarantee the successful prevention of aggression." Proclaiming that the Soviet Union will neither let the U.S. achieve military superiority over the Soviet Union, nor tolerate "any attempt to upset the existing military equality," he cites Gorbachev's statement at the 27th Party Congress: "The Soviet Union will not aspire [to attain] more security, nor will it go for less."[71] Although Sokolov does not use the word, it is possible to conclude that this article supports more or less the principle of parity rather than reasonable sufficiency.

Volkogonov is also presumed to oppose the concept of reasonable sufficiency. In the first place, his long article does not mention it. Instead, his central focus is on parity. To Volkogonov, a real possibility for peace was created precisely because the Soviet Union achieved strategic parity with the U.S. Although he also advocates that survival of mankind is possible only on the basis of compromises and mutual concessions, he immediately qualifies this by adding that "only the actual recognition of the principle of equal security gives the chances for the possibility of agreement." Finally, he concludes: "Military–strategic parity is not spiritual parity. We placed and are placing indisputable priority in this."[72]

After May 1987, it appears that the concept of reasonable sufficiency has become the most important dispute between those who support the new thinking and at least some in the military who feel dissatisfied with it. Colonel P. Skorodenko discusses the relationship between military parity and reasonable sufficiency. He at first defends the concept of reasonable sufficiency, defined as "such minimal quantitative and qualitative level of military potential of a state as to guarantee reliably its security and not to create real military threat to other countries."[73] Although he admits that military–strategic parity itself does not guarantee peace, he nonetheless defines reasonable sufficiency in terms of parity. In Skorodenko's opinion, the limit of sufficiency "under the conditions of parity" can be determined in three ways: first, by maintaining the present level; second, by reducing the level of military force through stages without offsetting the balance; and third, by increasing the limit of sufficiency as a response to the acquisition of military potential by the other side.[74] The Soviet Union would prefer the second option, Skorodenko argues, but ultimately the level of sufficiency will be determined by the other side, since the USSR will not allow imperialism to achieve military superiority over socialism.[75] It can be said that Skorodenko's article is an attempt to emasculate the concept of reasonable sufficiency by substituting parity for it.

Rear Admiral G. Kostev's formulation of the problem is even sharper. He argues that the level of reasonable sufficiency is determined first by the requirement to prevent unpunished nuclear attack "even in the most unfavorable conditions," and second by currently existing military–strategic parity, which remains a decisive factor in preventing war. Earlier Soviet military doctrine took the position that once imperialists began a war, it would inevitably lead to nuclear war where the major weapons would be nuclear missiles. This situation has changed, in Kostev's opinion. The U.S. and NATO are actively making preparations for a protracted war under the strategy of flexible response, using not only nuclear but also conventional weapons. From this it follows, Kostev argues, that "it is necessary for our country to engage in comprehensive preparations for military defense with the use of not only nuclear, but also conventional, highly effective weapons." Kostev concludes:

> Today war is a reality of our time and the integral part of a policy of violence by reactionary imperialist circles. The army and navy, which exist to carry out military struggle, perform their duty with weapons. Therefore, it is exceptionally important to support military–strategic parity by strengthening the Soviet armed forces, weakening all attempts by imperialism to disrupt the balance of force.[76]

Thus Kostev, much more forcefully than Skorodenko, insists on the need to maintain parity even with a unilateral military program.[77] It should be noted that there is a striking similarity between Kostev's argument and the one once advocated by Ogarkov.

A similar, less strident view supporting the thrust of the argument made by Skorodenko and Kostev is presented by General E. Ivanovskii, Commander of Ground Forces and deputy minister of defense. Relying on an article written by U.S. Secretary of the Army G. Marsh, Ivanovskii discusses in detail the malevolent U.S. military intentions. U.S. strategy continues to be based on deterrence [*ustrashenie*] through threat of punishment of assured destruction.[78] It also aims to take decisive measures to force the Soviet Union out of any part of the world, while it openly advocates U.S. intervention in revolutionary and national liberation movements. Marsh's views are tantamount to putting spokes in the wheels of Soviet–U.S. relations, particularly in terms of arms control. Ivanovskii concludes that the Soviet Union will be forced to "maintain its armed forces in such a composition and at such a level that will be able to repulse any aggression from outside."[79] It is important to note that this article was published only a few weeks before the summit meeting, and in the midst of the Yel'tsin affair.

Military and Political Opposition to Gorbachev

While military authors publicly state that they support the concepts of the new thinking, it is clear from the above analysis that they actually intend to undermine what the new thinking represents. The list of military authors examined herein is by no means comprehensive, but it is sufficient to show that there exist dissatisfactions and frustrations with the new thinking among at least some in the military. This is not to suggest that the military as a whole is united in opposition; there are undoubtedly some who enthusiastically support the new thinking.[80] But it is also true that the new thinking, which poses a difficult dilemma to professional military men, aggravates their frustrations.

One common thread that runs through these articles is a fundamental distrust of the intentions of the imperialist world. Spending their whole life studying the other side's military doctrine, strategy, force planning, and procurement patterns, the authors find it difficult to subscribe to the opinion that the nature of imperialism has become benign to the extent that their own security can be tied to that of the imperialists. It is on this fundamental point concerning the nature of imperialism that at least some military men and the advocates of the new thinking are diametrically opposed. If history offers some guide for the future, it is unlikely that the military will form an oppositional bloc to the political leadership, but the military probably will play an important role in the outcome of the power struggle that will inevitably be waged in the future.

Conclusion

The new thinking is not merely a tactical retreat of Soviet foreign policy; it basically stems from an approach to international relations that is quite different from the traditional Marxist–Leninist one. It is also integrally connected with the ongoing revolution in consciousness. The general direction in which the new thinking is attempting to steer Soviet foreign policy—whether it is toward interdependence or mutual security—is not adverse to the interest of the West in the long run, although its implementation in specific issues is likely to be difficult.

We have to bear in mind, however, that the new thinking is by no means a solid basis on which current Soviet foreign policy is anchored. In fact, it is still fragile. Various concepts of the new thinking that have arisen from the practical necessity of changing the previous course have led to a logical dilemma, the question of how to define the nature of imperialism. It seems that the discussions until now were merely preliminary skirmishes; the real test of the new thinking is about to begin where the battle line is clearly drawn.

The ultimate fate of the new thinking will be determined by the outcome of this decisive battle, which will be closely connected with the struggle on domestic reform. It is also possible that its outcome will be to some extent influenced by Western response to the new Soviet foreign policy initiatives; such response should be guided only by the principle of upholding and enhancing Western interests. Our interests themselves, however, will be ultimately influenced by the outcome of this conflict in the Soviet Union. To this extent, the new thinking expresses one universal truth of the contemporary world: interdependence and mutual security.

Notes

1. For a good treatment of the new thinking in the early stage of Gorbachev's regime, see Charles Glickham, "New Directions for Soviet Foreign Policy," *Radio Liberty Research Bulletin*, RL Supplement 2/86, September 6, 1986, but this article is somewhat dated. For ideological debates preceding the new thinking, see Stephen Shenfield, *The Nuclear Predicament: Explorations in Soviet Ideology* (London, New York, Andover: The Royal Institute of International Affairs, Routledge & Kagan Paul, 1987), *Chatham House Papers*, 37. The most important documents on the new thinking are the following: M. S. Gorbachev, "Politicheskii doklad Tsentral'nogo Komiteta KPSS XXVII s"ezdu kommunisticheskoi partii Sovetskogo Soiuza," *Kommunist*, No. 4 (March 1986), pp. 8–80; M. S. Gorbachev, "Za bez"iadernyi mir, za gumanizm mezhdunarodnykh otnoshenii," *Izvestiia*, February 17, 1987 (for English translation of this speech, see Mikhail Gorbachev, *For the Sake of Preserving Human Civilisation*. Moscow: Novosti Press Agency Publishing House, 1987);

M. S.Gorbachev, *Perestroika i novoe myshlenie dlia nashei strany i dlia vsego mira* (Moscow, 1987) (transl. as *Perestroika: New Thinking for Our Country and the World* (New York: Harper & Row, 1987).

2. For the ideological background of the new thinking, see Shenfield, *The Nuclear Predicament.*

3. Glickham, pp. 7–10.

4. Abraham Becker, Seweryn Bialer, Arnold Horelick, Robert Legvold, Marshall Shulman, eds., *The 27th Congress of the Communist Party of the Soviet Union: A Report from the Airlie House Conference* (New York and Los Angeles: RAND/UCLA Center for the Study of the Soviet International Behavior and W. Averell Harriman Institute for Advanced Study of the Soviet Union, December, 1986—hereafter referred to as *The Airlie House Conference*), pp. 58–61.

5. Gorbachev, "Politicheskii doklad," pp. 53–57.

6. A. Dobrynin, "Za bes"iadernyi mir, navstrechu XXI veku," *Kommunist*, No. 9 (June 1986), pp. 18–31.

7. "Deliiskaia deklaratsiia o printsipakh svobodnogo ot iadernogo oruzhiia i nenasil'stvennogo mira," *Izvestiia*, November 28, 1986.

8. Glickham, pp. 8–9.

9. See Gorbachev's Moscow Forum Speech, "Za bez"iadernyi mir," *Izvestiia*, February 17, 1987. Since the danger of nuclear war is not specifically identified as a global problem, there still remained a theoretical possibility that security and global problems are still separately treated. But this doubt was to be removed completely.

10. E. Primakov, "Novaia filosofiia vneshnei politiki," *Pravda*, July 10, 1987.

11. M. S. Gorbachev, "Real'nosti' i garantii bezopasnogo mira," *Izvestiia*, September 18, 1987.

12. *Izvestiia*, October 1, 1987.

13. Gorbachev, *Perestroika i novoe myshlenie*, p. 141.

14. Ibid., p. 144.

15. Ibid.

16. M. S. Gorbachev, "Oktiabr' i perestroika: revoliutsiia prodolzhaetsia," *Izvestiia*, November 3, 1987, p. 5; for English translation of this speech, see Mikhail Gorbachev, *October and Perestroika: the Revolution Continues* (Moscow: Novosti, 1987).

17. Gorbachev, "Oktiabr' i perestroika," p. 4.

18. Gorbachev, "Politicheskii doklad Tsentral'nogo Komiteta KPSS XVII s"ezdu."

19. See Tsuyoshi Hasegawa, "The New Thinking and Gorbachev's Foreign–Military Policy." Paper presented for a joint meeting between the Asia Pacific Association and the United Nations Association on "US–Japan Relations and the Soviet Union," May 20–22, 1987, pp. 7–10.

20. For a detailed argument on this problem, see Seweryn Bialer, "Soviet Foreign Policy: Sources, Perceptions, Trends," in Seweryn

Bialer, ed., _Domestic Context of Soviet Foreign Policy_ (Boulder, CO: Westview Press, 1981), p. 424; also see Shenfield, pp. 1–8.

21. For the organizational change in the Asian division, see Kimura Hiroshi, "Soron: sorenno ajia-taiheiyoseisakuno tenkan [Unfolding of Soviet Asia-Pacific Policy: An Overview]," _Soren Kenkyu_, 3 (October 1986), p. 23.

22. This information was revealed recently to the author by someone involved in this advisory body.

23. Glickham, p. 11.

24. See Hasegawa, "The New Thinking and Gorbachev's Foreign–Military Policy," pp. 17–18.

25. Dobrynin, p. 25; Glickham, p. 6.

26. Primakov, "Novaia filosofiia."

27. Ibid.

28. Haruki Wada, in his recent reportage, makes the point that Soviet intellectuals, who make an analogy between the Great Reforms in the 1860's and _perestroika_, liken Chernobyl to the defeat of the Crimean War. See Haruki Wada, _Watashino mita peresutoroika_ [_Perestroika Seen Through My Eyes_] (Tokyo: Iwanami shinsho, 1987).

29. _The Airlie House Conference_, pp. 58–59.

30. The following documents are crucial in understanding the key concepts of the new thinking as they affect the security policy: Gorbachev's Proposal to Eliminate Nuclear Weapons by the Year 2000 (January 16, 1986); Gorbachev's Political Report and the Resolution at the 27th Party Congress (February 1986); the Delhi Declaration (November 1986); Gorbachev's speech at the Moscow Forum (February 1987); Document on Military Doctrine adopted by the Warsaw Pact Organization (May 1987); Gorbachev's message to the United Nations (September 1987); Gorbachev's book, _Perestroika and the New Thinking_ (October 1987); and Gorbachev's speech at the 70th anniversary of the October Revolution (November 1987).

31. For the evolution of Soviet military doctrine, see Michael Mc-Gwire, _Military Objectives in Soviet Foreign Policy_ (Washington, D.C.: The Brookings Institution, 1987); Michael McGwire, "Why the Soviets Are Serious about Arms Control," _The Brookings Review_, Spring 1987, pp. 10–19; Stephen Meyer, "Soviet Theater Nuclear Forces, Part I: Development of Doctrine and Objectives," _Adelphi Papers_, No. 187, pp. 3–34.

32. This question is fully examined in Shenfield, Chapter 3.

33. Tsuyoshi Hasegawa, "Soviets on Nuclear-War-Fighting," _Problems of Communism_, July–August 1986, pp. 70–75.

34. Robin F. Laird and Dale R. Herspring, _The Soviet Union and Strategic Arms_ (Boulder, CO: Westview Press, 1984), pp. 121–122.

35. Hasegawa, "Soviets on Nuclear-War-Fighting," op. cit., pp. 75–79.

36. Jeremy R. Azrael, _The Soviet Civilian Leadership and Military High_

Command, 1976–1986, RAND Publication, R-3521-AF (Santa Monica, 1987), pp. 32–37.

37. We do not have to subscribe to the opinion, widely circulated in the West, that Soviet concessions have resulted only from the painful realization that their economic and technological backwardness would make it impossible for them to compete with the robust U.S. military program; in other words, that only our strength and resolve have induced their concessions. Recent studies by American specialists indicate that the Soviet Union is quite capable of matching the U.S. SDI challenge with both offsetting and emulative responses. See Stephen M. Meyer, "Soviet Views on SDI," *Survival,* 27, No. 6 (1985), pp. 274–292; Stephen M. Meyer, "The Near-Term Impact of SDI on Soviet Strategic Policy," Unpublished paper, August 1986. For the evolution of the Soviet view on strategic defense, see an excellent study by Bruce Parrott, *The Soviet Union and Ballistic Missile Defense* (Boulder, CO: Westview Press, 1987).

38. Gorbachev's message to the United Nations refers to the influence of Chernobyl on their view on nuclear weapons. See Gorbachev, "Real'nost' i garantii." Also see note 28 above.

39. Primakov, "Novaia filosofiia," Also see Shenfield, p. 52.

40. For discussion on universal peace and the class analysis, see Shenfield, pp. 40–47.

41. Gorbachev, "Oktiabr' i perestroika," p. 5. For the ideological debate on the nature of imperialism, see Shenfield, Chapter 7.

42. N. V. Ogarkov, *Istoriia uchit bditel'nost'* (Moscow: Veonnoe Izdatel'stvo, 1985), p. 9.

43. A. Bovin, "Novaia myshlenie—trebovanie iadernogo veka," *Kommunist,* No. 10, 1986, p. 116.

44. Mikhail Gorbachev, *Perestroika: New Thinking for Our Country and the World* (NY: Harper & Row, Publishers, 1987), p. 141.

45. Glickham, p.

46. Gorbachev, "Politicheskii doklad," *Pravda,* March 7, 1986.

47. Glickham, p. 8.

48. Hasegawa Tsuyoshi, "Beiso gunji baransu [U.S.-Soviet Military Balance]," Kimura Hiroshi, ed., *Joshikito shiteno gendai sobietogaku* [Soviet Studies as Common Sense] (Tokyo: PHP Institute, 1985), pp. 229–230.

49. Glickham, p. 8.

50. "Strategicheskaia oborona," *Voennyi entsiklopedicheskii slovar'* (Moscow: Voenizdat, 1983), p. 710. Also see Meyer, "Soviet Views on SDI," p. 285.

51. Primakov, "Novaia filosofiia."

52. "O voennoi doktrine gosudarstv-uchastnikov Varshavskogo Dogovora," *Krasnaia zvezda,* May 30, 1987; A. Kokoshin, V. Larionov, "Kurskaia bitva v svete sovremennoi oboronitel'noi doktriny," *MEMO,* No. 8 (1987), pp. 32–40.

53. "Vybor v pol'zu razoruzheniia i razvitiia," *Izvestiia*, August 27, 1987.

54. "Excerpts of Interview with Soviet Armed Forces Chief of Staff," *The New York Times*, October 30, 1987.

55. Gorbachev, "Real'nost' i garantii."

56. Gorbachev "Za bez"iadernyi mir."

57. Hasegawa, "The New Thinking and Gorbachev's Foreign–Military Policy," pp. 33–42.

58. Seweryn Bialer, *The Soviet Paradox: External Expansion, Internal Decline* (New York: Alfred Knopf, 1986), pp. 300–305.

59. For example, George G. Weickhardt, "The Soviet Military–Industrial Complex and Economic Reform," *Soviet Economy*, 2, No. 3 (July–September 1986), pp. 193–220; Mary C. FitzGerald, "The Strategic Revolution behind Soviet Arms Control," *Arms Control Today*, 17, No. 5 (July 1987), pp. 16–19; George E. Weickhardt, "The Military Consensus behind Soviet Arms Control," *Arms Control Today*, 17, No. 7 (September 1987), pp. 20–24; Dale R. Herspring, "On Perestroika: Gorbachev, Yazov, and the Military," *Problems of Communism*, July–August 1987, pp. 99–107.

60. Herspring, Ibid., p. 107.

61. *Literaturnaia gazeta*, May 6, 1987, p. 7. Adamovich's original article was published in *Moskovskie novosti*, March 8, 1987.

62. D. Volkogonov, "Imperativy iadernogo veka," *Krasnaia zvezda*, May 22, 1987.

63. *Literaturnaia gazeta*, May 6, 1987, p. 3.

64. Volkogonov, "Imperativy iadernogo veka."

65. For instance, P. Skorodenko, "Voennyi paritet i printsip razumnoi dastatochnost'," *Kommunist vooruzhennykh sil*, No. 10 (May 1987), pp. 15, 21.

66. Herspring, "On Perestroika," p. 107.

67. Ibid., pp. 6–7, 24.

68. S. L. Sokolov, "Pobeda vo imia mira," *Pravda*, May 9, 1987.

69. Volkogonov, "Imperativy iadernogo veka."

70. Jerome H. Kahan, *Security in the Nuclear Age: Developing U.S. Strategic Arms Policy* (Washington, D.C.: Brookings Institution, 1975), p. 33. Quarles stated as follows: "The buildup of atomic power in the hands of the two opposed alliances of nations makes total war an unthinkable catastrophe for both sides. Neither side can hope by a mere margin of superiority in airplanes or other means of delivery of atomic weapons to escape the catastrophe of such a war. Beyond a certain point, this prospect is not the result of *relative* strength of the two opposed forces. It is the *absolute* power in the hands of each, and . . . the substantial invulnerability of this power to interdiction."

71. Sokolov, "Pobeda vo imia mira."

72. Volkogonov, "Imperativy iadernogo veka."

73. Skorodenko, "Voennyi paritet," p. 15.

74. Ibid., p. 17.

75. Ibid., p. 19. A similar view is expressed by Lieutenant General V. Serebriannikov, "Sootnoshenie politicheskikh i voennykh sredsv v zashchite sotsializma," *Kommunist vooruzhennykh sil*, No. 18 (September 1987), p. 15.

76. G. Kostev, "Nasha voennaia doktrina v svete novogo politicheskogo myshleniia," *Kommunist vooruzhennykh sil*, No. 17 (September 1987), pp. 13–14.

77. Kostev presents an almost identical view in a newspaper article, "Dve politiki—dve doktriny," *Krasnaia zvezda*, November 26, 1987.

78. It is interesting to note that Ivanovskii uses the term *ustrashenie* here for deterrence. Deterrence is translated into Russian either *ustrashenie* or *sderzhivanie*. *Ustrashenie* has the meaning of intimidation, and thus more negative connotation. In recent years, *sderzhivanie* is more often used for neutral meaning of deterrence.

79. E. Ivanovskii, "Gegemonizm na marshe," *Krasnaia zvezda*, October 21, 1987.

80. For instance, see General Yazov's article in *Pravda*, July 26, 1987.

CHAPTER 8

Gorbachev's "New Thinking" and the Asian-Pacific Region

Hiroshi Kimura

New Political Thinking

Just as *perestroika* and *glasnost'* are catchwords of Gorbachev's domestic policy, new political thinking *(novoe politicheskoe myshlenie)* constitutes a key concept of the general secretary's foreign policy.[1] The three most salient propositions of the new thinking on international relations are: the growing tendency toward interdependence of the states in the world; the existence of global problems that can only be resolved by cooperation on a worldwide scale; and the limits of military means to ensure national security.

How seriously should the new foreign policy orientation under Gorbachev be taken? There seem to be three schools of thought on this question. One tends to dismiss the new thinking as another propagandistic ploy of the Soviet peace offensive. According to this view, the Soviets' main objective is to mask the weak position of the Soviet Union while buying time. The current leadership recognizes that the Soviet Union cannot compete, at least for the time being, with the United States in furthering the arms race, particularly in the field of space weapons. As a matter of fact, a Soviet troop commander was reported to have told another Soviet: "Your new thinking is fine for international consumption, but don't infect our troops with it."[2]

In contrast, the second school of thought argues that it would be stereotyping, and inaccurate, to continue to believe that the Soviet leadership persistently remains unchanged. Considering Gorbachev as completely different from his predecessors, the second school recommends that we take the new thinking more seriously and respond to what it has been advocating to the world. Needless to say, Gorbachev and his spokesmen themselves have tended to describe the new thinking as a brand new foreign policy orientation, thus indirectly criticizing "the traditional political thinking" [*traditsiia politicheskogo myshlenia*][3] prevalent during previous Soviet leaderships. Whereas the

149

first school of thought stressed the legitimizing or rationalizing function of Gorbachev's policy option necessitated under current international circumstances, the second school suggests that the new thinking serves the Gorbachev regime as a guide to action.

The third school of thought, to which this author subscribes, contains elements of both schools. It sees continuity alongside the changes in Soviet foreign policy. It seems that both Gorbachev's new thinking and the older outlooks associated with peaceful coexistence and détente (*razriadka mezhdunarodnoi napriazhennosti*)—characteristic of the Khrushchev and Brezhnev eras—constitute parts of current official Soviet foreign policy.

New thinking may be considered an ideology.[4] It is generally recognized among Western specialists that Soviet ideology performs several functions: a cognitive function, serving as an analytical prism; a normative function, providing specific policy prescription as a guide to action; a communications function, furnishing a common political language; and a legitimizing function, justifying or rationalizing the regime and its policies.[5] The commentator Alexander Bovin, reportedly an adviser to Mikhail Gorbachev, candidly acknowledged that "the verbal expression of policy can play a dual role: it either reflects or, conversely, conceals real political interests and intentions."[6] As an official ideology or expression of policy of the Gorbachev government in foreign affairs, the new thinking performs two major functions: a guide to action and legitimation.

The real test of its meaning is the *extent* to which Moscow's pronouncement of the new thinking is being translated by Gorbachev into actual policy and concrete measures. Generally speaking, the conduct of foreign affairs of any government is in fact a mix of continuity and change based on the conduct of previous governments. (No government can be totally different from its predecessors, nor can it be completely the same.) The Gorbachev regime provides no exception to this general rule, no matter how it may call its own foreign policy orientation in official pronouncements. To put it in a slightly different way, no state's conduct of foreign affairs can be entirely coherent. Even if top foreign policymakers are determined to pursue foreign policy consistently in accordance with their oral commitments, constantly changing international circumstances and other variables prevent them from doing so.

In this chapter, the focus is on Soviet behavior in the Asian–Pacific region as a test of the extent to which Gorbachev's words (expressing the new thinking) are being translated into actual deeds.

Is the New Thinking Global?

It is not yet clear whether the new thinking is a principle that Gorbachev intends to apply universally and indiscriminately to all the parts of the globe. There is little doubt that the new thinking is part of Gorbachev's foreign policy stance primarily in regard to the United States, and probably to other major Western powers, particularly those possessing nuclear weapons. Soviet foreign policy under Gorbachev has in fact demonstrated a major emphasis on reaching agreements on arms reduction and disarmament with the Western nuclear powers. It thus seems doubtful that Gorbachev's new thinking is meant to apply equally to relations with all the nations in the world, regardless of their size, political-economic systems, and military strength, particularly nuclear capability. It may not be completely irrelevant at this juncture to remember that the Soviet Union under Brezhnev limited the application of its détente policy primarily to its relations with the United States and some advanced Western countries, while it simultaneously conducted an aggressive, interventionist policy toward Third World nations. Furthermore, one wonders how high the Asian–Pacific region has ranked in Gorbachev's current list of foreign policy objectives, and how soon the Soviet leadership intends to apply the new thinking to this area. The official message that a Soviet spokesperson wants to convey is, of course, that the new thinking also applies to Asia and the Pacific. For instance, Sergei Razov, section chief of CPSU's Central Committee, made this point in a conference held in Tokyo in June 1987 by stating: "Mikhail Gorbachev's Vladivostok speech became synonymous with the new political thinking of the Soviet leadership."[7] Gorbachev's conciliatory Vladivostok speech in late July 1986 is considered, at least by the Soviets, to be the foundation of the Asian–Pacific policy of the current Soviet leadership. This brings us back to the question, To what extent is Gorbachev's new thinking being *put in practice* in foreign policy in the Asian–Pacific region? One clue to an answer lies in the Soviet interpretation of security interests in that region.

Global Security and Regional Security

Charles Glickham's article entitled "New Directions for Soviet Foreign Policy" has so far provided the best summary of Gorbachev's new political thinking. He incorrectly wrote, however, that Gorbachev "omits any reference to" and "shies away from employing" the phrase "equality and equal security" in his report to the 27th CPSU Party Congress.[8] The fact is that in that report the general secretary *did* mention "equal security" *(ravnaia bezopasnost')* and even "genuinely equal security" *(podlinnaia ravnaia bezopasnost').*[9]

The Party Program adopted by the Congress stated: "The CPSU will make every effort to have questions of arms limitations and averting the threat of war resolved . . . on the basis of *equality (ravenstvo)* and *equal security (odinakovaia bezopasnost').*[10]

Interpretation of the Gorbachev position becomes a bit complicated, because the General Secretary began to introduce the new concept of reasonable sufficiency *(razumnaia dostatochnost')* of military arsenals with the United States. In the report to the 27th Party Congress, for example, Gorbachev stated: "Our country is in favor of . . . confining military potential to the bounds of reasonable *sufficiency.*"[11] These two concepts, equality or equal security, and reasonable sufficiency, conflict with one another. Which concept, then, is emphasized more under Gorbachev? Some venture to argue that the Soviet Union has obviously changed the key concept of its military doctrine from the former to the latter. It still seems premature, however, to assume categorically that Soviet military doctrine and strategy under Gorbachev has shifted from a notion of equality or equal security to that of reasonable sufficiency. If we thus assume that equality and equal security remain a principle of the Soviet foreign and security policy, two questions arise: the first concerns the relationship between the new thinking and equality and equal security, and the second concerns the relationship between global and regional security.

What the Soviets seem to mean by the principle of equality and equal security is that the Soviet state needs to be as secure and strong as the United States. In light of the geopolitical handicaps it encounters (such as threats from China and from the independent nuclear forces of Britain and France, for example), the Soviet Union has not been content with possessing a number of weapons and armed forces equal to those of the United States.[12] In its most extreme form, this principle of equality and equal security seems to lead to the claim that, in order to compensate for such geopolitical handicaps, the Soviet Union should possess more weapons and armed forces than the United States does, or weaponry superior to that of the United States. Tsuyoshi Hasegawa was thus correct when he wrote: "If the Soviet Union insists on equal security, parity *[paritet]* cannot be realized, because pursuance of equal security— the notion that the Soviet Union has to possess military power equal to the aggregate military power of all its opponents—will inevitably lead to Soviet superiority."[13]

If this principle of equality and equal security were pursued to the extreme by the Soviet Union, it would lead to such a situation in which the Soviet Union alone would feel secure at the expense of everyone else, who would feel insecure. The Soviet claim of equality and equal security thus tended to lead to a dangerous demand of absolute security or perfect defense, which could be achieved only through annihilation of all adversaries, actual and potential, from the earth.

Particularly in the nuclear age, nations should not aim at achieving absolute security or perfect defense, but rather be content with living with a certain amount of insecurity. The Harvard Nuclear Study Group has concluded: "Like Sisyphus, modern man continually pursues an unreachable objective—absolute security—but perfect security is a goal that can never be achieved; it can only be approached."[14] In other words, any nation should realize that its security rests, in part, on that of others. Such is Gorbachev's concept of mutual security *(vzaimnaia bezopasnost')*. Emphasizing this notion, the CPSU's general secretary stated at the 27th Party Congress: "*Security,* if we are talking about relations between the USSR and the U.S., can only be *mutual,* and, if we take international relations as a whole, it can only be universal. The highest wisdom is not to be concerned exclusively for oneself, especially when this is to the detriment of the other sides. It is ncessary that everyone feel *equal security.*"[15]

In fact, Gorbachev simultaneously stressed two principles—namely, equal security and mutual security. How does one interpret Gorbachev's position regarding these two principles, which do not seem to necessarily coexist harmoniously? Four possibilities come to mind. According to the first, the Gorbachev leadership regards the increase of mutual security as the more important concept, and is likely to downgrade equal security, even to the extent that it will virtually abandon the latter principle and embrace instead the former. Second, on the contrary, still regarding equal security as a crucial Soviet claim, Gorbachev has been simply paying lip service to mutual security. Third, Gorbachev simply enumerated both principles without being bothered much by their incongruence, which may result in conflict only in extreme situations. Fourth, the general secretary stated the two principles because his leadership has not yet reached a final consensus on this matter. This last seems the most probable explanation.

The next question concerns the relationship between global security and regional (Asian) security in Gorbachev's foreign policy scheme. More concretely, it concerns the relation between the general secretary's new political thinking and his proposal on an all-Asian Security Forum. For the first time in the speech in which he welcomed visiting Indian

Prime Minister Rajiv Gandhi to Moscow on May 21, 1985, and for the second time in his Vladivostok address on July 28, 1986, Gorbachev proposed to hold an all-Asian (and Pacific) forum on security.[16]

There are two views on the nature of Gorbachev's proposal for an all-Asian Security Forum. The Chinese and most Western observers consider it to be similar to Brezhnev's concept of an Asian collective security scheme, and hence simply dismiss it as another unrealistic proposal, which is out of the question in view of the complicated power configuration and other complexities prevailing in the Asian–Pacific region. They doubt that anything specific has happened recently to prompt the Gorbachev leadership to revive Brezhnev's proposal. To be sure, normalization of Sino-Soviet relations is to be regarded as a new development in view of the fact that the Brezhnev proposal was virtually seen as a scheme to encircle China.[17] But the rapprochement in Sino-Soviet relations continues to be limited in scope. In fact, China's response to Gorbachev's proposal was again indifferent and cool. The New China News Agency, two days after Gorbachev's proposal to the Indian Prime Minister was made, simply reported that "observers have pointed out that the proposal (Gorbachev's) is similar to Brezhnev's scheme in 1969, in which Asian nations scarcely showed an interest."[18] According to this interpretation, Gorbachev's proposal is indicative of the fact that, despite emphasis upon the new political thinking, the basic scheme of Soviet policy in Asia under Gorbachev has not yet undergone significant change.

In contrast, however, Soviet spokesmen and some Western observers regard Gorbachev's proposal on an All-Asian Security Forum as different from previous, similar proposals. Brezhnev's proposal was based on the formation of a new grouping aimed at undermining the Western alliance: the late general secretary himself stated in 1969 that "such a system [proposed by the Soviet Union—H.K.] is the best substitute for the existing military political groupings."[19]

But Soviet spokesmen for the Gorbachev government have indicated that the Soviet Union no longer requires Asian countries to abrogate existing treaty arrangements. M. Isaev, for instance, wrote in 1985: "These treaties to be concluded among peace-loving nations [between the USSR and Asian countries—H.K.] shall not contain any paragraph or sentence detrimental to any third country."[20] This passage is interpreted by Professor Kuniko Miyauchi at the National Institute for Defense Studies in Tokyo to mean, above all, that any possible agreement between the Soviet Union and the People's Republic of China [PRC] must not offend the interest of their countries, such as Vietnam and Mongolia—a position that, of itself offers nothing new. More importantly, however, it also implies, according to Miyauchi's interpretation, that the conclusion of future agreements between the Soviet Union and Japan would be possible without offending interests of the United States, which already has a firm military security alliance with Japan.[21]

Dmitrii V. Petrov, one of the top Soviet Japanologists and the Japan Section Chief of the Institute for Far Eastern Studies, the USSR Academy of Sciences, indicated a similar position in an article that he wrote about fifteen years ago: *"This road* [Japan's improved relations with the Soviet Union—H.K.] *will not harm those U.S.-Japanese ties,* which both sides regard as necessary and mutually advantageous at the given stage."[22]

This statement by a relatively "dovish" Soviet specialist on Japan might be taken to indicate that, allowing the close U.S.-Japanese ties as a fait accompli, the Soviets are ready to improve their relations as much as possible, within the framework of Japan's close bond with the United States. A Soviet diplomat stationed in Tokyo, who does not want to be identified, recently said during a private conversation: "We are realistic enough to believe that even with the existence and continuation of the U.S.-Japan security treaty there still exists considerable room for improvement in our relations with your [Japan] country."[23]

It is unclear, however, whether Miyauchi's aforementioned interpretation reflects the real intention of the Soviets, particularly in view of the fact that Gorbachev made a statement which appears to contradict Miyauchi. In his Vladivostok speech the general secretary declared, "I would also like to state that the Soviet Union is a convinced advocate of disbanding the military groupings, renouncing the possession of military bases in Asia and the Pacific ocean and withdrawing troops from the territories of other countries."[24]

Accommodation with China and Japan?

Western specialists have long assessed the Soviet Union's policy toward Asia and the Pacific as unsuccessful.[25] There seems to be an almost unanimous consensus that Moscow's East Asia policy in particular has been a disastrous failure. Some have wondered why the Soviet Union has been pursuing such a counterproductive and self-defeating course there. The Washington-Tokyo-Beijing rapprochement in the 1970's to early 1980's, a similar movement between Washington, Tokyo, and Seoul in the early 1980's, and a possible resurgence of Japanese militarist tendencies, are a good illustration of the Soviet counterproductive and self-fulfilling prophesy. A self-fulfilling prophesy, according to Robert Merton, is a false definition evoking a new behavior which makes the originally false conception come true.[26] Concretely speaking, if a Soviet-discerned "anti-Soviet tripartite coalition" or the "revival of Japanese militarist tendencies" should come about, it will be due most of all to the Soviet Union's policies, particularly its own military buildup and hence so-called awakening to the "Soviet threat" in the Asian-Pacific region.[27]

In line with arguments put forward by George Breslauer,[28] an outstanding expert on the Soviet Union at the University of California at Berkeley, there is a possible scenario in which, prior to realization of a "crisis of survival" (Seweryn Bialer)[29] of the Soviet "empire," an able, enlightened anticipatory leader will appear. Whether Gorbachev is this sort of farsighted leader cannot yet be determined, but he does seem to be a leader who understands to some degree that the Soviet-Asian policy under Gromyko needs to be altered.

The major questions to address here are: Can any change be detected that the new political thinking may have brought about in Gorbachev's policy toward China and Japan, two major powers that the Soviet Union must deal with in Asia? And if the answer to this question is yes, to what extent has it been implemented? Is there any difference discernible in Gorbachev's policy toward Beijing and Tokyo? If the answer to this question is affirmative, is it because of Gorbachev's new political thinking or other factors?

To be sure, Moscow's efforts to improve relations with Beijing can be traced to the last years of the Brezhnev regime. Following Brezhnev's appeal for a Sino-Soviet rapprochement in his Tashkent speech of March 1982, the two countries gradually began to improve relations. This trend continued under Brezhnev's successors, Yuri Andropov and Konstantin Chernenko. But it was Gorbachev who appeared to have accelerated such efforts, apparently realizing China's importance in the overall Soviet policy toward Asia. The United States and China turned out to be the two important countries that were mentioned in the general secretary's major address to the Party Congress in February 1986. Stressing the particular significance of improvement in the USSR's relations with China in his speech in Vladivostok Gorbachev for the first time touched on two of Beijing's three preconditions for the normalization of political relations with the Soviet Union when he pledged the withdrawal of "a substantial number" of Soviet troops from Mongolia and of "six Soviet regiments" from Afghanistan. With regard to the longstanding dispute over the demarcation of the Sino-Soviet border along the Amur River, Gorbachev acknowledged for the first time, to the great surprise of outside observers, that the official boundary would be "the main channel of the river," i.e., China's official position. Ever since these proposals and statements were made, it has been debated whether and to what extent they represent any actual Soviet concessions to China. The Chinese have responded officially with both interest and caution.

To assess the extent to which Gorbachev truly intends to meet China's conditions for improved relations, it is necessary to look at what the Soviet Union has been doing in the three areas. The Soviet Union appears to have pulled about 6000 troops out of Afghanistan before the end of 1986, as Gorbachev had promised, although this constituted the removal of only a minor part of the estimated total troop strength of 118,000. After the Afghan government proclaimed a 6-month cease-fire in mid January 1987, the Soviet government indicated that it intended to withdraw all Soviet troops.

There are two views among Western specialists regarding these moves. One group believes that the Kremlin under Gorbachev is serious about a complete pullout from Afghanistan. The other school of thought does not rule out the possibility that the stated Soviet position since late 1986 is nothing more than propaganda. Whatever the Soviet intentions may be, the fact remains that as of this writing no further withdrawal of troops has taken place. On the issue of Soviet troop reduction in Mongolia, the Soviet government announced in January 1987 the removal of a division (an estimated 10,000 to 12,000 troops), also a mere fraction of the estimated 65,000 Soviet troops in Mongolia.[30]

As for a Kampuchean (Cambodian) settlement that would end Vietnamese occupation, the biggest obstacle to Sino-Soviet rapprochement, Gorbachev offered nothing new at Vladivostok, categorically stating that "it is unacceptable to prolong [Kampuchea's] tragic past." Speaking as though the Soviet Union had never been involved in the conflict, Gorbachev said simply that "much depends on the normalization of Chinese-Vietnamese relations." Here again, the Soviet Union's actions are more important than its pronouncements. Yegor Ligachev, widely regarded as number two in the CPSU Politburo, was invited to the Vietnamese Party Congress in October 1986; at a news conference he stated that rapprochement between the Soviet Union and China should promote better relations between Vietnam and China as well. Ligachev revealed at the same time that the Soviet Union would provide Vietnam with $11.7 to $13.2 billion in aid from 1986 to 1990, or approximately $2 billion a year, roughly doubling the level of aid of the recent past. This decision can be interpreted in two ways. The increase in aid might mean that the Soviet Union under Gorbachev is interested in providing Vietnam with economic assistance rather than military aid. This school of thought thus argues that some discernible change is taking place in the Soviet policy toward Vietnam. In contrast, the second school argues that since Vietnam can purchase more military weapons with the doubled economic aid from the USSR, no noteworthy change in Soviet policy toward Vietnam, and hence Kampuchea, is taking place under Gorbachev.

In his tour to the Asian-Pacific region in March 1987, Soviet Foreign Minister Eduard Shevardnadze did not appear to have used the Soviet Union's extensive economic aid as leverage to persuade Hanoi to stop Vietnamese aggression in Kampuchea. It is still too soon to draw any definite conclusion, but one can sense that, although the Soviet Union is not altogether satisfied with what the Vietnamese leaders have been doing toward Kampuchea, they do not necessarily intend to use their influence to stop Vietnamese aggression there.[31]

Since Gorbachev came to power, the Soviet tend to pay more attention to Japan and are attempting to woo the Japanese. Soviet newspapers, calling Japan "the Land of the Rising Sun,"[32] have carried numerous articles underscoring the Soviet need to "learn from the Japanese people's unique capability to creatively master technology."[33] In his Vladivostok speech Gorbachev himself called Japan "a power of top-level significance," and in his interview with the editor-in-chief of the Indonesian newspaper *Merdeka,* conducted on July 21, 1987, the General Secretary expressed his desire to visit Tokyo and referred to Japan as a "remarkable country that plays a great role in the world economy and an increasingly noticeable role in international politics."[34] In his 27th Party Congress address Gorbachev depicted Japan, along with the United States and Western Europe, as one of the three "principal centers of present-day imperialism."[35]

It appears that his government's assertion that it considers improving relations with Japan important is not mere lip service.[36] One indication is Soviet Foreign Minister Shevardnadze's visit to Tokyo in January 1986. This was the first such visit by a Soviet foreign minister in the ten years since Andrei A. Gromyko came to Japan in 1976. More surprisingly, the Soviet Union allowed Shintarô Abe, Japan's foreign minister at the time, to visit Moscow in late May of the same year. Gorbachev himself spared time to receive him at the Kremlin. At these meetings between the two countries' foreign ministers understandings were reached, with surprising rapidity, on the conclusion of a series of agreements on long-standing issues, including a trade payment agreement; a tax agreement; an agreement concerning cultural exchanges; an agreement on visits by Japanese families to the graves of their relatives in the Soviet Union, including two islands of the Northern Territories; and the reactivation of the Japan-Soviet Scientific and Technological Cooperation Committee.

Discussion of a Gorbachev visit to Japan also proceeded with surprising speed. While Japanese prime ministers have visited the Soviet Union on four occasions over the past 41 years (including attendance at funeral ceremonies), not one previous Soviet leader had ever expressed a desire to visit Japan despite strong and repeated requests from that country. Gorbachev candidly stated that his visit "is not only a hope but a necessity [*neobkhodimost'*]."[37] In December 1986, however, Tokyo and Moscow agreed that a projected visit early in 1987 was not feasible.

What caused the postponement of the general secretary's visit to Tokyo, which had been so publicized by the Soviet Union? The first thing that comes to mind is the rupture of the U.S.-Soviet "presummit" at Reykjavik in October 1986. Although Moscow's policy toward Tokyo is no longer—as it previously tended to be—simply a function or an extension of its policy toward Washington, it is likely that the Kremlin finds it difficult to decide how to deal with Japan while its relations with the United States are so uncertain. Another reason may well be that Moscow decided not to deal any longer with the Japanese government under Yasuhiro Nakasone, whose tenure ended in October 1987. A third reason may have to do with pragmatic diplomatic calculations of cost versus benefit of the visit, about which Gorbachev might have had second thoughts. A visit might be counterproductive if the Soviet leader went to Japan without any "souvenir" or "gift" in his pocket, thereby causing great disappointment and disillusionment among the Japanese. A fourth reason could be that the Soviets were not assured by Tokyo of what they would obtain from Japan as a reward for such an epoch-making trip by the general secretary.

Beneath these possibilities concerning the postponement of Gorbachev's visit lies the most fundamental reason: the diametrically opposing positions between Japan and the USSR on the so-called Northern Territories issue. Japan has been strongly requesting the Soviet Union to return Northern Territories seized by the USSR at the end of World War II—the islands of Etorofu, Kunashiri, Shikotan, and a group of Habomai islands off Hokkaido. The Soviet Union has flatly refused Japan's request. It argues that no territorial question exists between these two countries. When the Soviet leader goes to Tokyo, it is almost certain that the Japanese goverment will raise the territorial question. If the Soviet visitor flatly refuses to negotiate on this with his Japanese counterpart, the Japanese disillusionment with him would be great.

What, then, has happened to Gorbachev's new political thinking with regard to Japan? Shortly after his accession to power, notorious anti-Japanese Soviet Japanologist Ivan I. Kovalenko, deputy of the Central Committee International Department, started suddenly to stress the "new philosophy and new approach under the new leadership."[38] After the rupture of the U.S.-Soviet presummit at Reykjavik, however, Kovalenko began to shift back to the Gromyko-type old thinking, emphasizing that a top Soviet leader's visit to Tokyo cannot be conducted without some "visible, concrete achievements." It is crystal clear that by "achievements" Kovalenko and other Soviet spokesmen mean conclusion of a treaty of good neighborliness and friendship, an agreement on Confidence-Building Measures (CBMs) in the Far East and on the nonuse of nuclear weapons, and any other form of substitute treaty or agreement for a peace treaty containing a territorial clause. This is precisely the precondition that former Soviet Foreign Minister Gromyko used to attach to his trip to Tokyo. Some Japanese doubt that, except for the "smiling" approach, anything has really changed in Soviet policy toward Japan.

This doubt seems to reflect a misperception of "change" existing between Tokyo and Moscow. Moscow appears to feel that since Gorbachev's rise to power, the Soviet Union has already made several concessions to Japan, which included foreign ministerial exchanges (twice) and permission of Japanese visits to family graves on the northern islands. Regarding these concessions as a fee paid in advance for the General Secretary's visit to Tokyo, Moscow now requests Tokyo to prepare some "gift" that Gorbachev can bring home from Japan. In marked contrast, Tokyo regards foreign ministerial level visits and other accompanying agreements as overdue, as belatedly implemented by the Soviets. Thus Tokyo has contended that the Japanese will be, of course, hospitable enough to grant a favor to the Soviets, yet they would be greatly disappointed if the Soviet General Secretary came to Japan emptyhanded. More abstractly speaking, it appears that a misperception exists between Moscow and Toyko regarding the new political thinking. The Soviets believe that they are implementing the new thinking in their policy toward Japan; the Japanese disagree, particularly as long as the Soviets show no sign of change in their position on the disputed islands.

From an overall perspective, the momentum for improvement in Japanese-Soviet relations may be gone shortly. Why? A comparison between Japanese-Soviet relations and Sino-Soviet relations is instructive here.

It is almost certain that Japan is currently a much harder Asian country for the Soviet Union to deal with than is China, which thus appears to be the immediate target of Gorbachev's Asian peace effort. China is more vulnerable, or more manageable, than Japan in many ways. First, its underdeveloped economy requires cooperation and exchange with the Soviet Union, unlike the Japanese economy, which is one of the most advanced and most sophisticated in the world. For Japan, a country poor in natural resources yet highly industrialized, any resource-rich country is economically complementary. Hence Japan can choose almost freely its best trading partner in the world, depending upon its needs and other circumstances.

Second, China's geographical position and hence strategic military vulnerability to the Soviet Union obliges Beijing to take a conciliatory posture toward Moscow. Such considerations do not apply to Japan, which is separated from the Soviet Union by sea and is sufficiently well protected by both its own efforts through the Japanese Self Defense Forces and its close military cooperation with the United States based on the Japan-U.S. Security Treaty.

Third, being a socialist country, China has something in common with the Soviet Union that capitalist Japan does not. The Soviet Union and China have once again begun referring to each other as comrades, in marked contrast to the fact that the Soviet Union considers Japan one of the three principal centers of present-day imperialism.

Fourth, since the early 1980's, and particularly since the 12th Chinese Party Congress in 1982, Beijing has been pursuing an independent foreign policy, which means that China no longer leans excessively toward the U.S.-led Western bloc, as it had tended to do in the 1970's, and it has renewed efforts to improve relations with the Soviet Union. This is a position of which the Soviet Union can take advantage. In contrast, the Japanese government under Prime Minister Nakasone moved ever closer to the Western defense alliance, leaving no room for exploitation by the Kremlin.

Fifth, Beijing's three conditions for Sino-Soviet reconciliation are not as rigid as they appear. The Soviets are well aware that these demands do not necessarily constitute the real terms that the Chinese expect them to meet. They are, of course, partially genuine requests stemming from China's strategic-military interests, but they also serve as a signal to the West, including the United States and Japan, with whom China continuously needs good, cooperative relations in order to achieve its modernization scheme—a signal that Sino-Soviet rapprochement will remain, at least for the time being, "limited détente" (Donald S. Zagoria) or "normalcy without trust" (Robert A. Scalapino).[39]

Multidimensional Approach: Military Steps and Their Substitutes

In his speech to the International (Peace) Forum in Moscow on February 16, 1986, Gorbachev stated: "Since the nuclear disasters in

Hiroshima and Nagasaki, world war has ceased to be a continuation of politics by other means."[40] This is, of course, a denial of the famous dictum of Carl von Clausewitz, from whose teachings Lenin was reported to have learned a great deal.[41] Gorbachev subsequently expanded his rejection of von Clausewitz's dictum to include war in general.[42] Some Western observers have been tempted to take this and other Soviet pronouncements to mean that the Soviet Union under Gorbachev has at last come to realize the limited utility of military might as a source of national security. But two reservations need to be offered against such an interpretation.

First, it is necessary to examine to whom Gorbachev's statement was addressed. It is nothing new for Soviet politicians and spokesmen to criticize the U.S.'s heavy reliance on the military instrument in defense and foreign policy. However, such criticism previously was expressed exclusively to *other* powers, not to the Soviet Union itself. Georgii A. Arbatov, director of the Institute of the USA and Canada, the USSR Academy of Sciences, wrote in the Party journal *Kommunist* in 1973 that a situation now exists in which "the further accumulation of military power is not accompanied by an increase in political power."[43] As Thomas Wolfe at the Rand Corporation observed, however, Arbatov did not make it clear at that time whether he had in mind a universal phenomenon to which the Soviet Union also is subject, for his reference was to the restraint placed on the ability of the United States to exploit its power politically, thanks precisely to the military might of the Soviet Union.[44] If Soviet awareness of the limited utility of military steps, or to put it more bluntly, war, is now extended to the Soviet Union's *own* security and foreign affairs, it may certainly be considered a significant shift in Soviet foreign policy thinking.

The second reservation also concerns relations between words and deeds. To what extent has Soviet security and foreign policy actually been moving away from the previous heavy reliance upon the military factor in the Asian-Pacific region? Regrettably, it is an undeniable fact that ever since Gorbachev's ascent to the general secretaryship, the Soviet Union has not ceased building up its own military capabilities and those of its allies in that area.[45]

To be sure, the Soviet Union under Gorbachev agreed to a "global double-zero option," thereby expressing its readiness to remove all Soviet INF missiles from Asia. This policy was revealed first by the General Secretary in an interview given to the Indonesian newspaper *Merdeka* in July 1987, and then confirmed by Soviet Foreign Minister Eduard Shevardnadze in his meeting with his U.S. counterpart George Shultz in September of the same year. However, the Soviet Union's agreement to this became possible only as part of its global strategic considerations and disarmament policy.

The Soviet Pacific Ocean Fleet has been continuously strengthened with deployment of new advanced types of cruisers, destroyers and submarines. Ground and air forces of the Soviet Union in the Asian-Pacific region also have demonstrated a pattern of incremental growth and modernization. It hardly needs repeating that the Soviet military presence and use of Cam Ranh and Da Nang in Vietnam have been steadily increasing. As a result, Cam Ranh Bay is now the largest Soviet military facility outside the USSR. The Soviet Union recently obtained the right to use the ports of Kompong Som and Ream in Kampuchea as well.

The Soviet Union refrained for some time from delivering advanced weapons to North Korea in order to discourage military adventures by that country on the Korean peninsula. But this policy appears to have changed after Kim Il Sung's visit to Moscow in May 1984. In July 1985, a few months after Gorbachev's accession to power, it became evident that the Soviet Union had started to provide North Korea with substantial military aid, including MIG-23 fighters and SAM-3 surface-to-air missiles. According to Amos Jordan, director of the Center for Strategic and International Studies at Georgetown University, this decision was made by none other than Gorbachev himself.[46] In exchange for this and other military assistance, the Soviet Union seems to have obtained military overflight rights over North Korea, shortening the transit time for Soviet aircraft deployed at Cam Ranh Bay and for mounting surveillance flights off South Korea, Japan and China. Soviet naval vessels also have gained access to North Korean ports such as Najin, Chongjin, and Wonsan on the east coast of the Korean peninsula, and according to some rumor, even to Namp'o, a port on the west coast located opposite the cities of Qingdao and Luxun in China. In this new development of its military assistance and presence, however, Moscow is wary of adversely affecting Sino-Soviet rapprochement. Thus it still refrains from providing the latest generation of military equipment to Pyongyang.

Under Gorbachev the Soviet Union has continued not only to expand its military power but also to exert diplomatic pressure upon other nations using its increased military muscle. The Soviet proposal to Japan of "confidence-building measures" is an example. Japan does not want to conclude any treaty or agreement with the Soviet Union until the territorial question is settled and included. With the goal of shelving the peace treaty and hence the territorial issue, the Soviet Union has been tenaciously proposing a treaty or agreement that could serve as a substitute for a peace treaty.[47] Frustrated by Japan's negative reaction, the Gorbachev government threatened Japan, writing in *Pravda* that Japan's sea lanes could not be guaranteed. *Pravda* warned: "Japan depends greatly upon imported resources. Accordingly, Japan must be well aware that escalation of the arms race in sea-lane communication only increases Japan's vulnerability. The Soviet Union is ready to apply the proposed confidence-building measures to such sea lanes as the Indian Ocean and the Pacific Ocean. Japan's acceptance of the Soviet proposal will fit well with Japan's vital interests."[48]

If one regards the Soviet Union's incessant efforts to build up its military forces as a typical example of unchanged Gromyko-type old thinking in Soviet Asian-Pacific policy under Gorbachev, one ought to consider at the same time the flexible conduct of economic foreign relations as one of the changed aspects of the policy in the region, probably reflecting the new political thinking.

Gorbachev has made no secret of the fact that his major task is to revitalize the sluggish Soviet economy, and for this reason he has demonstrated a willingness to undertake all necessary measures short of abandoning the Soviet type of socialist system. Recently the Soviet Union has been approaching the Western bloc's international economic organizations, such as the International Monetary Fund (IMF), the World Bank, the Pacific Economic Cooperation Conference (PECC), and the Asian Development Bank (ADB), and has declared that it wishes to participate in the new round of multilateral trade negotiations under the General Agreement on Tariffs and Trade (GATT). The Soviet Union has also announced a policy of establishing joint ventures with Japan and advanced capitalist countries in Western Europe. Gorbachev has even indicated that his government would be ready to "open up" Vladivostok—previously, and for a long time, a completely closed naval port—for visits by foreigners as a major international center of trade and culture.

Abandoning its longstanding antagonism to the late Japanese Prime Minister Masayoshi Ohira's concept of Pacific Basin cooperation, the Soviet Union under Gorbachev has expressed its readiness to participate in the economic aspects of the concept. Such a stance represents a significant change for the Soviet Union, which in the past criticized this and similar concepts of a Pacific community on the grounds that they might lead to the formation of a new military bloc.[49] The Soviet government's Special Statement on the Asian-Pacific region, which formed the basis of a new Soviet policy there, surprised Western observers with its frequent use of terms such as "joint work," "division of labor," and "exchange." The term "cooperation" [*sotrudnichestvo*], mentioned seven times, was used in conjunction with fields such as economy, trade, science, technology, and information. For instance, the statement of April 22, 1986, says, "The Soviet Union proposes to start an extensive exchange of views among all the countries concerned in the region on a question of equal, mutually beneficial, smooth cooperation in the fields of trade, economy, technology, science, and culture." The Soviet Union is "ready to participate actively in such regional coopera- tion," which "is promoted, regardless of differences in social system . . . under circumstances of enhanced interdependence among nations."[50] Western observers were also astonished by the statement's resemblance to the report issued by the Pacific Basin Cooperation Study Group to Ohira in May 1980. Seven of the nine proposals in the Soviet statement duplicate proposals in the Ohira study group's report. The Soviet Union also stunned the Japanese and others in July 1986 by expressing a wish to send observers to the PECC meeting held in Vancouver in November of that year. This was in fact done, and subsequently Japanese members of that organization were reported to be persistently asked by the Soviet diplomats stationed in Tokyo to support the idea that the Soviet Union be admitted as a full-fledged member to the PECC, starting from its next meeting held in Osaka, Japan, in May 1988. Likewise, in April 1987 the Soviet Union sent an observer to the ADB meeting. These statements and moves of the Soviet Union appear to be in line with Gorbachev's new political thinking, which recognizes (1) that it is no longer enough to rely solely on military measures to increase its political-diplomatic influence; (2) that mutual interdependence between the Soviet Union and advanced Western capitalist states is inevitable.

The South Pacific

In recent years the Soviet Union has been trying to expand its presence and increase its influence in the South Pacific, particularly through lucrative fishing agreements with island nations. In August 1985 it concluded a one-year fishing agreement with Kiribati under which the Soviet Union paid an annual fee of about $1.5 million; the agreement was not renewed on expiration. After establishing diplomatic relations with Vanuatu in June 1986, the Soviet Union concluded a similar but more comprehensive agreement in early 1987 with this island state and has also been asking for port facilities for its trawlers and landing rights for Aeroflot. It is also reported that the Soviet Union has been approaching Papua New Guinea and other South Pacific island nations, perhaps intending to obtain similar fishing agreements, and that it has requested an Aeroflot route between Moscow and Suva in Fiji.

These developments make the following points evident. To begin with, the Soviet Union has been trying to make inroads in the South Pacific, taking full advantage of the island nations' economic discontent with their treatment by the U.S. The United States has turned down requests from some of the islands to recognize a 200-mile exclusive economic zone around their shores and to require American fishing companies to pay for fishing in these waters. Under the circumstances, it seems natural to some islanders that if American fishermen are not prepared to pay, Russian money will do just fine. What is more, the Soviet Union is not motivated simply by the economic benefits to be gained from access to a strategically important region. According to a U.S. specialist on the defense of Asia and the Pacific region, the military advantages the Soviet Union could obtain include proximity to U.S. territory, surveillance of U.S. missile and SDI research on Kwajalein, advantages in space and military operations, missile-testing advantages, support for seabed mining of strategic minerals, and trans-Pacific traffic capabilities.[51]

Conclusions

Why has the Soviet Union been adopting a more flexible economic policy in Asia and the Pacific? Desire to reinvigorate the stagnant Soviet economy is undoubtedly the primary reason. But it would be naive to regard the Gorbachev government's willingness to expand economic ties with Asian and Pacific countries simply as a sign of flexibility necessitated by the need to revitalize the deteriorating Soviet economy. Soviet efforts to increase economic contacts and exchanges with countries in the region could serve an important political function as well.

The Soviet Union has found it increasingly difficult to provide their military forces with everything they need. Moreover, recognition of the limited utility of military tactics—namely, a shift from the old thinking to the new thinking—must be occurring among the top political policy-makers. It may be misleading to conclude that such a shift has been completed, or that the new thinking denies entirely the utility of military measures. Recognizing only the *limited* utility of military maneuvers, the new political thinking means the contemplation of supplementing the military with other means. The ultimate objective of the Soviet Union has remained the same; i.e., to increase its political-diplomatic influence in the Asian-Pacific region. What has been changing since Gorbachev came to office is the balance between military and nonmilitary measures. It is thus misleading to contrast the continued military buildup and economic flexibility as mutually opposing trends; they are not contradictory but complementary, both serving the objective of increasing Soviet influence in Asia and the Pacific. Tia Bei sums it up well: "The Soviet Union has carried out *multidirectional, multilevel,* and *multichannel activities* in the Asian-Pacific region."[52] The Soviets themselves do not deny this interpretation. For instance, Anatolii Dobrynin, head of the International Department of the CPSU's Central Committee and the most influential foreign policy adviser for Gorbachev as well as a principal architect of the new political thinking, emphasizes as an important pillar of the new thinking what he calls a *"multifaceted"* [*mnogomer nyi*] approach; that is, an approach that mobilizes not only military but also nonmilitary measures, such as economic, political and humanitarian instruments.[53]

Notes

1. Charles Glickham, "New Directions for Soviet Foreing Policy," *Radio Liberty Research Bulletin* (Supplement 1/86, September 6, 1986), pp. 1–26.

2. Don Oberdorfer, "Glasnost: An Accident or a Rewrite of Marx? *International Herald Tribune,* April 30, 1987. For another example of the criticism made by a Soviet general with regard to the new political thinking, see D. Volkogonov, "Imperativy iadernogo veka," *Krasnaia zvezda,* May 22, 1987.

3. *Pravda,* July 29, 1986.

4. James P. Scanlan, professor at Ohio State University, regards Gorbachev's new political thinking as new ideology. Scanlan, "Ideology and Reform," Chapter 3.

5. William Zimmerman, *Soviet Perspectives on International Relations 1956–1967* (New York: Columbia University Press, 1969), pp. 282–283; Christer Jonsson, *Soviet Bargaining Behavior: The Nuclear Test Ban Case* (New York: Columbia University Press, 1979), p. 13; Vernon V. Aspaturian, *Process and Power in Soviet Foreign Policy* (Boston, MA: Little, Brown and Company, 1971), p. 337; Aspaturian, "The Soviet Union and International Communism," in Roy C. Macridis, ed., *Foreign Policy in World Politics,* third edition (Englewood Cliffs, NJ: Prentice Hall, Inc., 1967), pp. 162, 165; Michael P. Gehlen, *The Politics of Coexistence: Soviet Methods and Motives* (Bloomington, IN: Indiana University Press, 1967), pp. 22–23; Adam B. Ulam, "Soviet Ideology and Soviet Foreign Policy," *World Politics,* Vol. II, No. 2 (January 1958), p. 158.

6. *Izvestiia,* October 30, 1973.

7. Sergei Razov, "On Some Aspects of Soviet Policy in Asia and Soviet-Chinese Relations," a paper read at the Conference on "Security and Economic Development in Asia and the Pacific," held jointly by the Institute for Sino-Soviet Studies, The George Washington University and *The Yomiuri Shimbun* in Tokyo on May 28–30, 1987.

8. Glickham, op. cit., p. 20.

9. *XXVII s"ezd kommunisticheskoi partii sovetskogo soiuza: stenografi-cheskii otchet* (Moscow: Politizdat, 1986), Vol. I, pp. 87, 88.

10. *Programma kommunisticheskoi partii sovetskogo soiuza* (Moscow: Politizdat, 1986), p. 71. (Emphasis added by author)

11. *XXVII s"ezd kommunisticheskoi partii sovetskgo soiuza*, Vol. I, p. 90. (Emphasis added by author)

12. Iu. Lebedov, "Voenno-strategicheskoi paritet i realii iaderno-kosmicheskogo veka," *Mezhdunaronaia zhizn'*, No. 6, 1986, p. 25.

13. Tsuyoshi Hasegawa, "Beiso gunji baransu (U.S.-Soviet Military Balance," in Hiroshi Kimura, ed., *Jôshikito shiteno gendai sobietogaku, Soviet Studies as Common Sense* (Tokyo: PHP Institute, 1985), pp. 229–230.

14. The Harvard Nuclear Study Group, *Living with Nuclear Weapons* (New York: Bantam Books, 1983), p. 232.

15. *XXVII s"ezd kommunisticheskoi partii sovetskogo soiuza*, Vol. I, p. 87. (Emphasis added by author)

16. *Pravda*, May 22, 1985 and July 29, 1985.

17. Victor Zorza, "Collective Security," *Survival* No. 11 (August 1969), p. 248; Peter Howard, "A System of Collective Security," *Mizan* No. 11 (July/August 1969), pp. 199–201, 203; Hemem Ray, "Soviet Diplomacy in Asia," *Problems of Communism* (March–April 1970), p. 46; Ian Clark, "Collective Security in Asia," *The Round Table* No. 252 (October 1973), pp. 477–387; Alexander O. Ghebhardt, "The Soviet System of Collective Security in Asia," *Asian Survey* No. 13 (December 1973), p. 1076; Arnold L. Horelick, "The Soviet Union's Asian Collective Security Proposal: A Club in Search of Members," *Pacific Affairs* No 47 (Fall 1974), p. 269; Howard M. Hensel, "Asian Collective Security, The Soviet View," *Orbis* No. 19 (Winter 1976), pp. 1564, 1579; Alfred Siegel, "Moscow's Concept for Collective Security in Asia," *Military Review*, No. 57 (February 1977), pp. 3, 7, 11.

18. Yomiuri Shimbun, *Mainichi Shimbun and Nihon Keizan Shimbun*, May 23, 1985.

19. *Pravda*, June 8, 1969.

20. M. Isaev, "Aziia-mir: bezopasnost'," *Mezdunarodnaia zhisn'*, No. 5, 1985, p. 80.

21. Kuniko Miyauchi, "Gorubachofu no 'Zen-ajia foramu' Koso: Gunbikanri no sokumen (Gorbachev's Concept of All-Asian Forum: The Aspect of Arms Control), *Soren Kenkyu* No. 3 (October 1986), p. 55.

22. Dimitrii V. Petrov, "SshA-Iaponiia: novaia faza," *SShA*, No. 2 (February 1972), p. 25 [emphasis added by author].

23. For more detail on this point see Hiroshi Kimura, "Basic Determinants of Soviet-Japanese Relations: Background, Framework, Percep-

tion, and Issue, *Acta Slavica iaponica* (Slavic Research Center, Hokkaido University, Sapporo), Vol. 5 (1987), pp. 78–79.

23. *Pravda*, July 29, 1986.

24. See Donald Zagoria, "The Soviet-American Rivalry in Asia," in Marshall Shulman, ed., *East-West Tensions in the Third World* (New York: W. W. Norton, 1986), pp. 84, 88, 89; Paul Dibb, "Soviet Capabilities, Interests and Strategies in East Asia in the 1980s," in Robert O'Neil, ed., *Security in East Asia* (London: Gower, 1984), pp. 2, 3; and "An Air of Expectancy in Moscow," *Newsweek* (October 11, 1982), p. 60.

25. Robert K. Merton, *Social Theory and Social Structure*, Revised and enlarged edition, (Glencoe, IL: The Free Press, 1957), p. 423.

26. Hiroshi Kimura, "Soviet Military Buildup: Its Impact on Japan and its Aims," in Richard H. Solomon and Masataka Kosaka, eds., *The Soviet Far East Military Buildup: Nuclear Dilemmas and Asian Security* (Dover, MA: Auburn House Publ. Co. 1986), p. 113.

27. See George Breslauer, *Five Images of the Soviet Future: A Critical Review and Synthesis* (Berkeley: Institute of International Studies, University of California, 1978), pp. 27, 75.

28. Seweryn Bialer, *The Soviet Paradox: External Expansion, Internal Decline* (New York: Alfred A. Knopf, 1986), p. 169.

29. *The Military Balance: 1986–1987* (London: The International Institute for Strategic Studies, 1987), p. 46.

30. For Vietnam's military and nonmilitary significance to the Soviet Union, see Donald Zagoria's unpublished paper, "The Soviet-Vietnamese Alliance and Its Strategic Implications," and Hiroshi Kimura, "Soviet Focus on the Pacific," *Problems of Communism* No. 3 (May–June 1987), pp. 1–29.

31. *Krasnaia Zvezda*, March 28, 1985; *Pravda*, April 3, 1985, and January 12, 1986; *Izvestiia*, January 10, 1986.

32. *Literaturnaia Gazeta*, January 1, 1986.

33. *Pravda*, July 29, 1986 and July 23, 1987.

34. *XXVII s"ezd kommunisticheskoi partii sovetskogo soiuza*, Vol. I, p. 36.

35. On the first day of the fifth Japanese-Soviet high-level working consultations, which began on September 5, 1985, Deputy Foreign Minister Mikhail Kapitsa explained the political position of the Gorbachev government as follows: "The Soviet Union's new leadership puts emphasis on relations with Japan and is seriously thinking about an improvement in relations" (*Nihon Keizai Shimbun*, September 6, 1985). *Pravda* political commentator Vsevolod Ovchinnikov expressed a similar opinion (*Yomiuri Shimbun*, January 8, 1986). On July 11, 1986, Soviet Ambassador to Tokyo Nikolay Solov'ev, chatting with Nakasone during a courtesy call upon assuming his post, stated that "Japan is a great country, and the Soviet government pays great attention to Japan" (*Sankei Shimbun* and *Yomiuri Shimbun*, July 12, 1986).

36. *Yomiuri Shimbun* and *Nihon Keizai Shimbun*, August 12, 1986.

37. *Sankei Shimbun*, July 14, 1987; *Yomiuri Shimbun* and *Nihon Keizai Shimbun*, July 17, 1987.

39. Donald S. Zagoria, "China and the Superpowers: Recent Trends in the Strategic Triangle and their implications for Southeast Asia," a paper read at the Second Quadrilateral Project on Regional and Global Security Issues, Jogjakarta, Indonesia, on August 17–19, 1987, p. 10.

40. *Pravda*, February 17, 1987.

41. Nathan Leites, *A Study of Bolshevism* (Glencoe, IL: The Free Press, 1953), pp. 184, 254, 370, 434, 497; Raymond L. Garthoff, *Soviet Military Doctrine* (Glencoe, IL: The Free Press, 1953), pp. 53–56; Michael Howard, *Clausewitz* (Oxford: Oxford University Press, 1983), pp. 1, 54, 66.

42. Georgii Arbatov, "O sovetsko-amerikanskikh otnosheniiakh," *Kommunist*, No. 3 (February 1973), p. 105.

43. Thomas W. Wolfe, *Military Power and Soviet Policy* (Santa Monica: The Rand Corporation, 1975), p. 12.

44. Carl von Clausewitz, *On War* (London: Penguin Books, 1968), p. 119.

45. See *The Military Balance: 1986–1987* (London: The International Institute for Strategic Studies, 1986); *Strategic Survey: 1986–1987* (London: The International Institute for Strategic Studies, 1987); *Asian Security: 1986* (London: Brassey's Defence Publishers, 1986).

46. *Yomiuri Shimbun*, June 6, 1985.

47. See Hiroshi Kimura, "The Soviet Proposal on Confidence Building Measures and the Japanese Responses," in *Japan's New World Role*, ed., Joshua Katz and Tilly C. Friedman-Lichtschein (Boulder, CO: Westview Press, 1985), pp. 81–104.

48. *Pravda*, June 22, 1985.

49. See Hiroshi Kimura, "The Impact of the Afghanistan Invasion on Japanese-Soviet Relations," in *Soviet Foreign Policy and East-West Relations*, ed. Roger Kanet (New York: Pergamon Press, 1982), pp. 154–158.

50. *Pravda*, April 23, 1986.

51. *USSR Discovers Strategic Value of Pacific Islands* (text of testimony before the subcommittee of the East Asia and the Pacific Region of the Foreign Relations Committee, The U.S. House of Representatives on September 10, 1986, by Rear Admiral Edward B. Baker Jr., Director of the East Asia and the Pacific Region, Office of the Secretary of Defense, International Security Affairs).

52. In *Contemporary International Studies*, April 13, 1987, *Foreign Broadcasting Information Service: Daily Report: China* (Washington, D.C.: National Technical Information Service), Vol. 1, No. 93 (May 14, 1987), p c9. [Emphasis added by author].

53. Anatolii Dobrynin, "Za bes"iadernyi mir, navstrechu XXI veka," *Kommunist*, No. 9 (1986), pp. 24–25.
